My Passage to India

My Passage to India

a Life

Annabel Mehta

AS TOLD BY
GEORGINA BROWN

Published by Westland Non-Fiction, an imprint of Westland Books, a division of Nasadiya Technologies Private Limited, in 2024.

No. 269/2B, First Floor, 'Irai Arul', Vimalraj Street, Nethaji Nagar, Alapakkam Main Road, Maduravoyal, Chennai 600095

Westland, the Westland logo, Westland Non-Fiction and the Westland Non-Fiction logo are the trademarks of Nasadiya Technologies Private Limited, or its affiliates.

ISBN: 9789360456238

10 9 8 7 6 5 4 3 2 1

Typeset by Jojy Philip, New Delhi
Printed at Parksons Graphics Pvt. Ltd

To Anand,
without whom I would never have made the passage
in the first place

Contents

Preface

I MADE TWO MAJOR DECISIONS IN MY LIFE, BOTH AGAINST THE WISHES OF my parents. 'I took the road less traveled ... and that has made all the difference.' My mother loved this poem by Robert Frost, but she was less enthusiastic about my choices. At least in the beginning.

Leaving England in October 1966 and taking the boat to Bombay was a defining moment for me. But had I not abandoned the idea of becoming a professional pianist—my first, big, independent decision—I would never have gone to the London School of Economics, I would never have met Anand Mehta. And none of this would ever have happened.

I can picture the woman I might have become, dressed in a twinset and pearls, teaching my grandchildren to play Chopin Etudes in an airy drawing room in Worcestershire. Instead, I am wearing a fuchsia pink salwar–kameez and a mangalsutra around my neck. Today, Anand, my husband of nearly sixty years, and I will be going with our daughter Anjali and her husband Sachin Tendulkar to watch our grandson's team, the Mumbai Indians, play a match at the Wankhede Stadium in Mumbai.

Annabel Mehta
May 2024

Introduction

GEORGINA BROWN

> 'Biography is the mesh through which our real life escapes. It's only fact. Truth is quite another thing and is the work of the imagination.'
>
> — from *The Invention of Love,* Tom Stoppard

IN 2017, MY HUSBAND WAS OFFERED A JOB IN MUMBAI AS DEPUTY HIGH Commissioner (West of India) and HM Trade Commissioner for South Asia. His mother had been born in 1926 in Quetta (now in Pakistan) where her father served as a Brigadier General in the Indian Army. As a child, Crispin had listened to his mother and aunts speaking Urdu when they didn't want him to know what they were talking about. Bedtime stories were Kipling's *Jungle Book* and 'Rikki-Tikki-Tavi'. He spent his Gap Year 'teaching' at a school in Kalimpong. He was spellbound by this vast country. We had travelled there together and with our children dozens of times. How could he resist?

But what would become of me? For decades I had been a theatre critic on newspapers in London. I had never not worked. Dramatic as it may sound, I felt I must choose between my job and my marriage. Someone else would be taking my place in the stalls.

In October 2017, I flew to Mumbai with Quince, my beloved Jack Russell. Some months earlier, a wardrobe of summer frocks, paintings I couldn't live without, our bed and some goose-down pillows had been put on a container ship. The Foreign Office wanted us to feel at home in our little flat above the official residence.

The Residence of the British DHC in Mumbai is situated in one of the city's poshest streets. Outside our front door on the fifth floor were two armed policemen. Behind the coat of arms of the lion and the unicorn on our front door was a patch of Britain. Quite literally, because any diplomatic residence is deemed to be the territory of the country it is representing. A collection of pictures from the Government Art Collection hung on the walls as well as a photograph of our dear Queen Elizabeth II by Dorothy Wilding. Our balconies looked directly on to Antilia, the 27-storey skyscraper home to the richest family in India. Tiny figures cleaned the windows and swept the terraces all day long.

Every morning, my husband—aka 'Sir'—was collected by his driver in a black Range Rover. A policeman sat in front of him. Years ago, the then DHC, Percy Norris, had been shot dead in Bombay. Ever since, the city's police had provided protection for the DHC.

Madam—that was me—remained at the Residence to arrange flowers and menus for diplomatic receptions. No driver. No car. No protection.

Quince and I explored the neighbourhood. A Madam walking her own dog was a rare sight round these parts where dogwalkers, if required, were part of the household staff. We were soon on namaste terms with the banana-seller, a permanent fixture beneath a banyan tree. The heat of the tarmac scorched Quince's paws but she refused to walk in the boots I bought for her. Few kaali-peeli drivers were willing to take me and my fluffy pup to the nearest park. So I bought my own battered car.

A Madam driving herself in the mean streets of Mumbai was an even rarer sight.

I relished my role as the hostess with the mostess. I played the part of the trailing spouse with less conviction, though I loved dressing up for the endless receptions and parties—twice in a sari. And Mumbai was my oyster, all the more so thanks to having CC (Consular Corps) number plates on my car. I got to know this wild city and to love it. But I missed the theatre and I missed a sense of purpose.

One day, I had an idea. I would write a column: The Diplomat and the Doormat. And so I did. I gave it to the Diplomat to read. End of. I put it away in a drawer.

Then I met Annabel. She, like me, had been brought up in the Midlands, some twenty years before me. Our backgrounds were similar, though I was a country girl, not a townie like her. I knew where she was coming from. And now that I was in Mumbai, I knew where she had got to. She might have become a professional pianist but she hated being centre stage. While at the London School of Economics in the sixties, she fell in love with an Indian man. She married him in Bombay, wearing a sari, with not a single member of her family present. The young couple lived with his extended family.

Having had two daughters, Annabel threw herself into improving the lives of inhabitants in some of the city's worst slums. Her elder daughter, a doctor, married Sachin Tendulkar, the greatest-ever cricketer in the country where cricket matters most, making Annabel the mother-in-law of the most worshipped sportsman on earth.

Here was a woman who had one foot in the slums, the other in cricketing royalty.

'You have to write this story,' I said to Annabel. 'I couldn't possibly,' she replied. 'I am dyslexic. I can't write.' She is also very modest. 'Well, I can,' I said. 'And I need a project.'

We began talking. And talking and talking about anything and everything. Nothing was off limits. I recorded more than a hundred hours of talk. Present-day Mumbai was a very different city from sixties Bombay and in order to map that and create a context for Annabel's story, I researched, read, explored places for myself. I needed to describe the sights, the sounds, the smells, the tastes, the politics, the atmosphere.

Through Annabel, I learnt more about what it was to live in India than I might have otherwise been able to. Her passage to India became MY passage to India. Though, of course, I am all too aware that I have barely scratched the surface of this almost impenetrably complex country. A cliché perhaps, but true.

So here are a few chapters of Annabel's life as I have imagined it.

Thank you, Annabel. It has been a great adventure.

My Passage to India

1

Who Am I?

I BELONG TO THAT DISTINCTLY BRITISH GENUS OF WOMEN WHO WENT TO boarding school in the 1950s. I sleep with the window open; I would still win the Tidiness Cup; my posture is excellent for one in her ninth decade; I can knit, badly; I can pack, expertly; my hospital corners are second to none; I can eat anything put in front of me; I seldom make a fuss and I have never made a scene; and compulsory Sunday afternoon walks in the Malvern Hills have put me off walking for life. Occasionally, I catch myself using the word 'super'.

I was conceived before the outbreak of war in that fateful summer of 1939, and born while bombs dropped on nearby Coventry on 2 April 1940. The youngest of four—Gillian, Jeremy, Richard and me—my home was suburbia, a substantial, detached, red-brick Victorian house, bought for £1,685 in 1938, according to my father's meticulous records. It was on Hampton Lane, the smartest part of Solihull, which remains about the smartest part of the Midlands. Food-rationing had begun. My father, Norman Lancaster, had been called up, but after ten weeks of active service, he was recalled to Birmingham to run an armaments factory that made shell casings.

As for most of my generation, the war cast a huge, dark shadow over our early years. It had a brutalising effect on many of us, forcing us to be tough and to cultivate a stiff upper lip. Not that I suffered personally. In spite of rationing, there was always nourishing food on the table, and plenty of it. My mother, Betty, flirted with the butcher to get the best cuts of meat, and I developed a taste for tripe, pig's trotters, pigeon, brawn—and, best of all, oxtail soup. My mother was a good cook, possibly because it was one of the few ways in which she could express her creativity, which was otherwise stifled. We certainly weren't hard-up, but we didn't have any luxuries either. I don't think anybody was seriously wealthy in those days (no one we knew, anyway). We were solid upper-managerial Midlands middle-class. We had staff: a nanny, a live-in housekeeper, a daily cleaner and a gardener. We were privileged, but we didn't know it; I don't think we were spoilt brats. We were expected to make our own beds and clear away and dry up after meals. When our measly weekly pocket money ran out, that was that.

Summer holidays were a fortnight in Devon or Wales and, just once, in Scotland, until my father splashed out rather uncharacteristically on a holiday house in Devon. This was in the village of Shaldon, on the estuary of the river Teign, where my mother had grown up. From when I was ten, we all decamped there for two weeks at Easter, and a month in the summer. The house was let out for the rest of the year to cover costs. Clichéd as it may sound, those holidays in Shaldon were the happiest of my life. And, yes, the sun always shone. I burnt lobster-pink, blistered, and turned back to white. The days were spent rock-climbing on the red rocks, shrimping in rock pools, sailing in a dinghy named Tess of the d'Urbervilles by my pretentious brother Jem, mackerel-fishing and barbecuing our catch on the beach the moment we got back. Sometimes I sketched. It was heaven. School friends of my brothers turned up—one of them I remember, Joe Meynell, in an open-top Triumph TR2. When my friend Sue Davies, who lived not far away in Totnes, came to stay, it was even more enjoyable. We went off to the Shaldon Hop on Friday nights or to the cinema in Torquay, seven miles away. I have spent my life failing to find Cornish pasties as delicious as the ones we ate then.

My father, born in Yorkshire in 1906, was the piggy-in-the-middle, between overindulged Basil and suave Vernon. His parents had made sacrifices to send the boys to Rossall, a minor public school in Lancashire, after which my father studied chartered accountancy and moved to Birmingham, the successful candidate out of 700 applicants. His aspirational mother was delighted. She had worked as a milliner when times were hard, and she considered Birmingham to be 'Down South' and far superior to anywhere 'Up North'.

As a child, I used to watch my father shave with a cut-throat razor before he left for work, wearing spats, a stiff, detachable white collar and a bowtie. Like many of his type, he was a man of habit. Every month, he put on a bowler hat to go to a board meeting at the headquarters of Joseph Lucas in London. We—I—hadn't the slightest idea what his work entailed. My father wrote a memoir towards the end of his life, which, alas, records nothing personal, but details the anodyne aspects of his business life and my brother Jeremy's business career. He notes that when he left Tube Investments and joined Fillerys Toffees in Birmingham (suppliers of confectionery to Marks & Spencer), his salary dropped 50 per cent from £10,000 to £5,000. He records that he sold Sparrows Nest for £42,500 in 1978, ten times what he had bought it for. He seldom uses adjectives or adverbs, so I have no idea how he felt about these financial highs and lows.

My father had a peculiar relationship with money. You might call it money-itis, a sort of disease. He wasn't mean, but he was very careful. Money frightened him. He was suspicious of wealth and frowned on it. He routinely refused what he regarded as overgenerous pay rises because he was worried about upsetting the rank and file. He was undoubtedly conscious of the poverty caused by the Depression in the 1930s. When my brother Richard came home one day without his boots, which he had taken off in a field and forgotten about, my father beat him with a wooden crop, which must have been a relic from his army days when he learnt to ride. It was not the only time Rich was beaten, either at home or later at school at Rugby. My father always punished carelessness or waste. He was very anti-privilege, hated Old Etonian entitlement and abhorred conspicuous consumption.

In retrospect, I think my parents were far too frugal with themselves and with us all. As a result, I've always tried to be much more easygoing about spending, though my daughter, Anjali, doesn't see it that way. My granddaughter, however, might; in a moment of extravagance, I bought Sara a pair of ridiculously expensive Chanel high heels for her twenty-first birthday. She wanted a designer handbag, but that would have been going too far. I still can't stop myself being careful. I'm not generous by nature. I wish I was. I've tried to be more relaxed about money since coming to India, where I have often been struck by the fact that it's always the people who have the least who are most generous.

My father was also very anti-religion. I am not sure why. My mother had considered converting to Catholicism until my father's rigid atheism forced her to think again, and she became an agnostic. From that day, she refused to say the Creed because she felt that it would be a lie. As a child, my mother and her siblings had walked three miles to church every Sunday with their very devout Church of England mother. Or so she claimed. Fortunately, that stopped when her parents bought a motor car, the first in the village.

My father had been a keen rugger player; when he became a boss, he would always employ someone he rated as a team-player ahead of a public school toff with a First from Cambridge.

His judgement of people rested on how well they expressed their opinions and argued their case. Fiercely competitive and provocative, he loved sparking debate. I shall never forget one evening when my brilliant musical friend Caroline was staying with us. My father said that Mozart was too sugary, and Caroline surprised and impressed him with a spirited defence. That was the moment when I decided that Caroline and Rich should marry. Unfortunately, I failed to mention this to Rich until a few years later, by which time Caroline was happily married to Patrick. 'But I never thought of Caroline as a *girl*,' he said, surprised. 'She was just one of your friends.'

My mother automatically and unquestioningly took my father's position on everything. 'Your father wouldn't approve,' she would say whenever we tried her patience. It is only now that I realise he was a bully. She loved clothes and was one of the first women to wear trouser suits in the sixties, back in the day when Marks & Spencer didn't sell women's slacks. Her allowance didn't stretch to luxurious clothes and she was too intimidated by my father to spend her own money on expensive dresses. The moment he died, she splashed out on all the clothes she wanted, and continued to do so well into her nineties. She often bought rather smart 'pre-loved' frocks from charity shops on Bath Road in Cheltenham.

As far as I could see, my mother was content to fulfil the expected role of a wife and homemaker, having lunch ready for my punctilious father at one o'clock sharp, waiting on him hand and foot, running everything seamlessly on a limited housekeeping allowance. They were both creatures of their era. My father was quietly oppressive—these days you would call him a control freak—and my mother was quietly oppressed. My mother learnt German in secret, because she wanted to sing German Lieder and my father didn't approve. I can't imagine why. Was it a hatred of Germans because of the war? Or was it that my father simply regarded women as second-class citizens? He was certainly knotted with contradictions. He expected my sister Gillian and me to grow up to be as emotionally and financially independent as our brothers, but with rather unrealistic ideas about exactly how we would get there. From the moment I displayed the least bit of talent for ballet or the piano, he had visions of me becoming a prima ballerina or a concert pianist and achieving fame and fortune. And status. One of my brothers was certainly going to be prime minister. Our happiness was never the goal he had in mind.

My father and mother were an exceptionally good-looking couple. As well as warming the proverbial slippers (though my father was not a slipper man), my mother, every inch the fifties housewife, put on a pretty frock and lipstick to welcome Dad home. Then she would chase us off to bed so that she could have him to herself. My parents were so wrapped up in each other that I often felt excluded, perhaps more so than my siblings because I was the littlest.

My parents' marriage seemed strong in spite of their differences. Or so I thought until some thirty years after I had come to Bombay, when I found out about my father's affair with his secretary. None of us had an inkling of it at the time because we saw so little of our parents. Either we were away at school or we had already escaped from the Midlands. My sister Gillian told me about it. Apparently, my father had wanted to run away with the woman, but my mother managed to dissuade him. In those days, marriage meant marriage, for better or for worse. Divorce in Britain in the fifties was as rare as it is in Mumbai today, though even here, things are changing slowly. Gone are the days when men were seen in the company of a mistress while remaining unhappily married to a wife who remained out of sight and out of mind. Only one of my parents' friends divorced, and it was considered shameful, partly because it required sordid evidence of adultery with staged photographs of the rueful husband coming out of a Brighton hotel with Another Woman.

Evidently, my parents got over this uncomfortable marital hiccough because they seemed happy together, later in life. Not that one can ever truly fathom other people's marriages. Even one's own can be a bit of a mystery. According to my mother, my father did not understand girls, having had a very strained relationship with his own mother and grown up with no sisters. In so many ways, my father was an old-fashioned paterfamilias, almost a Victorian figure. He addressed his own parents as Pater and Mater. He thought men should be physically and mentally tough. Women baffled him.

When the war was over, my father had part of our garden converted into a tennis court, and he and my brothers played all the time. Gillian and I were not invited to join in, which was both odd and mean of him because my mother played well. When she and my father first married, the tennis club in Edgbaston was a terrific social hub. They were always going to tennis parties and playing mixed doubles.

My father didn't teach us girls to play chess either. Again, perhaps it was a girl thing, or simply that playing with us would have been no fun because he thought we were no good, too stupid or too meek. I still resent him for that.

Both my parents found boys less complicated, and I think they would have been happy to produce enough boys for a cricket team. Richard was my mother's particular favourite because he was blond and wicked and funny. My elder brother Jeremy was always more intense. Admittedly, when I showed an interest in photography, my father encouraged me, giving me a Box Brownie and patiently teaching me to develop and print in his own darkroom. I never felt the same need as he did to record the aperture of the camera for every one of the black-and-white photographs diligently stuck into two volumes that documented our childhood, including our outing to the Queen's Coronation in 1953. He was given tickets for seats in the Mall, and he took twelve-year-old me rather than my eighteen-year-old sister, Gillian, who was living in London; she was already becoming somewhat estranged from the rest of us. I can still remember the brand-new dress and the gorgeous pair of flat red suede pumps I wore for the occasion. A rare indulgence.

I have always liked cars, and my father loved them. My brothers were not the least bit interested. When I was little, my father's pride and joy was his MG 1.5 litre Drophead Coupé with beige leather upholstery. It was 'the most beautiful and pleasing car I ever owned,' he wrote in his memoirs. He bought it in 1938, when his annual salary had gone up to £5,000 and he must have considered himself quite well off. It seemed so unfair to me that Gillian, Jeremy and Richard were allowed to stand on the back seat with the hood down whereas I, the baby, had to sit on my mother's knee in front.

The cars my father drove later depended on where he worked. As a director of Tube Investments, he had a huge Austin Princess, which I hated because it made me carsick. As a director of Joseph Lucas, he was given a succession of smart cars, including the futuristic Citroen DS with its arrowhead design and hydro-pneumatic system that lifted the car up and down. I remember the advertising blurb describing it as 'stunning and improbably voluptuous'. I didn't understand the word 'voluptuous', but I found the car absolutely stunning. My mother hated it. Being driven back from a dinner party before strict drink-and-drive rules were enforced was evidently a nightmare and led to many acrimonious exchanges between them, which I overhead from my eyrie. One argument boiled down to a choice between my mother and the beloved Jag XK140. A rare triumph for my mother. In keeping with his characteristically frugal nature and his final, less well paid role as Chairman of Wolseley before he retired, my father made his office in a shed in the garden and drove a white Mini Minor station wagon.

My father's mother, whom we called Chum, was the only grandparent I ever knew. We weren't close, but she used to come and stay a couple of times each year, and she taught my mother how to dress a crab. I wish I had watched more carefully. Once, for Christmas, she gave me a doll with a china head and a rag body; that same Christmas, my friend and neighbour Rosemary Flood was given a walkie-talkie from America. I disliked dolls and much preferred playing with Ro's walkie-talkie or dressing my beloved and unusually compliant cat in dolls' clothes. But I made sure to get the dolly out whenever Chum was around.

My mother's father, Fred Theobald, was a planter of tea and rubber in Borneo. My grandmother, Agnes, was the daughter of General Sir John Campbell in the Indian Army. I have a lovely posed photograph of her in an exquisite silk gown, edged with lace, with two of her children, also beautifully dressed with little bonnets. I suspect these were photographs taken for the family she left behind in England when she went to live in the East Indies.

Fred died in his early seventies in 1936, just after they returned to South Devon; my grandmother, a neurasthenic, killed herself in the most desperate way by drinking formaldehyde and then throwing herself into a bonfire. My mother never spoke of it. I think of it now as a sort of sati, the Indian custom banned by the British in the early nineteenth century, when a wife immolated herself either on the funeral pyre of her dead husband or in some other fashion, soon after his death. It's like something out of a Victorian novel and all the more tragic because my grandmother was by no means penniless or destitute. She was quite simply heartbroken and suicidally depressed. She left my mother and all her siblings £3,000, a small fortune in those days. Their house,

Brookvale, was the grandest in Shaldon, complete with a billiard room, and the first to have electricity and a telephone, which my mother loathed because she was convinced the woman at the telephone exchange eavesdropped on her conversations. When my mother first came to Bombay, she said it reminded her of the England in which she had grown up, where everything was rigidly hierarchical and everyone knew their own place and everyone else's business.

When her parents travelled out East, my mother and her elder brother, John, her two elder sisters, Ethel and Mary, and her little brother, Wilfred, were left at home in the care of a housekeeper. The girls weekly-boarded at a Catholic convent across the estuary. They loved the convent, which was why my mother chose it for my sister Gillian. My mother adored children and trained as a Norland nurse in London's Holland Park Avenue—where girls are still trained to this day—though she gave up work the moment she married, as was expected. Having been pretty much abandoned by her parents throughout her childhood, she remained more than usually close to her sisters, which my father was always very jealous of. He discouraged her from visiting them in London, a hundred miles away, insisting that she could not leave until after breakfast and must always be home to make his supper.

My mother acquiesced. She was the kindest person imaginable, and I am afraid I wasn't nice to her. I resisted her desire to get close to me. She used to come up to kiss me goodnight and I would pretend to be asleep so that I didn't have to kiss her back. We didn't do girlie things together as she would have liked. She believed that one should always make an effort with one's appearance. I couldn't care less what I wore, though as a teenager I took to sewing my own clothes to make my dismal clothes allowance go a bit further. I never ever confided in my mother even though, oddly, many of my school friends did.

I preferred the company of my mother's unmarried sister, Aunt Mare—short for Mary—who trained as a Nightingale nurse at St Thomas's Hospital in her late twenties. She was clever, funny and wise, and was decorated for her work on hospital ships. She had a nervous breakdown after the war and was committed to an asylum where she was given electric shock treatment, after which she became fragile and inclined to depression. Not that this was ever spoken of.

I only got to know Aunt Mare well when I left school and moved to London to study at the Royal College of Music (RCM). Every Friday, often accompanied by my friend Caroline, I would go to her lovely Bloomsbury flat where she lived with her sister Aunt Prout (whose real name was Ethel) for the most delicious tea of tiny meringues and tarts filled with homemade lemon curd. They enjoyed hearing about our latest romances.

Poor Aunt Prout was an invalid, suffering terribly from scleroderma, a crippling disease of the joints. Aunt Mare used to wrap her swollen, pus-filled fingers tenderly and expertly in gauze dressings. Aunt Mare never married. Not for lack of opportunities, according to my mother. She had fallen in love with a man who went to live in New Zealand, and she travelled there to see if she could hack it, but decided it was too remote and feared she might lose touch with her family. I often thought about this when I was considering whether I could live in Bombay.

Following Aunt Prout's death, Aunt Mare bought a house in Bayswater in London, to share with my brother Richard, newly married to Helen, and they lived together and looked after one another until her death, almost like a traditional Indian family.

I don't really care for emotions like regret or guilt, but I wish I had been more loving towards my mother. As a child, I simply didn't feel a natural flow of affection for her. She was a much more emotional, loving person than I gave her credit for. I never even heard her snap at anyone. My friends recognised this, but I did not. Like so many, she had lost people in the war, including her younger brother, Wilfred, a gunner with the Royal Air Force (RAF). Our relationship improved when I moved to India, and especially when I became a mother myself. I always said that we got on better when we were 6000 miles apart.

In those early days, I went back to England only once in three years as it was so expensive, but I would stay for at least two months. My parents loved my two little girls. My father often said that the Indian–English mix was a good thing, though I don't really know what he meant by that. Physical beauty, perhaps? I like to think that I made up for my coldness towards my mother in her old age, for I spent as much time with her as I could when she fell ill in the last twelve or so years of her life.

My father died the day after his seventy-fifth birthday, when my mother was seventy-three, giving her the opportunity to emerge from his shadow and become more outgoing. To the dismay of some of us, and the great distress of her sister Mary, she married again when she was seventy-nine and three quarters. Her new husband, Forbes Horan, was a bishop, the son of a bishop and the grandson of a bishop, and the least Christian person I have ever met. He lacked humanity, yet was forever taking the moral high ground. My mother enjoyed singing duets with him. Maybe that was enough for her. In spite of being an absolute so-and-so, he had a very nice son, John, who remains a dear friend. Five or six years after their wedding, Forbes developed dementia, and although my mother felt guilty about not being able to look after him, he had to go into a home. Before he died, my mother bought a little house off Bath Road in Cheltenham, which I helped her make comfortable, and from then on, we grew much closer. She loved that house. She called it her 'mousehole', and she died there, just short of her ninety-ninth birthday.

While I failed to appreciate my mother's kindness either to me or to those less fortunate—she volunteered with the National

Society for the Prevention of Cruelty to Children (NSPCC) in Birmingham and the Disabled Club in Pershore, driving members all over the place in her van—I was well aware of my father's rigorous approach to public service. He had a rigorous approach to everything, actually. He had little money left after paying the school fees for the four of us, but gave 10 per cent of his annual income to charity and 25 per cent of his spare time to unpaid work. All this is recorded in his notebooks. He was on the board of both Birmingham University and Mosley Rugby Club—which involved dragging us off to watch rugger on rainy Saturday afternoons—as well as treasurer of Birmingham Children's Hospital.

The importance of public service was ingrained in me from very early on. At school, we didn't just pray for others, we were actively encouraged to help the poor. That it was harder for a rich man to enter the kingdom of heaven than for a camel to go through the eye of a needle was another early lesson. As was loving thy neighbour as thyself.

I remain a big fan of the Ten Commandments, at least the ones I can remember. I love the word 'covet' and can still recite: *Thou shalt not covet thy neighbour's house, thou shalt not covet thy neighbour's wife, nor his manservant, nor his maidservant, nor his ox, nor his ass, nor anything that is thy neighbour's.* I truly don't think I have ever been covetous, but I confess that as a child I used to steal three-penny pieces, and occasionally the odd shilling or florin, from a dish high on my father's chest of drawers. I would then go to the Co-op down the road and buy a peach or, my favourite, an OXO cube wrapped in silver foil, which I licked until it disappeared. I've always preferred savouries to sweets.

When I think back, there was always music in our house. As a child, I used to lie in bed listening to music on the Light

Programme on my beloved wireless, which sat on a high shelf next to my bed. BBC Radio has been my lifeline. Sometimes, at night, above the sound of my music—or below it—I could hear my father and the boys shouting at one another, and not playfully. If there was no one else to argue with, Dad would challenge my mother, and she would often reply: 'Do you want me to be a yes-woman, or to say what I think?' If she said what she thought, his voice became angrier. I never took part in these arguments. I made sure never to put myself in the firing line. I wonder now, what did I talk about with my father? Cars, perhaps?

From her first days at the convent, my mother learnt the cello and the piano, and she loved to sing. She had a beautiful soprano voice and dreamed of becoming a professional singer. It was not to be. But she did make sure that her children learnt an instrument. Jem learnt the bassoon and Rich the trumpet, but we were not like the von Trapps, and there was no family band. My mother sang songs from light opera and German Lieder, sometimes accompanied by Allan Hudson Davis, a business friend of my father, on the baby grand piano in the drawing room. I recall that my father didn't like that one bit. He thought they were flirting. They probably were.

I am not surprised by my father's reaction. The accompanist/singer relationship is a very sexy one. I have accompanied a few male singers on the piano and could easily have fallen in love with every single one of them. It was always as if they were singing only for me.

Although my father learnt the piano at school and took up the flute in his forties on the advice of a doctor—which always seemed a bit weird to us children—his love of music only came to the fore when his brother Basil gave him a sophisticated music system, which he installed in the small, low-ceilinged drawing room. His collection of LPs multiplied until he had every recording Maria Callas ever made, along with Elisabeth Schwarzkopf,

Joan Sutherland, Dietrich Fischer-Dieskau, all of Beethoven's symphonies, and I don't know what else. My mother shared his passion. Perhaps that was the glue that kept them together?

My early years in Solihull were quieter in every way than those in rural Worcestershire. In Solihull, I used to walk with my nanny to the private prep school, Windylow, which we all attended, and which was owned and run by Miss Hill and Miss Bagnall, a classic Laurel and Hardy pair. Miss Hill was tall and thin. We nicknamed short, round Miss Bagnall 'Baggy-fatlegs', which seemed very wicked at the time, but I was only five. Miss Bushall was my piano-teacher; she must have been good because, by the time I was ten and going to Hatley, Great Malvern, the junior school at Malvern Girls College (MGC), I had already flown through Grade Four. The teacher I adored was Miss Hammond, a former ballet dancer who wore a purple leotard and kept her black hair pulled back in a tight bun. I loved dancing. Naturally, I wanted to be the next Margot Fonteyn, but I was already too tall—hence my nickname, Lanky.

The teaching at Windylow cannot have been bad, because we all got into our chosen prep schools. I only shone at music and maths, but I remember being thrilled to have scored 100 per cent in the maths paper for the class above mine in my entrance exam.

My brothers were packed off at the age of seven to a boarding prep school, Durlston Court, miles away on the Dorset coast. When the school trunks came out, our dog, Brucie, went into mourning and hid under a bush in the garden. Jeremy invariably cried on the railway station platform. I was the one sobbing when Richard disappeared two years later.

I didn't shed a tear when I started boarding at MGC at ten, and the truth is, I never felt homesick. I made wonderful friends, four of whom have been friends for a lifetime. I often think that the survival and intensity of my friendships with the people I left behind in England can be explained by the fact that, though I didn't see them frequently, our get-togethers were very concentrated, just as it was when we were at school, which was a bit like prison with no escape for weeks at a time.

Boarding school suited me. I thrived on order. I liked getting up early. I even liked the food. Having grown up on wartime food, I was happy to eat the fatty bacon passed to me under the breakfast table. I was thrilled to have got away from two elder brothers who teased me, naming my miserably thin plaits 'Tinsy' and 'Winsy'. My parents had never given me much individual attention. I think they found me difficult, spiky and not very loveable. I suppose I loved them, because in those days one did, theoretically, even if one didn't. I adored my cat and my nanny, Doz, who doted on me.

My best school friends were in Avenue House with me. Cressida's father was in India, and she had a big black trunk with a Poona address painted on it in fancy writing that I envied. It was the first time I heard of Poona. Birdy's father was a doctor in the wilds of Wales; so was Sue Davies's father, but he worked in Totnes. Steph's father was with the Hong Kong Bank. Jenie was in the year below me. She loved listening to me play the piano, and I loved watching her paint. Amanda's father worked for the Ground Nut Scheme in Lagos, so she came home with me for the three exeats we were allowed each term. Other girls with parents abroad had to stay with grumpy maiden aunts in unheated Victorian houses.

Amanda never forgave MGC for deciding that she was non-academic. Quite wrongly. She didn't go to university, but had a brilliant career in television. As often as we were allowed to escape from school on Sundays, all six of us used to pile into my father's Jag and go home to Sparrows Nest for lunch, after which, weather permitting, we would strip down to our bras, slather ourselves with olive oil and lie in the sun. It was glorious, but hardly in line with today's health guidelines.

Sparrows Nest was a charming, cosy house created from two gamekeepers' cottages in fifty acres of wilderness, on a hill overlooking the Vale of Evesham. Water came from a spring, so it took half an hour to run a bath. There was a tennis court and an ornamental pool we could swim in, again fed by the icy cold spring. I hated it to begin with, cut off for weeks at a time up a rough track half a mile long, far away from neighbours. Until that time, I had been a townie, loving life in the suburbs, close to friends and the bus stop from where I would take the 155 to the Bull Ring shopping centre in Birmingham and wander around Corporation Street quite contentedly. Alone in Sparrows Nest, I played the piano for hours, a Bechstein with a fancy Victorian design, candlesticks at either end and a trelliswork front. Gradually, the garden at Sparrows Nest grew on me. Gardening became something of an obsession for my parents. The garden had been neglected and was more of an orchard with masses of assorted fruit trees. A great friend, Tommy Usbourne, advised them to create a garden as if it were a painting. My mother was in charge of the shrubs and my father of the trees. Roses thrived on the heavy clay soil and, thanks to my father being the chairman of Wolseley, which owned Webb's mowing machines and Merry Tiller cultivators, he had the latest equipment, and the lawn was very well manicured. Boys and their toys! I suppose I inherited my practicality from both of them.

Whenever I go to London these days, we meet at Steph's smart house in Kensington and reminisce about our schooldays, and Miss Brooks, our formidable headmistress. She had a large drooping bosom and a coil of snowy hair, and like so many schoolmistresses of that era, she was a spinster. We all believed their lovers must have died in the slaughter of the First World War. Brookie was a real personage. Every year, each one of us had to make a three-minute speech on a given subject with Brookie as the audience. Alone. One-on-one with the headmistress. I have seldom been so frightened.

My two closest friends from school are Amanda and Jenie. We have known each other inside out for more than seventy years. We have loved each other's mothers when we hated our own. I went to both their weddings, though they did not come to mine. We had children at the same time, and we have been through tragedies together such as the death of my daughter, Tara. They had daughters the same age, as did Caroline.

Caroline has remained my closest friend to this day. She was by far the best thing to come out of my two years at the Royal College of Music. She had been at Cheltenham Ladies College where, she says, all individualism was crushed and only the cleverest girls—which didn't include her—were taken seriously. We met in my first week at the Royal College, where she was studying organ, with piano as her second instrument, as we sat on a bench waiting to be auditioned for the Madrigal Group, which we both got into and absolutely loved. Caroline and I were quite literally in tune from the first moment. Later, we joined the Bach Choir together. One can live thousands of miles away from someone and not speak for months at a time, but a bond as strong as mine and Caroline's can never be broken.

Caroline was wholly unsurprised when I announced that I was moving to Bombay, where I would be marrying my Indian boyfriend, Anand, whom she had never met. She says it was completely in character, that I had always been a rebel and a free spirit and had never cared one jot about anyone else's opinion, least of all that of my parents.

I had never considered myself rebellious. Quite the reverse. I've always thought of myself as one of life's conformists. And a very practical person. I drove a Vespa in London because it got me around faster than a bicycle, not because I wanted to make a statement. I painted it in pink and purple, not to attract attention, but just because that was the colour of the paint pots I found under the stairs.

I was pretty well-trained when I went to MGC in 1950, at the age of ten, with a trunk packed with two-dozen handkerchiefs, a dozen vests, ditto liberty bodices. We all wore two pairs of knickers: a white knicker lining that I threw into the wash each day, and maroon over-knickers changed weekly. Our games shorts came down to our knees. The winter uniform was a hideous maroon and purple skirt and thick, mud-coloured lyle stockings, mine heavily darned and held up with a suspender belt. Our browny-beige summer dresses had three pin-tucks that stayed flat if you had no bosom, like me, and filled out massively if you were as well-endowed as my friend Amanda. My teenaged brothers once came to school to watch me sing, and having seen us all file past, they labelled us the Ugly 500. Our blazers were plain maroon until I became a Prefect and wore a striped one. Maroon felt hats with a band in house colours were compulsory for outings.

I conformed readily. I never wanted to stand out. We had an early Bendix washing machine at home and something maroon often found its way into a white load, turning all my underwear pink, which I found embarrassing rather than amusing. We were allowed to wear one of two mufti dresses after church at Malvern Priory every Sunday, but that was the only time when we were allowed to express our own personality.

We kept to a strict routine. First thing in the morning, we stripped our beds and folded the bedclothes into neat bundles only to remake the bed later with perfect hospital corners. What a ridiculous waste of time! We had a bath three times a week, which, like everything else at school, seemed normal, but also rather spoiling when compared to my father's generation, who had to take ice-cold showers. Every morning, we washed in the bowl of water on the bedside table. Birdy's mother once showed me a letter she had kept: 'Dear Mummy, the water in our bowels is frozen today!' It probably was.

I have always hated the cold, and I was cold for most of my childhood, which is somewhat ironic since my father's businesses included a central heating company. But he thought central heating was soft. It wasn't until we moved to Sparrows Nest that we had central heating, though not in our bedrooms. I took a hot water bottle up to bed if it was cold. If I was ill, my mother brought a two-bar electric fire up to my room. I gather the Queen had one just like it. Open fires were the joy of my life, and one of the few things that I continue to miss in India. I spent hours on a stool inside an enormous inglenook fireplace at Sparrows Nest, watching the flames and scorching my knees.

I hated games, partly because of the cold, but also because I wasn't sporty. I couldn't catch a lacrosse ball. I was always slipping on the icy-hockey pitch. I have not recovered from the trauma of being made to swim in an unheated pool, obediently diving in when the games mistress blew her whistle. The best thing about tennis was that the courts were so far away on the other side of the railway track that we could get away with lying down and sunbathing for a good quarter of an hour before the games mistress finally got to us. Amanda and I co-founded the Anti-games League, but it got us precisely nowhere.

I've always loved dancing and loathed walking. The British have always been strangely inclined to go for long walks in bitter weather. Just recently, I spent Christmas with Richard in his lovely house on the Camel estuary between Padstow and Wadebridge in Cornwall. After a gargantuan spread, we pulled on coats and hats and gumboots for a clifftop walk in horizontal rain. Within moments, we were blown inside-out and soaked to the bone. Anand, my darling husband, thought we were stark raving mad. I've often tried to explain to him that the British public-school system in my day was designed to train children at an early age to weather storms, quite literally, but also to prepare us to cope with the most challenging conditions in the farthest corners of the Empire.

It was certainly the case for me.

For the first two decades of my life, I occupied a very narrow, white upper-middle-class layer of society. I didn't really become aware of who or what was on either side until I left school and went to London, first to the Royal College of Music for two years and then, when I was twenty-two, to read Social Administration at London School of Economics. LSE in the sixties was a brave new world in every sense. Mick Jagger was there at the same time, though I didn't know him. Until then, all the boys I knew were white and educated at public schools in the Midlands such as Rugby, like my brothers, or Oundle, Stowe or Uppingham, or, if exceptionally brainy, at Charterhouse. Only aristocratic Midlanders went to Eton and Harrow, and if there were any, I didn't meet them.

My only exposure to anyone less fortunate than myself was through the people who worked in our house. As a child, my best playmate was Brian Briggs, who was my age and lived across the road in a dilapidated council house with no bathroom. Every week, the tub in the passageway was dragged into the kitchen and he was given a good scrub, sharing the water with his younger sister Wendy. Brian's mother, Glad Briggs, was my mother's right hand; she came in five days a week, endlessly putting clothes through the mangle. His father, Alf, our gardener, was called up in the war, and joined the Catering Corps. Brian had a lisp, which worried Glad, who thought it would prevent him from finding a wife. It didn't. He and his wife ran a successful building business. My mother kept in touch with the Briggs family long after we went to live in Sparrows Nest, and she left both Brian and Wendy a legacy in her will. When I met Wendy years later, she was driving a BMW and had bought the house next door to ours. That's social mobility for you. Both houses have gone now, replaced by smart blocks of flats.

Mrs Brain came in once a week to clean the silver and relay the local gossip. She had been in service all her life, as had her mother, a parlour maid in a nearby Downton Abbey–style pile. Next door to the Briggs lived Mrs Leason, a former bargee who had the most leathery, weather-beaten face I had ever seen. She grew vegetables for us in her garden and told wonderful stories. My darling nanny Doz, short for Dorothy, lived in. She sat knitting while I practised for hours on the baby grand piano. After the War, I ate oranges for the first time, peeled for me by Doz. It was from my mother that I learnt to appreciate and genuinely love the people that helped in the house rather than take them for granted.

My friend Ro—Rosemary—the one with the walkie-talkie doll, lived two doors away, and had a much bigger garden in what once must have been the Big House in this patch of Solihull. It had stables and Ro had a pony. I never learnt to ride. This was suburbia, not countryside, and therefore 'no place to ride' according to my mother, at least that was what we were fobbed off with. The truth probably was that it was considered too extravagant to keep horses or even have riding lessons. Ro and I kept white mice in her greenhouse, and that was how we learnt the facts of life. We saw them going at it, and watched them multiply rather alarmingly. We also had rabbits, and my brothers teased me about 'Wo and her wabbits'. I was transfixed by Ro's mother's dyed platinum-blonde Marilyn Monroe hair, and her grandmother's deep auburn, almost maroon-toned coiffure, which seemed so exotic and bold. According to my mother, their hair was evidence of the fact that they were from

Smethwick. It is only now that I know what that meant. British snobbery! There is nothing quite like it.

Britain was obviously much whiter then. My dentist and my cousins lived in Edgbaston, and it was on the way there from the car window that I first saw a brown person sitting on the pavement selling nylon stockings out of a suitcase. At MGC, Karen, from Turkey, had pale caramel skin and pierced ears, which we were all very jealous of. She was the only non-white person in the whole school. The only other 'foreign' girl was wild Gunilla, from Sweden, who was expelled for climbing out of a window at night and going into town to meet boys from Malvern College—thrilling for her, presumably, and certainly for us.

MGC has now merged with several private schools nearby, which we regarded as less academic and therefore inferior. Lawnside was full of girls who went hunting; at the Abbey School and St James's, the girls wore miniskirts and were taught how to get in and out of a sports car without showing their knickers. Or so we believed.

My poor sister Gillian, now well into her eighties, still recalls the shock she felt the day she arrived at her convent school in 1944 to find that the place was run by nuns. There were no nuns in Solihull as far as we knew. Her nuns were from the Convent of Notre Dame, and were dressed in black from head to toe, like women in purdah. Even for a girl from a reserved English family like ours, the nuns' stony remoteness and forbidding demeanour was chilling. All that Catholic stuff—long Latin masses every day, endless prayers and mea culpa guilt-tripping—made Gillian into the most rabid of all the rabid atheists in our family.

Gillian always claimed that she would have preferred to have gone to the local state day school rather than the convent, but my parents wouldn't have thought it good enough socially. Because Gill hated the convent, and because I was considered brighter than her, I was sent to MGC, where many daughters of Midland industrialists went (though not my Edgbaston cousins, who went to Roedean, much posher, like their mother before them).

After five miserable, furious years at the convent, Gillian went to the Sorbonne in Paris for a year and then got a job at Harrods—nicknamed Horrids—in the days when the salesgirls were as well-spoken as the customers. When she turned twenty-one, she left, claiming the pay was inadequate to live on. My father had made it clear to all of us that unless we were still studying, we were to be financially independent by the age of twenty-one. Storming out in disgust was typical of Gillian. My mother said that she had been stubborn and demanding from the moment she was born, prematurely.

It was not until my mother died, and Gilly and I spent a week together sorting out our mother's bits and pieces, that I finally understood her tricky relationship with our parents. Paris had given her a taste for life abroad, and she had worked in tourism, which eventually took her to Seattle, then San Francisco, and finally San Diego, where she opened a health-food shop in the Farmers Market. She screwed up her courage to ask my father for a loan against her inheritance in order to expand. He refused. A decision made by a shrewd businessman rather than a loving father. Gillian was devastated and never forgave my parents. Incidentally, my father had cheerfully given a loan to Richard when he wanted one to set up his practice after qualifying as a doctor.

It is only now, looking back on my upbringing, that I see that my sister's defiant spirit raised the bar for me. For years, she had a very charismatic Polish boyfriend. My father was appalled. Not because he was Polish, but because he was Catholic and an immigrant and didn't have a proper job. When she went to San Francisco, she met the only other real love of her life, Waldo, and she never told my parents about him because he was black.

He wanted Gilly to marry and settle into warming his slippers, but when she realised that, she moved on. My parents certainly failed Gilly, who disappeared from all our lives early on and never returned. Richard went to see her in California in the seventies and had a lovely time smoking pot, but she and Jem didn't get on as children, and they never became friends in later life. On the many business trips Jem made to California, he never once looked her up. She and I became close friends, but only in middle age.

By contrast with Gilly, my brothers were deeply conventional, though very different from each other. Richard and Jeremy did not appear close, and I'm not sure they even knew each other very well. When they were at Rugby, Jeremy seldom spoke to Rich, and referred to him as Lancaster Minor. Yet, Jem was clearly a major influence on him. He was a strange fellow, indeed a stranger in many ways, certainly to me. The name of our house, Sparrows Nest, embarrassed him. He would have liked his address to be The Manor or The Hall.

Although I hardly knew him, I believe his problem was that he yearned for grandeur. He would have liked to have gone to Eton. So much so that he sent his son Nick there, which made Jeremy very happy but made Nick miserable. Jem was aspirational in a way that none of the rest of us has ever been. British snobbery and the loathsome British class system were things I wanted to get away from, as did my sister Gillian.

Unlike Richard, Jem was interested in girls from an early age, and his first girlfriend at Oxford was the Lady Corisande Bennet, daughter of the ninth Earl of Tankerville. I never met her, but I shall never forget a name as exotic as hers. It was par for the course that the moment Jem met Serena, he fell in love with her. Serena had glorious cherry-gold hair and was doing A' levels at St. Clare's, Oxford. She was the daughter of Sir Anthony Rumbold, Old Etonian and diplomat, the tenth baronet in a line created for an earlier Rumbold who served as the Governor of Madras (now Chennai) in the eighteenth century. Her grandfather, Sir Horace Rumbold, was ambassador to Germany shortly before the war, and a distinguished diplomat.

Serena had been educated initially at St. Mary's, Wantage, coincidentally the same convent that my brother Richard's wife, Helen, went to. She got a place at Oxford to read English, but abandoned her degree after a year to marry Jeremy, which I think she later regretted. Not the marriage—though Jem was not the easiest husband—but not completing her degree. In later life, she studied Theology and became a lay reader in the Church of England, which is all the more commendable given the strength of Jem's atheism.

The Rumbolds struck us Lancasters as very grand. Serena had been brought up by maids and governesses and was only brought down from the nursery for tea. As a result, she couldn't boil an egg. When she married, she asked my mother for all her recipes for the kind of wartime stews Jem loved, and she dutifully cooked for him all his life. She was a devoted wife and mother, raising four delightful children, to whom I am much closer than I ever was to their father.

She and Jeremy married as soon as he graduated, with no job and little to recommend him as far as Serena's family were concerned. After a couple of years working in GKN, the automobile company, he followed my father into business, working in one of his engineering firms, which was clearly nepotism, though it then seemed very natural. They worked well together. He was a quietly brilliant, even visionary businessman who took Wolseley into the next realm, transforming a parochial company into a world leader. Like my father, he was involved in and supportive of the city of Birmingham, a member of the Council of Birmingham University (where my father had been Pro-Chancellor) and a long-serving trustee of the Barber

Institute of Fine Arts. As Chair of the Regional Committee of the National Trust, he had championed the survival of the last of the city's 'back-to-back' houses. Paintings were his passion, not people. Evidently, he had an extraordinary eye, for he assembled a most remarkable private collection of largely post-War paintings. It was truly tragic that, at the end, Alzheimer's left him unable to distinguish his Howard Hodgkin from his Bridget Riley. As an art historian, he was entirely self-taught. He kept meticulous notes about each work in his collection. When he died in 2019, part of his collection was auctioned at Christie's. It raised some £23 million. I daresay that even Serena's father would have been impressed.

The nature/nurture debate has always fascinated me. My two brothers were dramatically different, and yet their upbringing had been almost identical. When I moved to India, I was not close to either of them. However, Richard and Helen have visited Mumbai more than two dozen times, and all their children have been to stay several times, whereas Jeremy and Serena, after coming for the first time for my daughter's wedding, came just once more for a holiday without even telling me or seeing us. I was under the impression that Jem disliked people as much as Rich loves them. Richard has a thousand friends and no pretensions. As a boy, he was labelled 'thick', and he couldn't read until he was nine. Not even comics. He still can't spell my name correctly. He was a classic dyslexic in the days when children slow to read were accused of not trying and were beaten. I am dyslexic too, terrible at languages and a slow reader, but because I was good at maths and music, it didn't matter. Rich preferred cricket to maths, was bottom of the class and was advised to leave school after O' levels and become a farmer. Fortunately for him, his enlightened housemaster at Rugby recognised a spark and talked my parents into making him sit the A' Levels. He scraped into Cambridge on the strength of being an exceptional boxer (for which he picked up a Blue) and a fine cricketer, then read for a Natural Sciences Tripos, and halfway through changed to Medicine. I had always assumed that it was because a dear friend died from leukaemia, but it was actually because he had been to see that marvellous movie, *The Nun's Story*, with Audrey Hepburn as the nursing-nun sent out to the Congo where gorgeous Peter Finch is a missionary doctor. Romantic old Rich reckoned that would suit him very nicely.

Richard found his métier. He became a consultant physician at St. Mary's Hospital, Paddington, completed a PhD, and had a thriving private practice. He also found the perfect wife in Helen, a nurse on the ward, one of the many who were eyeing the eligible thirty-year-old Dr Lancaster. Helen was the eldest of six children, whose clergyman father died before she left school, leaving her mother struggling to bring up the children in the old rectory. I was sorry not to be at their wedding, which was held in a snowy December. The photographs make it look so romantic, but heavy snowfall meant lots of people couldn't get to the church.

Helen slotted happily into our family, and she and I got on very well from the very first time we met more than a year later. She is an excellent cook, as is Richard, and they are the most warm, generous and welcoming hosts. Well into his eighties, Rich remains a tireless enthusiast of life and of learning. After a couple of hours reading a book of history first thing in the morning, he turns to science at elevenses and then, when in London, sets off on his bicycle to meet a friend or on his mission to explore every single church in the vicinity or, when in Cornwall, into the woods beyond their rambling farmhouse to hack away at the undergrowth. He and Anand get along like a house on fire, spending hours talking and setting the world to rights.

I believe my parents were, in the end, proud of us all for being tough, independent, focused and driven in our sharply contrasting ways, which was surely what they wanted when they sent us away to fend for ourselves at such an early age. I often wonder if one of the intentions of boarding school is to deliberately weaken family ties and force children to stand on their own two feet, and whether that is a good thing or not. The best lesson I ever learnt at school was *Gnothi seauton*—know thyself—the inscription over the entrance to the Temple of Apollo at Delphi, which Miss Warry, our terrifying Classics mistress, drilled into us all those years ago. It has been my guiding principle.

2

Beginnings

I BECAME ANNABEL MEHTA ON 26 DECEMBER 1966, WITH NONE OF my family and not a single friend from England as a witness. The date was chosen so that Anand and I could see the Taj Mahal by the light of a full moon on our honeymoon. I wore a white sari of tissue-like organza with a wide orange and gold border. Behind my sixties fringe, I plumped up my hair with the pricy hairpiece I had brought with me from London. My mother-in-law provided the jewellery: pearls for the wedding itself, an emerald pendant and matching earrings for the reception the following day, heirlooms handed down from generation to generation of my new Indian family. From that day, Bombay became my home. I live here and I shall die here. As I soon came to realise about myself, I am both very ordinary and a bit different.

A year earlier, Anand Mehta, my boyfriend for more than three years, had returned home to Bombay with a Master's in Economics from LSE to work in his father's tin-can company. He had left me sniffling in Maida Vale with my flatmate Ruth, who was still at LSE. I had just swapped my Lambretta for a blue Mini, which I needed as a social worker with the Family Service Unit, caring for a dozen families scattered around the Elephant and Castle, South London. They were all variously deprived or not coping, many with mental health problems. In the evenings,

Ruth and I took it in turns to cook chops or sausages and mash or, best of all, Ruth's speciality of herring coated in oatmeal and fried in margarine. If I was on my own, I treated myself to fish and chips from the Seashell, Lisson Grove, which I passed on my way home from work, and ate straight from the newspaper. We still buy fish and chips from there when we're in London, but nowadays, it comes in a cardboard box.

I missed Anand. He wasn't much of a letter writer, and phoning abroad was unthinkably expensive. I missed him being around. Not all the time, because we both had our own friends and separate interests, and we still do, and we didn't do particularly exciting things together beyond going Dutch at the local classic cinema or at a cheap 'Indian' in one of the Warren Street restaurants. I liked his gentleness and quiet humour, and I got on well with all his friends, many from Bombay, who were studying or working in London. He was living on a very meagre allowance, the maximum permitted by the Government of India, so he was happy (or maybe not) to sit on the back of my Vespa, and later, when I started working, as a passenger in my Mini. After he left, I filled one empty evening each week with a carpentry class run by the local Education Authority. It was a long four months before one of those delicious blue airmail envelopes floated through the letterbox. 'Arrive in time for your birthday. I am sending your ticket,' wrote Anand. This was not a proposal—Anand was not a romantic. It was an experiment. He wanted me to find out if I could live in India. More specifically, if I could live with his family.

His father, having noticed that his only son was more than usually subdued, had forked out £500 for my plane ticket (the equivalent of an eye-watering £10,000 today). I asked my employers for two months leave and went to Harrods' 'cruise-wear' department, the only shop in London that sold swimming costumes in March.

Before 1966, I had only once been on an airplane, and that had been entirely unplanned. Aged nineteen, my friend Caroline and I booked a ferry to France, which was cancelled because of a strike, and we were transferred on to a little propeller plane. My Lambretta was put in the hold. Yes, I had progressed from my second-hand Vespa to an even more second-hand Lambretta. Caroline and I cruised along the Loire, me driving, Caroline sitting behind. We stayed in youth hostels. Such fun.

Going to India was my first time in a big plane, a BOAC VC10, a wonderful thing with its bent-up tail. It was super: masses of leg room, starched tablecloths, exotic food and endless drinks served by long-legged, well-spoken air hostesses to rows of businessmen in suits and ties—and also to me, an unsophisticated woman of twenty-six travelling alone. Becoming an air hostess was the height of glamour in those days. Only unmarried women aged between twenty-one and twenty-seven with a height between five-foot-two and five-foot-nine with a 'neatly proportioned figure with pleasing appearance' could apply. There was so much smoke from the cigar and pipe-smokers that I could barely breathe, and it was a relief to get out when we stopped to refuel. On the first of three stops in the Middle East—Kuwait, I think—a man in robes embarked, with a falcon on one arm and a harem of ladies on the other. They disembarked at the third stop, Dubai.

I landed in Bombay on 25 March. Standing at the top of the steps of the plane in a short, blue Mary Quant-style skirt, I felt a blast of humid Bombay air, hotter and wetter than any I had ever experienced. The sky looked like boiled milk. I was used to greyness, gloom and cold. I took my first breath of India: petrol fumes, sewage, rotting garbage, all rather intense and mildly nauseating. I quickly discovered that, like most things Indian, there is always a flip side to the bad—in this case, the heady scents of tuberoses, frangipani and jasmine in the garden at Anand's house.

Anand met me in a Chevy Bel Air, a ridiculously long turquoise-and-white car driven by Rama, one of the Mehta family's drivers. Rama's father had been the driver before him. I have always been a bit of an anorak about motorcars, so while everything else is a bit of a blur, I vividly remember noticing the cars on my first drive from the airport. Most were Ambassadors, very like the British Morris Oxfords I had left behind, and the traffic moved reasonably fast along the main roads.

In the garden of the bungalow on Warden Road in Breach Candy, the extended Mehta family had gathered to greet me, curious about the English girl Anand had invited to stay. Kripto, the family Labrador, lay twitching in the sun and didn't bother to introduce himself. Ever since Anand's return, his mother had been asking each morning: 'Baba, when are we going to meet Annie?' (Anand was twenty-six years old, and like so many eldest sons in India, he had been nicknamed Baba from birth.) Apparently, his youngest sister, Jill, used to tease him by stealing my letters to him from the breakfast table and refusing to hand them over until he gave her a rupee.

The family quite literally opened their arms to me, calling me Annie from the start. Anand's mother dipped her finger into a pot of thick liquid and placed a red spot on my forehead. Her welcome was as warm as could be, and I had to pinch myself to realise this was really happening to me. Already, faraway England seemed very chilly, and the English very literally buttoned-up.

Anand's smiling mother was known as Amru Masi to the younger generation. Always elegantly draped in pastel silk-cotton weave Chanderi saris from which her midriff bulged, she had prematurely snow-white hair, cropped short, unusual for an Indian woman then. His father, Jayantilal, was composed and quiet, leaving the women and girls to chatter away with me. Like my own father, he was a businessman. I took to him immediately. Only later did I discover that we had a common interest in cars, carpentry, do-it-yourself and mending things, which had earned him the nickname 'Fixit'. I had met him once before in London when he had taken a gang of Indian LSE Bombay boys—and me—out to supper, but he hadn't clocked then that Anand and I were dating. It was his business partner's brother who, on a visit to London, had spotted a lovestruck Anand and beetled back to Bombay to tell Amru Masi all about Annie.

The Mehtas' bungalow—unlike squat single-storey British bungalows—had three floors and was grand and spacious (by Bombay standards). It had a lovely garden and rooftop terrace. Warden Road, Breach Candy was—and still is—a smart part of what we now call SoBo (South Bombay). Not quite the smartest. That was—is—nearby Malabar Hill, where all the old money lived in splendid Indo-Saracenic detached bungalows. One of the most beautiful of these was Jinnah House, built by the future president of Pakistan, Mohammad Ali Jinnah, who moved out in 1946 following the partition of India to live in Karachi. The mansion became the residence of the British Deputy High Commissioner from 1948 until 1983. It was a splendid place for functions and parties to which Anand and I were often invited.

I was put in a spacious room in the front of the house, opposite an informal sitting room where Anand's middle sister, Chicken, chain-smoked and played cards. From my bedroom window, I could look out over Warden Road and the Maharaja of Wankaner's former palace, which had become the American Consulate in 1957, and beyond that to the sea. I have a vivid recollection of being woken every morning by the loud squawking of crows perched on the open windows. In those days, there were lots of sparrows too, just like in England, but I see very few these days.

The impressive ground floor—entered through an enormous reception room with twelve doors, no windows, marble floors and three huge chandeliers—was empty. Anand's uncle, his father's younger brother, and his wife and their sons occupied the first floor of the house and the back half of the ground floor. Anand's parents and three sisters lived on the second floor, reached by a lift and a main staircase, with the servants' quarters tacked on to the back.

Anand and his three younger sisters had grown up here. Chicken's real name was Mira. She had been a very scrawny baby, resembling a 'murgi' (chicken) according to Janabai, her ayah; the name had stuck. She was about to leave Bombay to study at Hollins College, Virginia, in America. Aged nineteen, Chicken had beautiful, large, deep-set black eyes and wore her thick mane of magnificent hair in a typical sixties beehive. Anand worried that all the backcombing was bad for her hair, which I found rather touching. He never made any comment about my hair.

The youngest, Jill, short for Janki, was at Walsingham School in Bombay. At fifteen, she was a typical teenager, more into clothes, boys and having fun than studies. Once Chicken left for Hollins, and with Anand's sister, Tulsi, in Oxford, Jill and I became close friends. I had first met Tulsi when she arrived in the UK on a scholarship to read PPE at Lady Margaret Hall. Anand asked me to meet her flight in my Mini and drive her to Oxford. We became the best of friends. I always felt so sorry for her, shivering in her freezing room in the college, stuffing the gas meter with coins to heat up the small gas fire. She lived on fried eggs on cold rice, the only 'vegetarian' option. At the end of each term, when Tulsi had to pack her trunk and vacate her room sharpish, she would come to stay with me, camping on the floor in the little rented flat I shared with Ruth in Maida Vale.

At the Warden road house, eight servants lived in, most of them sleeping on bedding-rolls on the floor, each with specific duties. I never got to know the cook or his assistant because they rarely saw daylight, toiling away in the kitchen. Walji, the bearer, was from Gujarat, and he always wore a topee. He laid the table, made breakfast, coffee and tea and washed napkins, and if required, would rustle up a sandwich, a smearing of green chutney made from mushed-up fresh coriander and ginger on white sliced bread. Delicious. Walji also prepared paan, the after-dinner digestif made of betel leaf and areca nut (or so I was told), which he placed in Amru Masi's cloth-lined silver box. Everyone else loved it but I found it absolutely disgusting.

Bansi was Anand's man Friday. He had been a tea boy in the palace across the road until Anand's mother brought him in as a so-called 'companion' for Anand when he was small. He did everything for him, including wearing-in Anand's new shoes. On our honeymoon, I discovered Anand's habit of dropping his clothes on the floor when he changed into his pyjamas. On our return, Bansi remained with Anand's parents, and I had no intention of folding Anand's clothes. Both Anand and I had a lot to learn. Bansi retired quite recently on a pension and returned to his village, having been with the Mehta family for more than sixty years.

Tukeram dusted and cleaned the floors and helped with waiting at table. Each of the girls had had an ayah as a baby, and they had stayed on because they had nowhere else to go. In time, I got to know their sad stories. Janabai, the sweetest of them all, had been thrown out by her husband because she was barren; Shanta had run away from her husband when he took another wife. Big Shanti, a child bride, had been widowed at the age of eleven. She was illiterate but a huge character, and she and my mother-in-law were great friends. It was a case of mutual respect. Despite being unable to read, she also worked as the moneylender in the immediate neighbourhood and could calculate daily compound interest in her head. She was the first person I had ever seen with leukoderma (patchy skin due to depigmentation). All the ayahs wore saris in what I came to recognise as Maharashtrian-style, a vast nine yards hooked up between their legs like a dhoti and, in Shanti's case, wrapped tight around her substantial buttocks. Two drivers, Rama and Anna, a mali and two silent Gurkha watchmen lived in the tiny servants' lean-to rooms above the garage, which still had an enclosure for a cow, a remnant from the days when Anand's grandmother would drink only the milk from her own cow.

Anand spoke to the staff in Hindi or Marathi, whichever they spoke, his tone warm but firm, with no chat. He was not good at either language. Between themselves, his parents spoke Gujarati and English. In the morning, Anand's mother sat in a big carved ebony chair at her telephone table, a semi-circular carved rosewood table now in my flat, the only piece of furniture I wanted from the family house when it was sold recently, because it is such a vivid reminder of her. For at least an hour, she chatted animatedly with her mother and her sisters, peppering Gujarati with English adjectives such as 'lovely' or 'pretty'. Then she summoned the cook to discuss the menu for lunch and dinner. Occasionally, but not often, she would go into the kitchen to vaguely supervise something, such as cleaning the fridge, or call for the upholsterer to measure up new cushions for the drawing room. If new fabric was required, she would shop for it herself, sometimes taking me along. We would be driven to Mangaldas Market, opposite Crawford Market, where she selected what she wanted. The upholsterer would then be summoned to collect it.

One of the many things I was amused by was that there was somebody very specific for each household job, unlike in England, where you did most things yourself; so, the chap who could attach a peg to a door could not also repair a broken leg on a chair, and the person who would run up a petticoat for a sari would not also make new cushions. Consequently, a memsahib's day was happily filled with appointments that generated considerable employment for the local workmen. Amru Masi would talk to all of them about their wives and children and what was happening in their village, and they often told terrible tales of huts collapsing and sick grandmothers; many would ask to borrow money. She would help when she thought it right to do so. Alas, I didn't generate the same amount of employment, preferring to sew my own curtains and fix the peg on the door, ignoring Anand's maxim: 'Never do anything that you can get someone else to do for you.' I love making and mending things.

My parents-in-law spoke beautiful English and, to my shame, knew their Shakespeare and Milton rather better than I did, as well as their British history, which Anand's generation had also been taught at school. I tried my best to learn Hindi, first from Jill's school tutor and then as part of a class for foreign wives, but I didn't make much progress as the household was filled with Marathi and Gujarati, as well as Hindi, and I couldn't make out one from the other. Being dyslexic certainly didn't help.

The house at Warden Road was filled with chatter and comings and goings and to me felt very warm and relaxed. Indian time, I discovered, is much more elastic than British time, but every evening, the family gathered for dinner around the big dining-room table.

I had eaten plenty of Indian food in London because Anand preferred it to a burger and milkshake at a Wimpy Bar. A watery thali lunch cost two shillings at the cafeteria inside the Indian High Commission in the Aldwych across the road from LSE, and I was introduced to dosas at the India Club in the Strand. But my favourite was tandoori chicken, which we ate at one of London's many tandoori restaurants that opened in the early sixties around Warren Street, such as Quality, Gaylord and Taj Mahal. Real Indian food, cooked with fresh spices and fresh herbs rather than the powdered approximations used in England, tasted completely different with many more layers of flavour and much more chilli. Anand's family were vegetarian, though some more strict than others, and Anand cheerfully ate non-veg outside the house. The food was completely different from anything I had eaten in London and luckily, by and large, I loved it. But after a week or two, I found myself dreaming about meat. Anand took pity on me and sent for some chicken curry; Amru Masi permitted it to be served to me. She had been brought up to eat vegetarian food, though she still ate fish occasionally. But her own mother-in-law had not permitted even eggs to be cooked in the main kitchen. They were always prepared for the children in a separate pantry. Gujaratis are oddly ambivalent about eggs, something I have never quite cracked.

The biggest adjustment was how I ate rather than what. In Anand's house, as in nearly all Indian homes, food was served on thalis—the metal trays with katoris for different vegetables and dal or dahi khadi. I had to learn to eat with my right hand but, thankfully, I was given a spoon. Though I soon got the knack of scooping up the vegetables with a bit of chapatti, I have never mastered eating rice with my hand. When my father eventually came to Bombay, thalis delighted him more than almost anything else. The precision and neatness appealed to his sense of order.

On weekdays, Anand went off to work at around 9.30 a.m., which seemed rather slack to me but was normal for India. I often ate breakfast in my pyjamas, looking out over the courtyard at the back where, if I was lucky, I could watch the barbets pecking a hole to make a nest in the lovely old mango tree. Walji would bring me a bowl of skinned grapefruit segments mixed with sugar syrup—I have never eaten such delicious grapefruit since—and a plate of soggy toast and scrambled eggs, which were watery because he cooked them on too high a flame. His masala omelette with tiny chopped onion, tomato, chilli and fresh coriander was much nicer. There was delicious freshly squeezed watermelon juice or sweet lime to drink.

I taught Walji to make tea the way I liked it, with boiling water poured on to the tea, which had been spooned into a teapot (always called a kettle) and served with a jug of cold milk. I have never liked masala chai, but I loved his lassi, flavoured with salt and powdered jeera, rather than the sweet sort. I tried the so-called cornflakes, but they were hard and horrible, nothing like Kellogg's (which didn't start manufacturing in Mumbai until 1994), and in any case, fresh milk was scarce because it was rationed and unpasteurised and had to be boiled—so, a problem on several counts. What's more, I learnt that it came from buffaloes, not cows, which gave it a slightly sweeter taste. India is now the biggest milk producer in the world, but back then, there was a government-run milk distribution system, and a servant would join the 6 a.m. queue to collect the ration. No cheese was made in India, but I didn't miss it because we had had so little during the War anyway. Paneer wasn't a big thing then because of the milk shortage. The only food I ever longed for was all savoury—kippers, or smoked haddock with a poached egg on top, or crispy bacon, or a nice cold cut of ham. I had always enjoyed cooking but was occasionally frustrated by what I couldn't get. Alas, no suet for mince pies at Christmas, and only Indian raisins and sultanas, full of flavour but also with pips.

Toast from bread bought from Bombelli's, the 'Swiss' bakery nearby, spread with butter (a luxury because it was scarce) and lashings of Rose's lime marmalade was pure home away from home. As was crème caramel, one of many items left over from the Raj. I missed Marmite but only until 2017, when it appeared on shelves. Rice and wheat were rationed, but there was never a shortage of Rose's lime marmalade. Or Rose's lime juice cordial for one's gin. Prohibition meant no alcohol, though there was never a shortage of gin and bootlegged whisky in the house. It was important to have a reliable bootlegger because bad stuff could be lethal. A bottle of Scotch whisky cost more than my cook earned in a month. That made me feel terrible because I was very conscious of the fact that my lovely cook Ganpat had a wife and three children in the village, and his elder daughter suffered from rheumatoid arthritis. But we always had one in case we had an important visitor.

Anand returned in the early evening for a cup of tea before driving himself off to the Willingdon Sports Club for a rubber or two of bridge, unless there was a bridge tournament his team was playing in. The Willingdon was another leftover from the Raj, founded in 1918 by a Brit, Lord Willingdon, then Governor of Bombay, when he was refused permission to take an Indian maharaja to any of the British clubs in the city. These days, only the crème de la crème of Bombay society belong, and membership is passed from generation to generation, though top foreign diplomats on postings in the city are allowed membership and charged top dollar for the privilege. Anand might possibly have sacrificed playing bridge for the first two or three days when I arrived, but I am not one hundred per cent sure that he did. For as long as I had known him, he had played contract bridge very seriously—fanatically even—for both the LSE and London University, so I had long been accustomed to being neglected every evening and often at weekends too. His mother, too, was chauffeured to the Willingdon every afternoon to play cards. Her game was high-stakes poker, and when she got much older, rummy. I had never played cards and I was not about to start.

I didn't feel homesick at all for England, or my family, but I did miss the BBC. I couldn't get anything but a crackly Radio Ceylon, the Indian equivalent of Radio Luxembourg, which played a mix of Hindi film songs, some jazz, and the Beatles for an hour or two in the evening. It may surprise many readers, but no one stared at me—a white woman—in the streets. All of us at LSE had rejoiced at the end of Empire, and I had expected to face a barrage of anti-colonialism here. On the contrary, it was all smiles and 'welcome memsahib'. Anand's uncle was one of dozens of people eager to tell me that India had gone to the dogs after the British left and that he wished they would come back and sort things out, install law and order and crush corruption. Anand's grandmother, Motimama, had been part of the Establishment during the Raj, her husband having worked alongside the British as Collector in Benares, Uttar Pradesh. In spite of being steeped in Indian culture, she had adjusted to many British lifestyle habits, including tea poured from a teapot into cups and saucers and served on a tray. The dinner table was prepared for a party with cutlery laid out in order for each course with wine glasses to match. She wore her saris with crocodile leather sandals and a matching handbag, her nod to British style. By the time I came, she had been widowed for years and only wore simple white saris and chappals.

Had Anand come from a lower-middle-class Bombay family, I might have found it very alien, perhaps too strange to have felt at home so readily. But it was home away from home in so many ways, including a shared sense of humour and a shared love of P.G. Wodehouse. I ate at a table and I slept on a bed with a mattress, sheets and pillows, things I took for granted as 'normal' but which I learnt only later were not the norm for the vast majority of Indians.

When Anand had been a small boy, his paternal grandmother celebrated Hindu festivals such as Diwali with everyone sitting on the floor and eating from thalis with a glass placed on the left, because they drank with the left hand. Anand's maternal family were more Westernised because so many of them, as well as their relations and friends, had been abroad to study in England and America. Anand's adventurous parents had also taken the entire family on holiday to Europe and to Japan.

Life in Bombay in the fifties was more lavish for the likes of the Mehtas, with their two gas-guzzling American cars and hot and cold running water, than it had been for us Lancasters in frugal post-War England. When I arrived in the sixties, the atmosphere in Bombay was a world away from the bra-burning and the protests against the Vietnam war that I had left behind in London. Not least because few Indian women wore bras. Or knickers for that matter. Underwear, I soon discovered, was considered unnecessary by many and largely confined to the middle classes.

No one told me what I should do or how to do it. I was encouraged to do exactly what I liked. I stopped wearing white waffle miniskirts and my Mary Quant A-lines very early on because mosquitoes attacked my lily-white legs, leaving them hideously pocked and pink. I had loved my minis, but I quickly clocked that I was the only woman, other than very young or unmarried girls, wearing Western-style short frocks. The moment an Indian girl becomes marriageable, she covers her legs with a salwar-kameez or a sari. I quickly took to wearing trousers and a blouse.

Anand's mother could not have been sweeter to me. She wanted me to be happy, possibly having the good sense to realise that, should I choose not to settle in Bombay, her darling only son might abandon her for me and for England. She welcomed Anand's friends, who dropped in at any time, and we often went to movies in one of the many huge Art Deco cinemas such as the Eros, Liberty or Regal. And so began my introduction to Bollywood movies and stars, such as Raj and Shashi Kapoor, Sharmila Tagore, Dilip Kumar, Asha Parekh and Dev Anand. The television didn't arrive until as late as 1982, and even then, it was only in black and white with one government channel, but there were plenty of Hollywood movies to see, even though the kissing had been censored. I wasn't surprised, because while still in London, I had had to come to terms with Anand's refusal to hold my hand in public. It had bewildered and upset me at first until he explained that any public display of affection was considered improper in India. Indeed, kissing is still considered to be 'obscene' by Indian law. Arrests are rare but it is unusual to see any PDA even between young married couples.

My new friends, Didi and Indu, were eager to show me their city. Didi had studied art at St Martin's in London and Indu was the well-travelled daughter of a delightful Cambridge-educated judge. I was amazed to find much here that seemed familiar. Everywhere, there were echoes of England. The Victoria Terminus, which twenty years after Independence, still had a statue of Queen Victoria, erstwhile Empress of India, on the front, reminded me of St Pancras station. The Gothic law courts were just like Lincoln's Inn, round the corner from LSE. The Rajabai Tower in Bombay University was a mini chip off Big Ben, doubtless the intention of the British architect Gilbert Scott. On little parks and large maidans with burnt, patchy grass, hundreds of barefoot youths, some wielding sticks instead of bats, were simultaneously playing a bewildering number of overlapping cricket games. From the boughs of towering trees, albeit banyans and rain trees rather than the plane trees of London, hung bats, humungous compared to the pipistrelles I was used to. Biggest of all was the ginger Giant Indian Flying Fox, which swooped and screamed at dusk, like something out of a horror film. When my daughter Anjali moved north to Bandra after her marriage, I saw hundreds of these monstrous creatures hanging upside down all day long at certain times of the year from the trees in her compound. Marigolds had never been my favourite flowers in England, but it was oddly reassuring to see their bright orange faces, not sticking out of vases but beheaded and threaded in garlands or afloat in bowls of water.

Occasionally, Amru Masi would say to me: 'Annie darling, I have got lots to do today. I need to buy a bucket.' So, off I went with her to bustling Crawford Market to buy a bucket or, better still, fruit, vegetables, groceries and rare smuggled goods, such as Kraft cheese. Over the entrance to this red-and-buff-coloured Gothic building, she pointed out friezes of Indian rural life made by John Lockwood Kipling, Rudyard's father. Kipling was born in Bombay in 1865 but was sent back to England as a little boy of six and wrote, poor little chap, of being scared by a Bombay chicken, 'a winged monster as big as myself' on the grounds of the Bombay art school where his father was the dean. Somewhere, Kipling mentions the 'far-going Arab dhows' and 'gaily dressed Parsees wading out to worship the sunset' he saw in Bombay, but I have never spotted either.

Of course, much was startlingly unfamiliar. Often, almost surreal, such as the legless grand piano being transported on ten turbaned heads—a sight I'll never forget. The sheer numbers of traders and shoppers crammed into the narrow streets around Crawford Market, each lane specialising in spices, kitchenware, stationery, luggage or clocks. You name it, they sold it. Similarly, Chor Bazaar, where you could buy antiques, which may or may not have been taken from temples or ancient sites, or every imaginable second-hand, third-hand or maybe tenth-hand car part, from an odd door to a single windscreen wiper. Everywhere, there were so many people. Squeezed in behind the stalls were construction sites swarming with women, thin as crickets, in splattered saris. On their heads they carried bowl-shaped containers filled with mixed concrete or piled high with blocks and bricks. When my mother came to Bombay for the first time, the building next door to our bungalow was under construction, and she spent hours gazing at these women as they negotiated the flimsy scaffolding made of bamboo and tied with string. Elsewhere, on pavements and in doorways, I saw rows and rows of still, near lifeless bodies, sleeping in broad daylight.

It took quite some time for me to pluck up the courage to drive my Morris in the market areas, where cars fought for space with pedestrians, bullock carts, three-legged one-eared pye-dogs, the odd lackadaisical holy cow and hundreds of heavy handcarts loaded with bulging sacks and pulled by scrawny men in dhotis. And there, amidst all this chaos, I was astonished to see red double-decker buses making slow progress along the wider roads. I might have been in Piccadilly Circus rather than in Bombay. Nipping between them were dozens of Bombay's idiosyncratic yellow-and-black taxis—'kaali-peelis'—tiny, tinny, motorised wasps, either Ambassadors or an indigenous version of a Fiat 1100 called the Premier President, engaged in a never-ending game of dodgem cars. It was not the organised chaos of the Bombay streets, nor the occasional child defecating on the side of the road, nor the raw eyes of the beggars tapping at the car window, but the deafening sound of the city that made the most immediate and piercing impression. The cacophony of beeping, pooping, blaring, hooting, tooting and honking here was like no other, though it took a while before I could distinguish between the exuberant Mr Toad-style poop-poop and the impatient blaring of a serious road-rager. Once I started driving my beloved Morris, the only thing to wear out early on was its high-pitched and distinctive horn.

It took me a long time to figure out what to do when a pitiful beggar held up a limp baby to my car window. I recoiled from taking a rupee or two from my fat purse full of cash to dole out until one day I saw Vatsal, Tulsi's husband, do just that, explaining that he felt obliged to help a little. After that, I would feel mean if I didn't. And I still do, though there are fewer beggars now.

The population of Bombay in 1966 was a mere five million—today it is more than 20 million—but even then, many parts of the city were already overcrowded, and most streets pulsated with life and noise. As a people person, I revelled in the diversity, the vibrant colours, the sounds and sights, the endlessly different faces and clothes, and the many different trades being touted in the streets. I loved hearing the flute seller, playing expertly as he walked up the street with a quiver of homemade bamboo flutes on his back. From behind, he looked like a porcupine or, to me, Beatrix Potter's Mrs Tiggy-Winkle. The twang of the mattress-seller's long metal hook was a new, strange musical sound, like a vibrating bowstring. He sat plucking out the ancient cement-hard cotton filling, fluffed it up and added new stuffing, leaving it plumped and comfy. The arrival of foam in Bombay in the 1970s has rendered him almost extinct.

It is a long time, too, since I have seen a canewallah, ever ready on the pavement to restore chair seats and chair backs. A high-pitched whine alerts you to the presence of the local knife-sharpening man, still a regular astride his specially adapted bicycle, which pedal-powers the whetstone, sparks spraying like a Catherine wheel. Similarly, nothing has changed about the peripatetic barber with his own chair and the mirror he hangs in the shade of a wall or on a branch of a tree, before sharpening his skinny cut-throat razors and following up a shave with a head massage. There are plenty of shoe-shiners and cobblers resoling shoes, often using rubber from old car tyres. Ear-cleaners are much rarer. The neighbourhood ear-cleaner was always easy to spot in his traditional red turban, carrying a stool and a little satchel filled with tools and potions. I used to watch in horror as he wound a wad of cotton around the tip of a steel pin, dipped it into a bottle of some unknown liquid and proceeded to scrape out the dust and grime from a customer's ears. Not mine. Though I am sure he was expert.

The sound of the double-headed drum played by the monkey-man as he came along Warden Road would send my little daughters running to the gate. For a rupee, he would bring his dancing monkeys dressed in a hat and coat and attached to a piece of string through the gate and into the garden and make them dance for us. Dancing monkeys are no longer commonplace. Nor snake charmers, who appeared on Hindu high days and holidays. I have remained stubbornly resistant to the charms of a musical cobra, but how could I not be captivated by life on the streets?

Most workmen of every trade had a rolled bidi leaf between their stained teeth. Others chewed paan, which contained a corrosive and carcinogenic mix inside the rolled betel leaf and which they eventually spat out in an expert arc. I tried it once; never again. It accounted for the bloody looking splatter on every pavement and wall in Bombay, like the scene of a brutal crime, despite the numerous signs saying, 'No spitting'. There are fewer paan-sellers now, possibly because of the massive gory posters illustrating the monstrous mouth cancer it causes. India remains the oral cancer capital of the world.

There were few tourists in Bombay in those days because foreign exchange controls were strict. UK citizens, like me, were allowed to bring £20 out of England with them, which didn't go far even in dirt-cheap India. I had searched for a guidebook to Bombay before I left London, something to explain some of the sights, smells, sects and superstitions I encountered on every street. In vain. Travelling in India was challenging and finding a good hotel even more so. Goa got its first five-star hotel in 1974, and tourism took off properly only in the eighties. The Beat Generation poet Allan Ginsberg had come here in the early sixties, in search of the mystic and exotic and some sort of understanding of God, as well as to experiment with drugs. He found it to be more like a shabby Victorian-era London with some Art Deco edges, but he did get to hang out with some Marathi poets who took him to a real opium den. The hippy trail in India only got going in 1968 when the Beatles famously came to learn transcendental meditation at the ashram of the Maharishi Mahesh Yogi up in Rishikesh. But the Beatles themselves were already well known in Bombay. I was able to buy their latest single—'Eleanor Rigby', I think—at Rhythm

House, a wonderfully hip record store in Kala Ghoda, where you could listen to music on headphones in booths. Alas, Rhythm House stands empty now having been sold to the jeweller Nirav Modi. Soon after, he fled the country to escape the long arm of the law for defaulting on vast loans taken from an Indian bank, and he is now languishing in prison in London, fighting to escape extradition back to Mumbai to stand trial.

Before my marriage, having accompanied Amru Masi on her errands, we usually finished up at her mother Motimama's old bungalow on Malabar Hill. Moti means big—actually, it means fat—though not in this case. At five-foot nothing, Motimama was the *tallest* in her family of miniature women. She lived with her only son, Kumi Mama, and his wife Vasu Mami, and her two divorced daughters, Moon Masi and Nandini Masi, which was unusual because divorced women in India are frequently shunned by their families. Not the Mehtas, fortunately. Motimama's third daughter, Pupul Masi, lived in Delhi with her husband, Jaki Masa, and they owned a flat across the road, where they stayed on their frequent visits to Mumbai.

After a morning of shopping or visits, we used to go back to Warden Road for a lunch of dal and rice. After lunch, everyone in the house, including the servants, settled down for a siesta, which in parts of India is something taken rather seriously, not only by the rich, who don't need to work, but by farmers, shopkeepers and housewives too. In Goa, which was a Portuguese colony for more than 450 years before its liberation in 1961, the shops still close, European-style, for two hours after lunch. I found this very annoying when trying to shop for all the things I needed for the house we built there in 1995.

When I first arrived, it was summer and very hot indeed, and the heat made me sleepy. But I have never been one for afternoon naps, so I read a book and often ended up falling asleep anyway. To this day, I never sleep in the afternoon.

I couldn't enjoy walking as I found the pavements too crowded and the sun too hot to walk until later in the evening, as the sun went down. Then I would love strolling along the waterfront from Chowpatty beach to Nariman Point. I have always loved the sea, and even in the heat, this boulevard somehow breathed in the way the coast always does. It gives this frenetic city its lungs. At one end is Wilson College, a typically English Victorian Gothic building. Then there is the scruffy Taraporewala Aquarium, which I have still not visited, and then dozens of pastel-painted Art Deco apartment blocks built in the thirties, with balconies from which the lucky residents could—still can—watch the sun drop into the sea at night. Some are lovingly restored, others are stained and mouldy, battered by the monsoon rain and shamefully neglected. Further along, Marine Drive, known as the Queen's Necklace because of all the lights that make it sparkle from dusk, never fails to exhilarate. People say it's the second-longest stretch of Art Deco buildings in the world, bettered only by Miami. I've never been there, but I don't believe Bombay could be upstaged. However, all this is changing now with the coastal road under construction from Colaba up to the distant northern suburbs. Hated though it is by most of those living in South Mumbai, it's decades overdue and, along with the metro lines being built and the many connecting highways, essential for a rapidly expanding and already overcrowded city.

The Bombay streets were seething in the sixties, though there was possibly less colour then than there is now. I had left a London where the palate was fifty shades of grey. The sky, the rain-stained pavement, the coats, the shivering faces. India woke me up to colour, and it is probably what I love most about it. Never have I seen two people dressed in identical saris.

I have always admired the way in which even the poorest people come out of the slums looking so neat and clean, the schoolgirls in pristine uniforms, their thick, glossy hair neatly plaited and tied with bows. My little daughter Anjali once came running up to me with tears pouring down her cheeks saying, 'I don't have plaits. How can I ever go to school?' Long plaits seemed to be an essential part of the school uniform in the sixties.

Working men invariably wore white starched cotton shirts. I recognised them from V.S. Naipaul's description in *An Area of Darkness*: 'The hundreds of thousands who poured in a white stream in and out of Churchgate station as though hurrying to and from an endless football match.' Indeed, Anand wore a white shirt with white drill trousers, which, like all his clothes, were stitched by his darzi, the family tailor. There were no washing machines. A dhobi collected the household washing once a week, bundled it in a blanket that he balanced on his bicycle and pedalled off to the Dhobi Ghats, the world's largest open-air laundry.

Built in 1890 by the British, it gives a new spin to the notion of washing one's dirty linen in public. In row after row of concrete washing pens, each with its own flogging stone, 5,000 men (you have to be male and born there to work there) pounded the city's laundry and hung it out to dry on thousands of washing lines. Powdered detergent and bleach could be bought by the ounce, weighed out in little bags. A dark blue powder called Blue was added to the final rinse to create the dazzling whiteness.

Presswallahs slogged away with weighty coal-filled irons for a rupee per shirt. Somehow our clothes, none with a nametape, found their way back to the house, delivered on a towering pile precariously balanced on a bicycle rack. Fewer saris and more jeans are washed today, but the Dhobi Ghats remain largely unchanged, a medieval and miraculous business, possibly run by some sort of mafia. I don't know this for a fact, and I should be shot if I am pointing fingers! All I can say is that one could not buy a new washing machine in India until many years later. After my second daughter was born, I managed to buy a second-hand twin tub. Until then, my ayah Julie literally beat the dirt out of our dirtiest clothes with a large wooden block with a handle.

That first May in Bombay, the entire family decamped to Anand's aunt's tea estate, Glendale near Coonoor, high in the Nilgiri Hills in Tamil Nadu. In their magnificent bungalow, built in 1880 by a British planter, I might just as well have been in England. Familiar flowers were in full bloom around the manicured lawn where tea was served in English china. From there, Anand and I and a couple of his friends, regarded as chaperones by his parents, were driven in the Plymouth by Rama back to Bombay via Mysore and Bangalore. Thundery showers battered the vivid orange-blossomed gulmohar trees lining the roads, turning the pavements into ginger mud. When the car broke down on the way, we spent a sleepless night in a roadside inn. There was no bed linen on the rusty iron bedstead. I heard rats scuttling all night. It was called a hotel, but it was a hovel. It was one of the most challenging nights of my life, a true test of my ability to adapt to life in India.

We arrived back in Bombay in early June, and it was now unbearably hot and sticky. I had been assured that the monsoon always started by 20 June when colleges reopened. But that day came and went, so did the rest of June, and there was no sign of rain. With potential disaster looming, there was talk of evacuating 'non-essential categories'—which meant women and children—from Bombay. But where to? The drought in the villages was even more serious than in the city. I learnt then what it was like to look up at a cloudless sky and feel terrified. Everywhere, people were doing pujas with mounting panic, pleading with the rain gods to precipitate a downpour. The fear was almost palpable. I vowed never to take water for granted again.

Nearly two months had passed, and I liked Bombay well enough. Now I had to decide whether I could spend the rest of my life here. Then, one day, I caught myself singing, '*Ae dil hai mushkil, jeena yahan, zara hatke, zara bachke, yeh hai Bombay, meri jaan,'* a song from *C.I.D*, a Hindi movie, which translates as 'Oh my heart, it's very difficult to live here, be careful, be warned, this is Bombay, my love', which had recently become the city's unofficial anthem. Was it because it was sung to the familiar British tune of 'Oh my darling Clementine' or that Bombay was beginning to get under my skin? Both, perhaps. My only worry was boredom. I didn't even have to make my own bed, never mind shop or cook. As a dyslexic, I've never been a big reader. As a girl, I had spent hours playing the piano and making silly crafty things such as sandals out of raffia or cooking. Here, there was no piano, nothing to make, and no place for me in the well-staffed kitchen. I found myself wondering if I could be happy living here long-term. I must have wondered about this out loud at some stage, and possibly even grumbled about being abandoned, because Anand suddenly told me with a smarting frankness that if I was to marry him, I would have to make my own life here and not rely on him for company since he would be busy with work and bridge and had no intention of changing his habits. It stung at the time, but once I recovered, I felt grateful that he had called a spade a spade—exactly what you would expect from a bridge champion.

In a flash, the two months of leave from my work in London was up, and I was still uncertain about committing to living in Bombay. One of my overriding concerns was where we would live. When Anand's father told me that a flat would be created for us out of the empty ground floor of Warden Road, my heart sank. The thought of living under the same roof as one's in-laws was anathema to a girl like me. At home in London, my impoverished newly married friends, Caroline and Amanda, were living in tiny, rented flats, with babies sleeping in drawers. It was testing for them but at least there was no one snooping or listening or bossing them around. Anand's dear father saw my face crumple, and he explained that renting a flat was prohibitively expensive in Bombay. Should Anand and I marry, he said, we could try living in Warden Road for a year before committing ourselves. He didn't add that I should consider myself extremely fortunate because most Bombay brides, even well-off ones, move into a modest bedroom in their in-laws' already overcrowded flat or, if less well-off, sleep like sardines next to sisters, brothers, parents, grandparents, nieces and nephews. There is no such thing as privacy in Bombay. I decided I needed longer to make up my mind.

I can't remember when I did eventually do so. Somehow both of us just drifted into certainty. Anand didn't go down on one knee and give me a ring. I always say he just assumed I would marry him, and he was right, as he always is! We became engaged on 16 July. His parents were delighted but not surprised. I had stayed for so long that I suppose they had taken our marriage for granted. The rains arrived on the eighteenth. Like a blessing. I was booked to fly back on the twentieth, and I suddenly realised that I would need a ring to go home to England as proof of my engagement. But engagement rings are not traditional in India. There was no romantic trip to the jewellers to choose a ring. Instead, Anand turned to his mother and said: 'Ma, give her a ring.' And from my future mother-in-law's glittering jewellery box, I chose a marquise diamond in a simple setting, so traditional it might have come from London's Burlington Arcade. I boarded a flight back to London two days later.

There had not been a lightbulb moment. Just a calm, firm realisation of my love for Anand and how much I liked India and Indians. I had already found out that you only have to smile at an Indian in Bombay and you've got a friend for life, be he the banana-seller squatting under a tree or the chowkidar outside the Consulate across the road. It was a world away from British reserve, and I felt at home.

But I knew I had to find something useful to do here. I had loved my job as a social worker, and I had not been brought up to be a lady of leisure. I needed to find a sense of purpose. I needed to be needed.

3

Mothers-in-Law

WHEN I WAS GROWING UP IN ENGLAND IN THE FIFTIES, THE WIFE'S disapproving or overbearing mother was a mainstay of harmless if tasteless and sexist low-grade comedy, the butt of endless bad jokes.

In Bombay, I quickly discovered that mothers-in-law are no joking matter. It may sound like an absurdly sweeping statement but I truly believe that Indian sons are invariably Mummy's Boys, overindulged and over-entitled. Being a good son is infinitely more important than being a good husband. But an even bigger problem for any wife is that when she marries an Indian man, she marries his mother as well. And it is with her that all happiness rests.

In some big business families with lots of sons, there is a vast extended family of married sons with wives and children all living under the same roof, eating together and sharing a kitchen, with the sons' mother ruling a very large roost and holding a very important position within the family, which she can exploit. Often, she stirs up trouble and rivalry between the daughters-in-law, but she can also keep the peace, as in the fantastically bitter feud, well-documented in the papers, between the richest men in India, Mukesh and Anil Ambani. Following the death of their rags-to-unbelievable-riches father, Dhirubhai, in 2002, their mother famously sorted them out. In the absence of the patriarch, the matriarch had taken over. As Indians would see it, the family may be fractured—but it was not broken.

My friend Veena had been a well-paid physiotherapist before she married and was told by her mother-in-law that she could no longer work because she was needed to look after her husband's elderly grandmother and his sick aunt who lived with them. She was not allowed to go out alone. Her mother-in-law was a Bollywood cliché, a sari-clad battle-axe who routinely tyrannises and humiliates the timid young bride who has come to live under her roof. The girl is never good enough for her Baba. She is not pretty enough. She smiles too much and, unforgivably, reveals her teeth. She can't cook. She fails to touch her mother-in-law's feet first thing every morning. Her mother-in-law never fails to remind her of her flaws.

Another friend, Pushpa, married into a strict Gujarati family at the tender age of sixteen, also had a classic domineering mother-in-law. While Pushpa was happy to knuckle down to the domestic chores, she didn't get pregnant immediately, which put a strain on her relationship with her mother-in-law. Failure to conceive is always the fault of the daughter-in-law, never the Baba's. My own lovely mother-in-law couldn't resist glancing at my stomach whenever we met until the day I told her, two years later, that I was pregnant. Pushpa's miserable early years were made mildly less so by the companionship of her two unmarried sisters-in-law still living at home and of a similar age. Some aspects of the extended family can turn out to be an unexpected salvation.

Pushpa 'redeemed' herself in her mother-in-law's eyes eight years later by producing a baby, then three more and, fortunately for her, two of them were boys. Once the children were at school, I asked her to come and teach sewing at Apnalaya, the charity I later got involved with. Her mother-in-law insisted that she get home by midday, in time to put lunch on the table. (Which reminded me, in a bad way, of my own father's jealous insistence that my mother return from visiting her sisters in London in time to make his supper.) Pushpa didn't complain. She was home by noon each day, on the dot. She had no choice.

I hadn't known Pushpa for long when she showed me an evergreen house plant with sharp leathery leaves, which I had often seen and never liked. It is believed that its leaves miraculously purify the air and are poisonous to insects. Its juice causes a rash on one's skin. Apparently, it thrives in a dark corner, requiring little light, water or feeding. Its common name is Mother-in-law's Tongue, which, to my mind, makes its name simultaneously appropriate and inappropriate. Many of the Indian mothers-in-law I've met deserve their reputation for being prickly. Some have tongues that can be lacerating and truly toxic. All tend to be feared, but I suspect that few like to be stuffed into a dark corner and ignored.

When I arrived in Bombay in the sixties, I met a handful of foreign women living here with their Indian husbands, including Jinx from New York and Iddamarie from Switzerland, all blessed with easy-going mothers-in-law with whom they lived happily, which is why they are still here sixty years on. My German friend, Helga, had a more formidable, controlling mother-in-law who insisted on continuing to choose clothes for her thirty-year-old married son and for her grandchildren. Helga returned to Germany, taking her husband with her.

Few Indian women have that option. I used to take lunch into JJ Hospital for Anjali when she was working in what was known as the Suicide Ward, but is actually the burns ward, filled with pitiable women, many with blackened flesh. It still haunts me. Some had set fire to themselves because the mother-in-law made their life unbearable. Others were set alight by the mother-in-law because their dowry was less than promised or they didn't get pregnant or produced only girls. These injuries and, often, deaths, were always called 'accidental'. It is, after all, easy for the kerosene stove on an uneven floor on which the mothers-in-law is cooking to be knocked over inches from the daughter-in-law's sari, which 'accidentally' catches fire. Through my work for Apnalaya, I've come across women who have been pushed into prostitution by their mother-in-law in order to supplement the family income. I was lucky in so many ways. My mother-in-law, Amru Masi, did everything imaginable to welcome me into the family. Partly because she was a genuinely sweet person but also because she knew that if I was unhappy, I might flee, taking her darling Baba with me. I knew better. If pressed, Anand would have put his mother before me. I knew that he would never, ever, under any circumstances, leave India. His obligation to his family was, from the get-go, stronger than his obligation to me. I was the outsider. In India, the family is solid, impregnable, and nothing and no one, especially a young woman from a foreign country, must be allowed to threaten it. A son stays with his mother not just physically, under her roof, but also emotionally.

I accepted this early on and without resentment. Anand loved me and he loved England, but he could never have settled there. He loved his mother and India first. Not better, perhaps, but first. He did not pretend otherwise. He was also working for his father, which added more layers of co-dependence and complication. One of the many reasons I fell in love with Anand was that he always made his feelings clear while being simultaneously laidback. From the moment we met, it was obvious that he was different from the white upper-middle-class, grey-legged, conventional, public-school types I had been expected to marry. When I joined LSE, the whole world opened up to me, and I was soon good friends with Michael from Nigeria; Tony, who was Chinese and from Singapore; African-American Waldo from New Orleans; and West Indians Bert and Bert's friend Jacques, through whom

I met Anand. It may sound like an absurd generalisation, but I have loved nearly all the West Indians I have ever met because they were so laidback, loved music, rhythm and dancing, all my favourite things. Sachin aside, Brian Lara has always been my favourite cricketer, and one of the greatest thrills of my life was meeting him. He is absolutely gorgeous.

When my friend Caroline met Anand for the first time, a couple of years after we married, she said I had fallen in love with him because of his Indian eyes. She was partly right. It was also his legs. Anand's legs were fabulous and they still are, and he is over eighty. English men's legs have never appealed to me. They are greyish-blue, flecked with black hairs and not improved by the knobby knees so many have. At least, that's how they were in my day. Indian men's legs are straight and long and brown, for those who are not carrying too much weight. Their hands are even better. Soft, narrow, slender, made for slipping through bangles. As for Indian skin, it's smoother and less lined. I also envy Indian hair, so thick and strong compared to mine.

In sharp contrast to my father and brothers, Anand has never felt the need to assert himself. I have never heard him shout or lose his temper. He has always been happy in his own skin. Perhaps because he has seldom been crossed. He excelled academically; he played cricket for LSE's second team and bridge for the University of London, but he has always been quietly competitive rather than noisily cut-throat. As were all his Bombay friends.

Anand calmed me down. One day, when we were students in London, my scooter disappeared while we were seeing a movie near Liverpool Street station. I loved my Vespa. It had cost me £50 and was my most precious possession. I got terribly het up and burst into tears. 'Getting upset isn't going to help,' said Anand, snippily. 'Either you will get your scooter back—or you will never see it again. Crying won't make a difference.' It was a lesson to me. It's a Hindu thing, I think. Anand is more accepting because he knows that he is not so powerful that he can change the course of history. His cards, my cards, everyone's cards, have been dealt. If the gods have ordained that my scooter has been stolen, then so be it. That is the way Anand has lived his life, resisting futile confrontation and only fighting battles he can be certain he will win. Incidentally, I got my scooter back a few days later.

Anand had a very uncomplicated relationship with his mother, whom he simply adored. I found her easy to love from the start. She never made me feel beholden or inadequate. She often said: 'Annie darling, you are like a daughter to me,' and she truly made me feel beloved.

She had not been so fortunate. Her mother-in-law had been the stereotypical, restrictive, controlling, bitter old dragon who would not let her paint, play tennis or sing bhajans. Amru Masi obeyed her own mother-in-law to the letter while under her roof—and then disappeared every afternoon to the Willingdon Club, ostensibly for tea but actually to play poker. With considerable success. Being a good card-player is in Anand's genes, inherited by Anjali. When she met Sachin, she taught him to play several card games, but she always won—a result that Sachin, who is highly competitive, never enjoyed.

I have been astonished that even when an Indian lives on a different continent from his parents, they continue to exert a major force on his life. Indian children—especially sons—take it for granted that parents will take care of them when they are young and until they marry or start earning. In return, they will look after the parents when they are old, sending money from abroad, visiting several times a year, dropping everything and catching the next flight over if a parent is ill. With no social security in India, the family is its own welfare system. In 2007, a law was introduced that made daughters as well as sons legally bound to take financial responsibility for their elderly parents. It was partly done to encourage parents to value their daughters more. The law, called the Maintenance and Welfare of Parents and Senior Citizens Bill, also includes grandsons and granddaughters. In 2018, it was amended to make sons-in-law and daughters-in-law similarly responsible for their parents and in-laws. But I don't think many people know about this law because, in India—to my mind—no one takes much notice of laws unless it suits them. Traditionally, when the daughter marries, her parents wash their hands of all obligations. From then on, she 'belongs' to her husband's family. That is why, in the villages, so many girls, regarded as just another mouth to feed, are married off as children, in spite of the legal age being eighteen for girls. Moves are now being made for this to be raised to twenty-one. It is already twenty-one for boys. That law was made in 1978, updating the Sarda Act made in British India in 1929, which permitted marriage for girls of fourteen and for boys of eighteen.

I soon learnt—and it was quite a lesson—that every sensible Indian wife tries her best to reach a modus vivendi with her mother-in-law. I seldom heard daughters-in-law complain. The interdependency seems to be part and parcel of life. Some will sink; others will swim. I floundered a couple of times. Once, I came home from a holiday to find that my mother-in-law had completely reorganised the space outside my kitchen. It was a tiny thing, but impossible not to regard as a criticism of the way I did things. At the time, it was difficult for me to understand why I felt so angry, and I knew that if I told Anand, he would side with his mother, so I didn't say a word. No Indian wife can afford to forget that every man is, first and foremost, a son, and only after that a husband. Even Anjali has had to accept this in her marriage to Sachin. I dared to stand up to my mother-in-law when she wanted Anjali's ears to be pierced as a newborn baby, for I considered it barbaric. I suspect that I was only able to summon that courage because it concerned Anjali, not me.

In another instance, when Anjali was a baby and not yet walking, Amru Masi cut up an old sari and made her a chanya choli, a little top and a long skirt for her to wear on her birthday. I was exasperated because a child can't crawl in a long skirt. Many years later, she used what I thought of as unnecessary pressure to make Anjali wear a white Gujarati sari for her wedding. Anjali was her first grandchild to marry, and she bought a beautiful traditional white sari with a gold border, which she wanted her to wear with festoons of family jewels, Gujarati-style. After all, she said, Anjali was getting married from the house of a Gujarati family of note and should do things properly. 'Wear it for my sake, just to please your old grandmother,' she wheedled. Anjali resisted. She was marrying a Maharashtrian and wanted to get married in the Maharashtrian style, in red, yellow, orange or green, not white, and with just a few simple gold necklaces rather than decked in diamonds and emeralds. Anjali put her foot down and I supported her, and on the day she looked radiant in a traditional red Paithani sari. Amru Masi got over it. There is a marvellous photograph of Anjali's grandmothers and Sachin's grandmothers, four little old ladies together at the wedding. His mother's mother was stone deaf and spoke only Marathi, yet somehow managed to communicate with my English-speaking mother. Smiling went a long way, as it always does in India. Sachin's father's mother was called Moti Moti Aaji, and her body was bent at a right-angle. There were no surviving grandfathers.

When some Indian women get married, I was told that even visiting their own family is discouraged by their husband's family. However, it is universally 'permitted' for the daughter-in-law to return to her mother for forty days following the birth of her first child so that the daughter can be nurtured, given the right food and taught how to manage the baby. In some communities, staying under the same roof as your married daughter even for a short visit is considered improper. My friend Indu, a Mathur from Delhi, lived in Bombay with her husband, as did two of her three sisters. When visiting her from Delhi, her very proper, traditional father—a Cambridge-educated retired judge—always stayed in a hotel rather than with one of his daughters.

Sachin's mother had become so disabled by the time Sara was born that she could not hold a baby, never mind care for her as she would have liked to. I worried, unnecessarily as it turned out, that she would resent the fact that we were more involved with Sachin and Anjali and Sara than she was because we often accompanied them on holidays or on tour to help with the children. We have, in fact, had some wonderful holidays in Australia and South Africa. While Sachin was playing in a Test match, we would take the children on a trip elsewhere so that he wasn't disturbed. Had Anjali married someone else and lived a more traditional life, I don't believe that our relationship with Sara and Arjun would have been anywhere as close. Because Sachin was off playing cricket when they were little, we all lived in a strange bubble.

Anjali and Sachin spent their early marriage in a flat one floor down from Sachin's parents, so they saw lots of Sara in the first couple of years. Sadly, Sachin's father died before Arjun was born. Shortly afterwards, Sachin and Anjali moved into a new, spacious flat, taking Sachin's mother with them. Later on, they moved into their own house, where she has a room on the ground floor and 24-hour nursing care under Anjali's watchful eye, with family and friends constantly visiting. Until the Covid-19 lockdown, Sachin's brother Ajit came over every night to spend time with her, usually eating dinner in her room. As a boy, before Sachin went off to school or to play cricket, he would always go into his mother's room and touch her feet and say goodbye. He still does, first thing in the morning and when he leaves the house. My grandson Arjun, too. He often spends time in her room in quiet companionship, lying on the sofa at the foot of her bed, gaming or watching cricket on his cell phone. Even though she seldom leaves the room, and Anjali runs the household, she is free to invite whoever she wishes to stay, and informs the kitchen of the numbers to be catered for. Anjali would never overrule her. It is the Indian way.

Perhaps it's because of the lack of privacy in India, but I have never felt truly alone here. Even as a newly-wed, my bedroom was not considered sacrosanct. 'Bed tea' would be brought in by the servant every morning without so much as a knock on the door. Ditto when I came home from the hospital with my newborn and was breastfeeding in bed.

In the same way, I have had to come to terms with the idea of sharing and joint ownership. I realised very quickly that within a typically Indian extended family, there is no clear-cut ownership of space or possessions. Seven family members owned 'our' house in Warden Road. It was like the Church of the Holy Sepulchre in Jerusalem, which is shared by multiple Christian communities—Catholic, Coptic, Syriac Orthodox and Armenian—each with much in common but also their own particular idiosyncrasies. When we went there in 1987, we were told that even something as simple as changing a lightbulb had to be debated at length by all concerned. Here, bank accounts were—and are—joint accounts. Some of Anand's were shared with a parent or a sister or two. I had no idea if the furniture in our flat belonged to us or if Anand shared it with his parents and sisters. Even children were shared. Anjali was my mother-in-law's first grandchild, so the first child of the next generation. I never felt that she was truly mine because she seemed to be everybody's—the whole extended household, including maids and drivers and malis. I felt very low down in the pecking order when it came to rights over my own child. It was hard, but again, I had to deal with it.

The grandparent-grandchild relationship is a special one—or can be—but perhaps it's even more special in India. It certainly is for Anand and me, and for Sara and Arjun. The younger generation happily spend time with the elderly because they have grown up with, and sometimes been brought up by, grandparents and great-grandparents. My friend Shanta, the first president of Apnalaya, was eighteen when she married Prem. He was studying in America, so Shanta joined him. Dimpu was born within a year and sent back to India to be brought up by his grandmother, Shanta's mother-in-law, while she went to Johns Hopkins and Prem took up a job. Dimpu didn't live with his parents until he was twelve, when they returned to India and his younger sister was born. He was no less loving or dutiful a son as a result.

In India, it seems very normal for grandparents to stand in for parents. When Anand's sister Tulsi was widowed, she brought her children back to our house in Warden Road, and my mother-in-law then had four grandchildren to enjoy. Physically, she didn't do much for them, any more than she had when her own children were small, and she had ayahs to help, but she loved having them around. Anand's sister Jill had a daughter quite late in life, and as a child Aliya always came to our house after school and stayed until Jill collected her after work. She too grew up in our house with Anand's mother supervising. Had she grown up in England, Aliya would have been sent to boarding school or cared for by an au pair.

Recently, I heard the actor Rupert Everett on '*Desert Island Discs*' discuss the 'heart-breaking experience' of being sent to boarding school at the age of seven. 'It cauterises some emotional thing,' he said. 'I think these schools were made for Empire because they calcified the hearts of the Empire rulers. They would never be as hurt again as they were hurt by the abandonment of their parents.' Which is my opinion exactly, and why I wouldn't have dreamt of sending Anjali to boarding school. Being brought up with grandparents is, I think, the best thing about living with your in-laws here in India. They are older, calmer versions of parents, and a child raised by his or her grandparents will not, in my opinion, feel hurt or abandoned by absent parents. And they love their parents nonetheless. Look at Dimpu. When his mother developed dementia, he moved her into a flat in the same compound as his in Delhi. He provides 24-hour care for her and also visits her each day.

My own mother-in-law was a loving and proud grandmother but, to my dismay, she didn't quite 'get' the babysitting thing. The first time I wanted to go out after Tara was born was to the wedding of a close friend. She agreed to babysit Anjali and Tara. When I got back, she had gone to the Willingdon Club to play cards, leaving her maid to put the children to bed, which was fine, but she was unable to read them a story, which was not.

After the initial shock of sharing a roof with the in-laws, I began to enjoy the advantages. My parents-in-law were out of sight but available and useful if I decided, for example, to host a coffee morning or have a party, and needed to borrow three dozen cups and saucers or fifty glasses. Unlike my servants, my mother-in-law never barged into my flat without knocking and calling out 'Annie darling, can I come in?' and waiting until I answered before doing so. When she was ill, it was so easy for me to take up cauliflower cheese, her favourite dish, or some nourishing soup. The day she died, she was feeling unwell, so I made her cauliflower cheese at eight o'clock and she ate it all up. Sadly, she expired—as they always say in India—within a couple of hours. I hope she took with her fond memories of my cooking.

Certainly, she was never lonely. There was always a daughter or two—or me—for company. These days, when rich Mumbaikars downsize from the shared family bungalow, they often buy flats in the same building so that the upstairs/

downstairs arrangement continues. If they can share a front door and then go their separate ways, so much the better, not least because there are considerable tax advantages. No wonder there are few care-homes for the elderly in India. Indian families take care of their own. Though that is changing too. For the worse, I believe. Retirement homes or 'senior living residences' are getting more popular.

Early on, when Sachin and Anjali moved to their lovely flat in Bandra, he asked us to live with them. We were happy where we were in Warden Road, so we declined. When Sachin built his own house, he not only created a room for his mother but another for us. Before we too moved to Bandra, we often stayed the night, but now we live nearby, and his niece or aunts sometimes use 'our' room.

Indian homes are always open to relatives who need a roof. If the rooms are full, then space is found on a floor. When we were thinking of selling the family house in South Mumbai, Sachin offered us his flat in Bandra where we have lived very comfortably ever since. Who could ask for a sweeter, more caring son-in-law? And how different from England. When my father died in England, my friends in Bombay could not understand why my mother did not immediately move in with one of her two sons, choosing instead to live alone until she died a month shy of her ninety-ninth birthday. I don't think the thought of inviting her occurred to either my brothers or to my mother.

Nor do I believe that my mother would have wanted it. In a very British way, she valued her independence, and fortunately my father had left her comfortably off. And even if he hadn't, at least her medical care would have been free in the UK. Whatever age you are in India, medicines and doctors' bills soak up much of the average income. Recently, the son of my driver's cousin-brother needed two surgeries on his deformed hand. We helped, but so did my driver, who has next to nothing to spare.

Whenever someone in my office needs something urgently, such as the deposit for a place in school for their child or a train fare to visit a sick relative, everyone chips in with what they can. There is no moaning and groaning. A person asks for help loudly and clearly, and graciously and gratefully accepts it. Usually with thanks implicit rather than spoken out loud.

In my experience, people will readily ask for money but won't trust one another with their more intimate secrets, possibly because they know that it will not remain a secret for much longer. That's because everyone has a mother or a sister or someone they play cards with, and even if people think telling just one person isn't breaking a confidence, in a flash, someone's private troubles become the talk of the town. Having been trained in counselling in England, I personally believe it is usually best to unload one's burdens and bring problems out into the open. At least, up to a point. But that is not always the way here.

Only once has Anjali discussed her marriage with us. She has always shared her concerns about the children, but even that is quite unusual in India. In Apnalaya, we opened a counselling service for drug addicts—but nobody came, because they didn't want to be seen going to a place with 'Counselling Centre' written above the door. We discovered that the best way to get someone talking was on a street corner, never at home or at a place where they could be identified as having a problem.

The first time I went to California to see my sister, I got the impression that everyone was terribly self-obsessed and all too willing to share their addiction/depression/obsessive compulsive disorder with anyone who would listen. India is the reverse of that. The lack of personal property, wealth and financial independence may not in itself be a good thing and the strong influence of the family can be stifling, but it often means that there is always someone willing to help. While few in India live alone, or die alone, things are changing here with the breakup of the joint family, people living in smaller homes, and migration. The only person I know who lives alone is my ninety-seven-year-old Parsi friend whose children live abroad.

If Anand's family hadn't spoken good English, I would have of course found it much tougher to fit in. I am a hopeless linguist, and though I can muddle through in Hindi now, my fluency doesn't stretch to conversations about politics or complex emotional issues—not that these are much discussed. Had Anjali not learnt Marathi in order to be a doctor, she would never have had a proper conversation with her mother-in-law. My sister-in-law, Tulsi, could barely communicate with her mother-in-law, who spoke only Tamil while Tulsi spoke Hindi and English. My other sister-in-law managed rudimentary French with her Arabic and French-speaking Lebanese mother-in-law. By the time I met nineteen-year-old Sachin, his English was perfect, and by the time he and Anjali married, I had seen more of him than most mothers-in-law because he had spent so much time with us in Warden Road. Not that I feel I know Sachin in a personal way even now. I know he is gentle. I know he is honest. He is a wonderful husband, father and son-in-law. But he is such a private person that I think only Anjali really knows him. Real heart-to-heart conversations are seldom, though once, when he and I were driving back from dropping Anjali and the children at Heathrow for their return trip to India, he told me that he would have loved to have had four children of his own; however, it would have been a bad example to others in India, where people are told to have no more than two. Like Prince Harry. And I agreed. Car journeys are very good for candid conversations for two reasons: both parties can avoid eye contact and neither party can escape. That includes mothers-in-law.

4

Caste, Creed and Colour

MY MOTHER SAID THAT VISITING INDIA WAS LIKE GOING BACK IN TIME to the village in England where she grew up. Social and financial distinctions were clear and rigid and everyone knew their place. She was always convinced that the woman on the local telephone exchange listened in on everyone's conversations and knew precisely what was going on in every single household. Indian villages are still like that. Everyone knows who you are, what caste and sub-caste you belong to, and what you are up to. Funnily enough, my convent-educated mother observed that both Hindus and Catholics expressed themselves through the little shrines to deities that people have in their houses, to which flowers would be brought, and by observing all the special feast days or festivals when everyone had a day off at school. There is, however, a major difference between class in the UK and caste in India. The 1944 Education Act in the UK made it possible to move out of one class and into another through education. These days, an exceptionally fortunate Indian can move from poverty into relative wealth—but no Hindu can move out of the caste they have been born into.

I describe myself as liberal, Westernised and socialist; to my mind, caste is the dark side of Hinduism. It seems that caste in India is a bit like social class in Britain in the 1920s, but much more pernicious as Hindus are born into a caste that determines their status, their occupation and, most of all, their marriage options. Hindus appear to know instinctively what caste everyone is because it is so integral to daily life. I seldom know and I don't really care. When I asked Anand about caste, his answer was, why on earth was I interested. Caste, he explained, was of no consequence whatsoever to him or his family. My own fundamental belief is that everyone is equal. No one can claim to be socially superior to anyone else. Morally superior? Perhaps.

I had never thought about caste before I came to India, so I was appalled the first time I heard about a Brahmin priest running off to bathe because the shadow of a servant from the lowest caste had fallen on him. And astonished. I simply could not work out what was going on. Anand sighed and told me that there would always be things about India that I would never fully understand. Caste is certainly one of them.

It is reported that there are currently almost 200 million Dalits in India, and human rights abuses against them are frequent. According to a recent newspaper story, in Maharashtra, two Dalit children were murdered by neighbours for defecating in the open. As Dalits, they were not permitted to use the public latrines, so they had no option. Those children were beaten to death.

It is, of course, illegal to discriminate on the basis of caste, but it doesn't mean that it doesn't happen. Whenever government forms ask what caste an employee of Apnalaya may be, we leave it blank. Unfortunately, the caste system cannot be similarly blanked, abolished, dissolved or eradicated, even by an Act of Parliament. Not that any modern politician would risk addressing such an incendiary subject. There is no head of Hinduism who can implement change in the way that the Pope can as head of the Church of Rome. A recently published research paper delved into more than 42,000 households and concluded that 'social change is invariably slow' but added that 'notwithstanding the likelihood of under-reporting of the practice of untouchability, 70 per cent of the population reported not indulging in this practice. This is an encouraging sign.' And probably rather optimistic, if you consider that this means 30 per cent are still willing to admit 'indulging in this practice'. Civil rights were granted to Dalits and the practice of untouchability was abolished by Article 17 of the Constitution seventy years ago. The 'invariably slow' bit of this is a massive understatement.

Sachin is a sincere, devout, practicing Saraswat. My grandson Arjun is also Saraswat and, like all good Saraswats, he had a thread ceremony or Upanayana, the sacred rite of passage before formal schooling begins. One might compare this to the Parsi Navjote, the Jewish Bar Mitzvah or the Church of England Confirmation. Though, unlike in the Anglican ceremony, Arjun did not have to make any promises to believe in this or that. The caste system itself appears intractable, but somewhat paradoxically, Hinduism is wonderfully liberal in terms of belief. It is up to you and God (or gods or goddesses). All I hope is that whatever individuals choose to believe, it entails tolerance. As far as I am concerned, everything else is discretionary.

My granddaughter, Sara, is of course also Saraswat, but Hinduism errs on the side of patriarchy and so there's no thread ceremony or anything else equivalent for girls. Quite what being a Brahmin means to a bright young woman like Sara, educated in Mumbai and graduating from University College, London, I do not know—I should love to understand this better—but being a Hindu is definitely part of her identity.

Anjali went to college with a bag printed with the slogan, 'Thank God I'm an atheist', which always amused me. At the age of about sixteen, she had a boyfriend, and one day, I asked her what on earth she talked to him about every evening on the phone; she answered: 'School and God and things. Because he believes in God and I don't.' Anjali did not go to the temple as a child because Anand never went. In the sixty years I have known Anand, he has wanted to go to a temple only once. That was in Puri where the very famous Jagannatha temple has some association with a relation of his. We were travelling with my brother Richard and his wife Helen; non-Hindus were not allowed into this holy temple, so we arranged to meet an hour later. Anand went to get an entry pass and was refused. He was told that 'he had been seen with foreigners' so he obviously was not Hindu. He was furious. The guards asked for a bribe, which Anand refused to pay. It was raining, and by the time we came back to meet him, he was a very forlorn and bedraggled figure. He has not been near a temple since.

I have a theory that one of the many reasons I slipped so comfortably into the Mehta family was because it was so similar to the Lancaster family in terms of the social pecking order. Mehtas, like Lancasters, are solid, liberal, educated upper-middle class, and not landed gentry. There was no inherited wealth in my father's immediate family, though there certainly had been in the past before it sank due to unfortunate investments in shipping. My mother's father was a planter 'out East', as she always put it, and my mother was the proud owner of a few shares in the Hong Kong Bank; she called it her nest egg, which, mercifully, she never needed.

Anand's grandfather was one of three brothers and a cousin running the once prosperous Century Mills in Bombay. A hostile takeover bid of the mill led to reduced circumstances after the First World War, and when the business was sold, each of the four Mehta offspring was given a sizable property. The bungalow in Warden Road was the legacy of Anand's father, where a flat was created for us when we got married.

When money got tight in the seventies, the ground floor was let out to the American School to bring in some income.

Anand's other grandfather, Vinayak Mehta, his mother's father, had been a distinguished civil servant, a magistrate and collector of several districts, including what was then known as Benares, where there is a statue of him in the museum. His marvellous obituary in *The Pioneer* in 1940 states: 'There was no one who did not highly esteem Mr Mehta's rich qualities of heart'. I wish I had known him.

In the vast majority of the families I have come across in my work with Apnalaya, parents still control their children's marriage. Few want their children to marry out of their own caste or outside their own community or out of their own religion. My parents probably felt the same way all those years ago when I married a Hindu but they didn't actually say so out loud. People like what they know. In England and in India, people tend to employ others like themselves to work in their businesses, often educated at the same schools or universities, and of the same religion. That awful 'old boys network' is the same the world over. It may be wrong, but it is human nature.

Going back a long way, I can see that for the Mehta family, a prospective son-in-law's education and his ability to provide for a daughter were the only concerns. Anand's mother, the youngest of five children, one boy and four girls, was from a Brahmin family; His father's family are Vaishyas. Clearly, the difference in caste was immaterial, not least because Amru Masi's sister Nandini was already married to a cousin of theirs, so the family had obviously been 'approved'. Amru Masi's eldest sister Poornima (I love the name but she was always called Moon) had studied at LSE, as had her brother Kumaril and her other sister, Pupul. Moon married a brilliant Punjabi of her own choosing, and Pupul had a love marriage with a Maharashtrian whom she met while at LSE. Anand's sister Tulsi married Vatsal, a Brahmin from Tamil Nadu with a Master's from Stanford University. Brahmins from that part of South India are often referred to as Tam-Brahms, and I quickly got the impression that they had earned their reputation for being brainy. Vatsal was documentary evidence. He was a friend of Anand's from college in Mumbai, as was Chicken's husband Juggy, a Brahmin with a degree from LSE and a doctorate from Princeton. Neither had much money, but I don't think Anand's parents gave a damn. All they cared about was the happiness of their children. (Unlike mine!)

Teaching me about Hinduism was not something Anand felt was necessary. Indeed, much of what I learnt came from the servants. I couldn't help but notice if they were fasting or feasting, and sometimes they would tell me why. One of the many things I like about the Hindu calendar is the way the many festivals mark the passing of the months, rather as the seasons do in England. Working for Apnalaya, I met countless people who had no idea of their date of birth or when they got married. These dates would be remembered as being 'just before Dussehra' or 'after Holi'. In a land where most people do not go away on holidays, festivals mark a break from the normal work routine and are celebrated with lots of colour, noise (sometimes awful electronic tuneless droning) and, of course, special food for each occasion. I love the diversity. By contrast, the British Christmas, Lent, Easter and Whitsun seem rather dull.

Of the many festivals throughout the year, my favourite has to be Diwali, the nearest to Christmas, as schools are on holiday and families gather from far and wide to celebrate the festival of lights. Homes are decorated with oil lamps and strings of blinking, twinkling bulbs. But I could do without the deafening firecrackers that are lit and thrown around pretty madly to drive away the spirits of bad luck, so we usually escape to the relative peace of Lonavala with the family for a few days. For the first few years I lived in India, Anand's uncle, who lived on the first floor of Warden Road, organised a puja to Laxmi, goddess of wealth, prosperity and good fortune, when the new account books for the next year, each bound in red cloth, would be symbolically opened. Anand had to sit cross-legged on the floor and write a few words in Gujarati, both of which he found challenging. I remember, too, that he adamantly refused to wear a dhoti.

Hindu religious rituals and ceremonies have never been even a small part of Anand's life, but we are both happy to be included in those observed by the Tendulkar family. Most important of these is Ganesh Chaturthi, which falls at the tail end of the monsoon. In line with tradition, Sachin and his brothers bring a Ganpati into his house and invite all their family and close friends for the puja. Sachin's married brother, Nitin, hosts on alternate years. This festival has a long history, but I was quite surprised to learn that it gained new significance in the freedom struggle more than a century ago. The Indian teacher Lokmanya Tilak had a clever idea; he transformed it from being a simple household ritual into a national movement to generate nationalistic fervour against British colonial rule.

Ganpati idols can be huge, but Sachin keeps a small clay idol in his house for one and a half days, after which it is taken away and immersed in water. If not a stream or the sea, even a bucket will do, like last year, when I watched it disintegrate in a bucket in his garden. A priest officiates, and only he and the older women in the family seem to know what to do during the ceremony. I'm encouraged to join in the puja even though I am not a Hindu. Sachin and Anjali then invite the family priest to stay for lunch.

The relationship between a Hindu family and their priest is a bit like the English-style 'tea-with-the-vicar'. Sachin's priest comes to his home for all the significant Hindu events throughout the year, and the same priest will probably carry on doing so from one generation to the next. When my grandson Arjun marries, he will eventually take over from Sachin the tradition of bringing a Ganpati into his home each year—I hope!

The whole city of Mumbai goes mad for Ganesh Chaturthi because Ganesh is the city's presiding deity. Some communities keep their idol in their immediate locality for a full ten days and then, on the last day, parade these spectacular towering idols on huge trucks through the streets of Mumbai to the sea for immersion, followed by bands of riotous musicians and devotees chanting, 'Ganpati Bappa morya, purchya varshi laukariya'. When I first came, I witnessed the scene on Chowpatty beach where the biggest idols are immersed. It attracts crowds in tens of thousands and is an extraordinary sight, quite overwhelming and difficult to describe. The immense crowds form a seething mass, and the fervour, the colour, the noise are unimaginable. In Mumbai alone, more than 150,000 idols are immersed each year. For weeks afterwards, the sea shore is littered with technicolour debris.

One festival particularly looked forward to by Anand's family was Raksha Bandhan, in which a sister ties a thread, or rakhi, around the wrist of her brother or cousin-brother to protect him from evil and wish him long life and happiness. In return, her brother gives her a present and a promise to protect her. I loved this idea, of brothers promising to care for their sisters. When Anand was younger, his sisters and cousin-sisters, and sometimes very close female friends, used to tie rakhis on his wrist and he would grudgingly hand out hundred-rupee notes in return—and in his youngest sister's case, pinch her cheek in a rare display of affection.

When I first came to India, I was somewhat surprised to learn that there were something like twenty-seven bank holidays. I left an England where there were just six. Then Mrs Gandhi cut them to a dozen, but the number has gradually crept up again. Independence Day and Republic Day are universal holidays and calendars fill up with the birthdays of Gandhi, Guru Nanak, Krishna and several other Hindu deities, saints and heroes, as well as with Good Friday and Christmas, both Muslim Eids and Navroz, when Parsis celebrate their new year. But most shops and traders continue to do business regardless of who is celebrating what.

I tried to learn as much as I could about the many different faiths and practices around me because what people believe in interests me. But there is just so much to take in, and I am still learning. And sometimes, curiosity meets a dead end. No non-Parsis are allowed inside Parsi temples, and I have not been into many mosques in India, except for the major ones that tourists visit, such as the Jama Masjid in Delhi, which we visited on our honeymoon. I loved the simplicity and calm of mosques, which contrasts with the busy and sometimes messy Hindu temples, thronging with devotees bringing offerings of flowers and coconuts and noisily exuding religious fervour. The temples themselves are usually dark inside, and often noisy, as bells are rung and prayerful Hindus chant and sing. Even then, I prefer this noise and bustle to the monumental stillness of some of the beautiful ancient temples one visits as a tourist. Only in the Golden Temple in Amritsar, the holy of holies for the Sikh community, have I felt a strong feeling of spiritual calm. Not that it is lacking in activity, as devotees queue for hours to go inside the temple, while others volunteer to sweep the complex clean or help prepare food for thousands every day.

To me, Hinduism seems to be a vast, all-embracing religion, the complexity and diversity of which I can't even begin to understand after more than fifty years in India. I like that Hindus are free to choose their deities and methods of worship according to their nature, preferences and lifestyles, though most people follow their family tradition. Temples are demarcated for different gods, in the same way that churches are dedicated to a particular saint or the Virgin Mary—like the Siddhivinayak temple in Mumbai is dedicated to Ganesh. Sachin, being a devotee of Ganesh, often drives there in the early hours of dawn in order to be alone with his god.

As in my childhood when we were brought up on the parables in the Bible, many Indian children are brought up on the Panchatantra, which tells wonderfully imaginative animal fables. Anjali grew up with Amar Chitra Katha's marvellous comic adaptation of the Mahabharata, the great Indian epic poem; in the early days of television in India, almost everyone in Bombay used to watch B.R. Chopra's serialised dramatisation of the Mahabharata every Sunday evening, including all the Warden Road servants and Anjali. Indeed, people never held parties on Sunday evenings because no one would have turned up. For my grandchildren, Sara and Arjun, Hinduism is as much a part of the family tradition as breakfasting on poha and lassi.

I find it difficult to understand the Hindu belief in destiny or karma, that a person's position in this present life has been determined by their actions in a previous life. Karma provides an explanation for the tragedies as well as the good things. I know now that a Hindu's spiritual salvation should, and often does, come before everything else, which means that theoretically, it is quite acceptable in the latter stage of your life to devote yourself to your faith, even if that means leaving your family and going away to the mountains to do so. If Anand has any such plans, he has not mentioned them. Yet!

To my atheist mind, all faiths have some pretty strange ideas. It is fascinating to me that we all feel passionately about different things. Long ago, when I was at LSE in the days of the Vietnam War protests, I asked an Indian friend, Qaid, what cause he would be prepared to die for if necessary. Nothing at all, he answered. I don't know why, but I was really surprised. I felt there were many I would have died for without nailing any particular one at the time. But I also remember my mother saying during the Second World War that if the Nazis had come to her door, she would readily have risked her own life for her children. Since living in India, I have often wondered how far I would go for the things I believe in. I am all too conscious of the fact that I am part of a family and what I say may affect others. I consciously do not discuss my sometimes controversial views on politics or other matters outside a small circle of family and friends. I never shall.

Nor do I discuss religion. Perhaps my reserve is one of my more enduring British characteristics. But what is the point of trying to persuade someone who believes that the god Ram was born in a particular place that he was born elsewhere, or maybe he wasn't born at all? I only notice someone's religion if it affects what they wear or what they cannot eat. Not that everyone sticks to the rules. Not all Sikhs wear turbans or have a beard, in spite of the teaching that says hair should not be cut. I know Hindus who eat beef and Muslims who enjoy a drink.

I do myself reflect occasionally on the strongly held beliefs of some old missionary friends of mine who lived here for years. They always referred any important decisions they had to take to God, secure in the belief that He would provide the right guidance. One day, we had twenty-two inches of rain in twenty-four hours, and their wooden house in a missionary compound in Bombay was submerged, so I took them food and dry clothes. They knew I was an atheist but as far as they were concerned, the cake, the curtains and the casserole had actually come from God. I was merely the delivery person. It became a great joke to us all. I used to tell them that I was entrusting my soul to them and in case I had got it all wrong, I would be relying on them to get me through the Pearly Gates. I hope they will remember.

As a student, I read the Bible—New Testament and Old—and the Koran from cover to cover; also parts of the Bhagavad Gita, the 700-verse Hindu scripture that is part of the epic Mahabharata.

So I know they do not tell you what to do and what not to do. Instead, they hold up examples of what is good and what is bad. If there is a God, I do not think He or She is very interested in all those rules and prohibitions. He/She would surely have more important things to do—such as performing miracles.

In my early years here, we had an Irish friend whose twelve-year-old son had serious epilepsy—grand mal—and he was cured after a visit to a Sikh faith healer in Bombay. The faith healer presumably believed it was God's doing. Perhaps it was, though the boy's father did not believe in God. Perhaps the boy's natural repair mechanisms kicked in. Had we not known the family well and witnessed what happened at first hand, I would not have believed it to be true. His healing was a truth. But whose truth?

I would hope that most people in Mumbai are tolerant of each other's faiths. Many participate in the Ganpati festival regardless of their religion. During the Mount Mary fair in Bandra, an eight-day carnival to celebrate the birth of the Virgin Mary, fewer than half of those streaming up to the church and lighting candles are Christians. I am told that Hindus believe that blessings can come from any god and it does not matter which one.

For those who go to church in England, it's very different. Faith is not obligatory. At school every Sunday, we went to an Anglican service at the Malvern Priory, held by the most stupefyingly dull vicar, where we sang hymns, said prayers and listened to his sermon. In India, you sometimes see the fervour in people's faces. Faith in evidence. Before going to Varanasi, the spiritual capital of India, the nearest I had come to experiencing a profound sense of communal faith was in Rome. In 1965, my parents noticed that I was rather miserable because Anand had gone back to India, and to my astonishment, they invited me to go with them to Rome for a week's holiday. It turned out to be rather wonderful. The high point was going to the Vatican where, the moment I entered the Sistine Chapel, I was hit by the feeling of unquestioning, utterly sincere faith. There were relatively few tourists then, so we had time to gaze at the ceiling and drink in the atmosphere without being hustled on.

In Varanasi, years later, I experienced that feeling all over again, and more. Pilgrims visited in order to bathe in the sacred waters of the Ganges or, better still, to die there and be cremated immediately on the sacred ghats. Eric Newby explained it in his 1966 book, *Slowly Down the Ganges*: 'To drink the water, having bathed in it, and to carry it away in bottles is meritorious. To be cremated on its banks, having died there and to have one's ashes cast in its water, is the wish of every Hindu.' I had been told in advance about the floating garbage and raw sewage, but it didn't seem to worry any of those bathing. For true believers, there is no water purer than the Ganges, and most visitors carry at least one bottle of the precious liquid back home with them. As our small sightseeing boat drifted along the Ganges in the early evening light, the sight of shrouded corpses burning in full view on towering funeral pyres along the bank—some roaring bonfires, others tapering embers—filled me with both fascination and a mild repulsion. The heightened atmosphere of religious intensity was in itself deeply affecting. Cows and goats wandered among the many sadhus with ash and markings on their foreheads. Hawkers sold clay lamps set in plates filled with rose petals, which the pilgrims set alight and afloat on the water. Accompanied by the ceaseless ringing of bells, it was inexpressibly moving and somehow beautiful. One day, I saw a cycle rickshaw on the road with a corpse tied to a bamboo stretcher propped up behind; another rickshaw dragged a Christmas tree. Mortality meets immortality in Varanasi, one of the oldest continually inhabited cities in the world.

I knew so little about the country I was coming to, but one of the few things we were all familiar with about India in the England of my youth were the maharajas, with their great wealth, exotic turbaned headgear and chests adorned with jewels, often depicted returning from a tiger shoot with a number of trophies. Indian society has been shaken up quite a lot since I arrived here in the sixties. Then, each one of the former maharajas, rajas and nawabs of the 565 princely states benefited from the Privy Purse, a generous government allowance to help them keep up princely appearances, which was guaranteed to them under the Constitution in return for acceding to the Indian Union and surrendering their powers.

I was here when Indira Gandhi took away their Privy Purses in 1971, and many went off to Switzerland. She wanted to tax the rich to give to the poor, so income tax was very high, just as it was in England at the time (99 pence in the pound on unearned income as I remember). Inheritance tax here was crippling, and I knew one or two widows who had to sell up in order to pay death duties. That was abolished by Indira's son Rajiv Gandhi in 1985, by which time some maharajas had turned their palaces into hotels, some really luxurious, others dusty, old-fashioned and uncomfortable.

Anand and I did not hang out with maharajas, but we were good friends with Pat Sisodia, the erstwhile maharaja of a small state in Rajasthan and one of the handsomest men I have ever met. In colonial days, the grandest maharajas got a 21-gun salute on official occasions; Pat's ancestors were awarded a perfectly respectable 15 guns. He lived with his second wife, Parveen, in Bombay, and as far as I know, he did not actually do very much beyond battling alcoholism for much of his life. I daresay many maharajas suffered a similar fate, having lost first their status and then their income. The legendary Nizam of Hyderabad was one of the richest men in the world, reputed to have used his father's £50 million Jacob diamond as a paperweight; yet he lived a very simple life in Hyderabad for twenty years until his death in 1967, smoking Charminar cigarettes and rarely dressing up. Incidentally, maharajas were far more likely to be from the Kshatriya caste than Brahmins, because they had probably got where they were from conquering territories at some stage or through patronage and favour, just like the British aristocrats.

One of many things I loved about Bombay from the start was the vocal and visible representation of multiple religions, sects and inter-marriages. Although there are very few Jews remaining in India, there are at least four synagogues in Mumbai, of which the Knesset Eliyahoo Synagogue, built in 1884 by Jacob Sassoon for the Baghdadi Jews in Kala Ghoda, is one. It has been beautifully restored recently to its original glory, including exquisite stained-glass panels, with money raised by people of all faiths, including Hindus which, to me, powerfully sums up the multifaith community spirit of Mumbai.

All the major religions, Christianity, Islam, Judaism and Hinduism, are represented in our own family. Of Anand's cousins, Pupul Masi's daughter, Radhi, is married to a German Jew; his sister Jill's husband is a Lebanese Muslim, and his aunt Moon Masi's daughter Shyama married Nihal, whose mother Rani was a South Indian Catholic and whose father was a Sinhalese Buddhist. His stepfather, Bobby (we called him Bobby Uncle) was Parsi. Nihal was brought up a Catholic, baptised and confirmed, and then stopped practicing for four decades. He returned to Catholicism in earnest sixteen years ago, and he and Shyama founded St. Jude India ChildCare Centres in 2006 to care for children undergoing cancer treatment in Mumbai. Of the next generation of cousins, six married Indians and seven married foreigners from Canada, the USA, the UK, Sweden, Belgium and Australia!

I often sat on the floor for meetings in the office of Apnalaya in the early days with Arni Antia, a Parsi; Shanta, a North Indian Hindu; Pushpa, a Jain; Pat, an American married to a fellow American who was the third generation of Christian missionaries to India; Fakira, a Muslim, married to a Tam-Brahm—and me, an atheist married to a Hindu. Quite a mix! Everyone got along very happily together in an atmosphere of total acceptance.

I had met dozens of Hindus and Muslims and Jews at LSE, but I had not come across any Parsis before I came to Bombay, where many of the leading lawyers, judges, scientists and doctors tended to be Parsi. I soon noticed that people often announced that So-and-So was a Bombay Parsi, such as the brilliant Rohinton Mistry, author of *A Fine Balance*, who now lives in Canada, and the famous conductor Zubin Mehta, who was born and went to school here. I have seen a photo of Zubin taken in his twenties and, oh my, what a heart-throb.

Some Parsi families who settled in Bombay made their fortunes two centuries ago, a few through trading opium with China, and many have since become generous philanthropists, possibly out of gratitude to India for taking them in as refugees from Iran. It is only thanks to huge handouts from Parsis that many of the best institutions in Mumbai exist at all, such as JJ Hospital, where my daughter studied medicine, the Tata Institute of Social Sciences (that Apnalaya has worked with throughout its fifty years) and the National Centre for the Performing Arts (NCPA), an amazing addition to Bombay's cultural life, showcasing the best of the arts, both Indian and Western. I am a regular at their Western music concerts, and hope to be there when Zubin Mehta comes to conduct the Symphony Orchestra of India for what will probably be his last concert.

But not all Bombay Parsis are rich and successful. At Apnalaya in the 1980s and 1990s, we found a very high incidence of drug dependence in the Parsi colonies hidden away in Tardeo where many of the not-so-well-off Parsis continue to live. People are born Parsi just as they are born Hindu. There can be no conversion to Zoroastrianism, and most Parsis do not recognise the children of mixed marriages. There are 60,000 Parsis left in India, and many families have reached the end of the line. I hope that the community will embrace marrying out before it is too late.

Actually, the Parsis who cling desperately to their religious purity remind me of those people who, in my childhood, used to refer to those of mixed race as 'half-caste', usually in a whisper because it was something vaguely taboo. It's not a word one ever uses today. My uncle John, my mother's brother, a planter in Java, fathered a child with his cook's wife and had a daughter, Juanita. He brought her up as his own until war broke out, when they were both interned as prisoners of war by the Japanese. On his release, he asked the Red Cross to find her, and they returned to England where she had a very tough time; England in the late forties and fifties was not an easy place for people from her kind of background. Eventually, she moved to Vienna and worked as a skilled scientific stenographer for a United Nations body. But I don't know if she ever found true happiness and felt truly at home.

When Anand and his Indian friends were students at LSE in the sixties, they all experienced racial prejudice—being pushed off pavements and ignored in pubs when trying to order a pint. Signs saying 'No Irish, No Blacks, No Dogs' were still to be seen in those awful days. In fact, it was one reason why Anand did not want to stay in England. When I married him,

I realised that had we lived in South Africa or in some states of the USA, our relationship would have been banned. We would have had to wait a year to marry in sixteen states in the USA when, in 1967, the Anti Miscegenation laws in Virginia were ruled unconstitutional in the *Loving v Virginia* case, making the laws forbidding interracial marriage in all sixteen states unconstitutional. We could not have married legally in South Africa until 1985, when the Prohibition of Mixed Marriages Act of 1948 was repealed. One of the many things I loved about Bombay was its embrace of diversity. So I was both surprised and disappointed to discover that colour prejudice was rife in India, if in a different way. I once observed to another white woman that skin colour means nothing to me, and she said that was my white privilege speaking. What she meant was that, as a white person, I have never had to consider my colour because, subconsciously, I have known I would never be unfairly or racially stereotyped as a result of it. I suppose that is true—and a very sad fact of life.

Another difficult truth in India is that 'fairness' has always been a measure of beauty, hence the ever-burgeoning cosmetics industry for lotions and potions promising to lighten brown skin. I once caught myself describing Anjali as fair, and I realised that I was sounding just like one of the matrimonial ads that appear in the Indian papers. Some are even more specific about skin colour and say 'wheatish' or 'milky white' or 'light white'. The lighter a girl's complexion, the more attractive and therefore marriageable she is considered to be. Recently, the skin whitening cream 'Fair & Lovely' decided to drop 'Fair' from its name. It is now 'Glow & Lovely'; I can't say I think that's a great name, but it's the best the advertising agency could come up with. Years ago, every Indian girl used Fair & Lovely, marketed as being 'The key that'll get you the man of your dreams' despite allegations that it was dangerous because it contained bleach. Now there are men's whitening products advertised on television with before and after shots showing startling results.

As a student, Anjali was always being asked where she was from. Kashmir? Spain? Italy? When we went to Egypt, everyone spoke to her in Arabic, presuming she was Egyptian. When she was about eight years old, my niece Radha, aged four, said to me: 'Annabel Mami, when I grow up, will I be fair like Anjali?' I felt sad because I realised that, even at that age, she was taken in by the idea of fairness. Radha is strikingly beautiful, with brown skin, like her dark and handsome father.

The dishy, dashing movie star Shashi Kapoor married the lovely blonde Jennifer Kendal (sister of Felicity, the English actor who co-starred in Merchant Ivory's wonderful film *Shakespeare Wallah*). Their daughter Sanjana was at school with Anjali, and she had the most striking pale eyes. At one stage, I had hoped for a light-eyed child because the combination of light eyes and dark skin is so striking. My research revealed that the Mendelian theory gave me a one-in-four chance of a light-eyed child, more likely if I had a boy. I could not have been more delighted with my two dark-eyed daughters.

I count my blessings daily that my Indian family have very little time for either gurus or superstitions. I have known people who will not choose the name of their child without consulting a guru and will not consider a marriage proposal until the horoscopes are matched. Sadly, if a horoscope cast according to the moment of the birth is considered inauspicious, a girl might never marry. The minute at which Anjali was born was noted carefully by the hospital staff but not by me. She and Sachin celebrated their twenty-fifth wedding anniversary in lockdown 2020, so I can only assume that their horoscopes must have been perfectly aligned. Sachin's father was tasked with finding an auspicious date and a prescribed time for Sachin and Anjali's wedding, but I think he had to make do with Sachin being in the country and not away on tour somewhere. Some Hindus have strong feelings and beliefs about certain numbers and good and bad omens. When my father came to Madras with the chairman of Tube Investments for the opening of the Hercules Bicycle factory in 1953, he was amazed that auspicious dates had been chosen first for the laying of the inaugural stone for the factory building and then for its opening.

I do not believe that astrology is scientific and I do not like fortune tellers. I would not even have a test to tell if I was predisposed to get cancer. I know there is Alzheimer's in my family, so every time I have a 'senior moment' and can't remember a word or a name that I know, I think this is it. But I do not want that confirmed by a predictive test. Until it happens, there is a possibility that it will not happen. I have a very dear Indian friend who was told by a fortune teller that she would die in childbirth. When the birth of her son was long and difficult, his words returned to haunt her. She did not die, but she was reluctant to risk it again.

I am old enough now to have reached some conclusions about what is necessary to live happily in India: optimism, patience and a sense of humour. Optimism is probably the most important, and I am a true optimist. It also helps to take things in very small bites. And to concentrate on things that I can control. I can't change the bigger picture, but I can tweak tiny things and so improve the lives of a few people. And live in hope. Hoping for the best rather than fearing for the worst is the way I want to live my life to the end.

5

The Music of My Life

MUSIC WAS NEVER MY OVERARCHING PASSION IN LIFE. I WASN'T A musical genius. But I had perfect pitch. As a small girl, I could sight-read expertly and play by ear better than most. I loved singing. I drifted into the Royal College of Music at the age of eighteen. Had someone suggested I should become a doctor, I would almost certainly have thrown myself into that, and I might have been a good one. But no one made any such suggestion. On reflection, I think I should have liked to be a neurologist because the human brain fascinates me. My doctor brother, Richard, once wrote the sentence: 'The flower has white petals' and only 'the' and 'has' were correctly spelt; despite his dyslexia, he became the youngest consultant at St Mary's Hospital, Paddington, completed a PhD and wrote a book on pharmacology. Clearly, his brain is differently wired from most others when it comes to spelling, but there is nothing important missing. Or is there?

I would love to be able to map the brain and to learn how the brain of an outstanding sportsman such as my son-in-law, Sachin, differs from that of an exceptional bridge player such as Anand or that of a musical maestro such as Zubin Mehta. I might even have considered studying maths at university. But times were different back then, and while my parents always took education very seriously, they did not believe in studying for the sake of studying. They thought of it as a means to an end, and that end was employment. When they heard me play the piano, I think they also had stars in their eyes. Their little Annie was obviously going to be the next Clara Schumann or maybe Cornish-born Moura Lympany.

At first, I didn't disappoint. It was a great accolade to be a UK gold medallist, having got top marks for playing Beethoven's 'Appassionata' for my Grade 8 piano exam at the age of seventeen, an immediate springboard into the Royal College of Music. Now, when I listen to that piece, I marvel that I ever was able to play it. I suppose that I had the technique that came with practice, which I did tirelessly because, at that age and stage, I enjoyed the challenge of getting on top of something. But I must have also had an emotional response to the piece, which the judges at my exam heard loud and clear. Where that came from, I do not know. I did feel passionately about things: about injustice, about the Vietnam War, about my friends. But even then, I don't think I wanted to be the one in the spotlight.

Playing the piano for the rest of the school as they marched into assembly was great fun. I wrote the score for an operetta that we performed in our last year. It was titled *The Rose and the Ring*, based on the classic fairytale by William Makepeace Thackeray. My friend Amanda wrote the lyrics and the whole class took part. I loved the way music could bring people together.

During my first couple of terms at the RCM, I shared a tiny flat in Queen Alexandra's House with my old school friend, Helen Rennie, who was doing a secretarial course at Pitmans and, somewhat predictably, went on to work for the Conservative Party before she got married. Students could use the music rooms at the top of the building. The warden of the hostel was Miss Grace, a member of the formidable Grace family, of whom fourteen members played first-class cricket, many for England, including W.G. and his three brothers. Large, no-nonsense, with short grey hair, she made sure we were in by ten o'clock every night, which, frankly, I found rather petty. I was always quietly anti-authority.

It was not until I went to the Royal College that I met people for whom music was the be-all and end-all of life and I found many of them a bit narrow-minded and dull. It was a shock to me to be told to wear skirts for lessons. Trousers were not allowed. I didn't much like the Royal College, except for my new friend Caroline Maurice, and singing with her in the choir of the church in Lancaster Gate, the Madrigal Society and, best of all, the Bach Choir. Truly, there is nothing quite so wonderful as singing in a good choir.

After two terms, I had had enough of Queen Alexandra's House, and I moved with Sonia Westrup to a scruffy basement in Holland Park. Sonia had been in the year above me at school. Flute was her first instrument and piano her second; mine were vice versa. My father, thrilled that I was at the Royal College of Music, bought me a little upright Bechstein piano from Harrods, a Model 8, smaller than normal and of superb quality. After all the school pianos and practice-room pianos, it really did make a difference to play on a genuinely good piano. Years later, Caroline gave the London Bechstein a home and now her daughter, Rebecca, my godchild, has it in Oxford. Neither Reb nor her children play, but I am glad it has stayed in the family.

The piano was in the main room of our flat and the boiler was in the kitchen next door. First thing in the morning, the boilerman would come in and stoke it. We didn't mind. It made the room wonderfully cosy at no expense to us. Unfortunately, the bathroom was at the back and icy cold, as was the separate loo where we always did flute practice so as to not disturb the one playing the piano. A Pakistani woman lived in the flat next door, my first close encounter with someone from the Indian subcontinent, and the acrid and all-pervading stench of dried fish she cooked most days permeated the loo. It haunts me still. I can eat dried fish now in a Goan curry, but never without thinking of those days.

Things perked up a bit when I met a flautist named Jimmy Galway (now the legendary Sir James, best known as 'the man with the golden flute'), a Belfast boy with a strong accent and a glorious sense of fun, refreshingly different from the rest of the snooty, Pringle-and-pearl types at the Royal College of Music. Jim used to come to the flat in Holland Park to practise the flute, with me accompanying him on the piano. He had extraordinary eyes, always on the move, darting from side to side. I subsequently discovered that it was a condition called Nystagmus, which, amazingly, did not affect his brilliant musicianship. I had seen nothing like it before, or since.

Sometimes, we went to a Wimpy Bar or to see a film at the Classic for one shilling and three pence; we always went Dutch. Like everyone else, Jim called me Annie. It was when he recorded John Denver's 'Annie's Song' that he shot to fame. My friends always assumed that this song was written for me, but I had gone to India in 1966 and imagine I was long forgotten. That Annie was his then wife, another Annie. When I knew him, Jim played a simple silver flute. His golden flutes, fortune and knighthood came much, much later.

I remember our relationship as an innocent, uncomplicated summer romance, but I must have been quite keen on him because I took him home to Sparrows Nest one weekend. Perhaps it was because my father also played the flute that I thought they would get on. In Jimmy's autobiography, he recalls being collected by my father in a Jag from Stroud, Gloucestershire. At the risk of sounding like Hermione Gingold singing 'I Remember it Well' with Maurice Chevalier in the film *Gigi*, we were actually picked up from Evesham station, Worcestershire, though my father might well have been driving a Jaguar. My brother Richard misremembers it too. Just the other day, he said he was convinced that Jim had proposed to me; he most certainly hadn't.

Years later, my father sent me Jimmy's first autobiography, written in 1978, with the mentions of me underlined in pencil. I hadn't actually given him a thought since leaving in 1960. I don't think he will mind me quoting from it.

> There were other traumas that summer. Largest of them all, perhaps, was the fact that I fell in love.
>
> Her name was Annabelle [sic] Lancaster and she played the flute and the piano and for a few weeks it was cloud nine. I got to know her by accident. I had telephoned a flat to talk to one of the girls I knew at college and Annabelle [sic] answered instead. So I invited her out for a beer and to my surprise we got on like a house on fire. She was my first introduction to girls as girls, if you know what I mean, and for the few weeks that the affair lasted even my precious flute had to take a second place. She invited me to meet her parents one weekend, so we went down to Stroud in Gloucestershire where her father, a company director picked us up in his Jaguar—very impressive as far as I was concerned. Annabelle meant the whole world to me and we spent every moment we could together, just holding hands and mooning about. That summer I took a job at Bexhill, playing in the local Pavilion with an orchestra, but I was hardly ever off the telephone to Annabelle and I was back in London every weekend.
>
> I had taken the job in Bexhill because I was fed up with the flat in Notting Hill. It proved a happy decision and that summer will never fade from my memory. The weather was glorious, Bexhill pleasant, the people in the orchestra marvellous—and I was in love with Annabelle.

At this point I vanish and Jimmy goes on to write about flying a box-kite on the beach and living in the flat where Dickens wrote *Little Dorrit,* until four pages later, when he takes up the story again.

> Suddenly the happy days were over and James Galway was plunged into the dumps. Annabelle had drifted away and I was inconsolable. I really lost heart for a while and for the first and only time in my life since I had first picked up a mouth organ and penny whistle, music ceased to mean anything to me. For weeks the flute lay there unplayed and I not once plucked a string of the guitar I was messing about with at the time. Instead I painted. For the next month or so, I endeavoured to drown my sorrows in paint. Finally, however, I decided I would never make a painter. Technically I was good, but I soon realised I had nothing original to say. So it was back to the flute.
>
> Two things helped to lift the depression and enabled me to bounce back. The first was a bunch of girls to whom I was introduced by my friend Robert Dawes; the second my lessons with Geoffrey Gilbert and my tuition at the Guildhall.

The flautist Geoffrey Gilbert was Jimmy's great mentor. My flute professor was Eddie Walker, a pretty hopeless teacher but tremendous fun. I spent all my flute lessons with him playing the flute and me accompanying him on the piano. He was plump and jolly and flirtatious, not in an uncomfortable, #MeToo way, though I became adept at keeping my distance. He lived in Pinner, and to this day, when I pass Pinner on the train out to visit Uday, an old Bombay friend who lives in Rickmansworth, I remember Eddie and hear in my head the music of Elgar, which he and his father recorded.

At the end of the first year, I became an ARCM, Associate of the Royal College of Music, in both piano performance and teaching. In my second year, I embarked on the graduate course, which was more academic. The magnificent—if terrifying—

Herbert Howells was my professor for composition, but while I enjoyed composition, I already knew my ambitions lay elsewhere, and I felt myself to be undeserving of him. Only yesterday, the morning radio graced me with a Magnificat that he wrote. Exalting stuff. But I felt no regrets.

My piano professor was Angus Morrison, who I have since discovered had a reputation for taking on only the most talented students. He was highly regarded and I liked him, but he did nothing for me musically. It had happened to me very gradually, but I had hit a point where I knew I did not want to spend every waking minute perfecting a particularly tricky page of demi-semi quavers. I once watched a television programme about Jimmy Galway when he had already had dozens of solid gold flutes and he said he continued to practise for at least six hours a day because he was never ever satisfied with his performance. The same applies to my son-in-law. It is the difference between a performer of genius and someone, like me, who merely has an exceptional facility.

By now, I was travelling to college on my beloved scooter from a very tatty first-floor bedsit on the back of 22 Powys Square, off Portobello Road, living alone and loving it. A nice woman lived in the front flat with its big bay window. She would sit in the open sash window in the nice weather and talk to passing gentlemen, some of whom dropped in on her. One day, the penny dropped that she was a prostitute—or sex-worker, the modern and much better word. I didn't care a jot. I loved this area and I had nothing against this woman. I spent all my spare time singing in choirs or volunteering at the Rugby Club in Notting Hill, which was founded by an old Rugbian in 1884, playing with disadvantaged kids rather than practising the piano by myself.

My friend Caroline could see how miserable I was in college. She had known from when she was young that she didn't want to be a performer but wanted to teach. As soon as she left the

Royal College of Music, she began teaching the piano at home, and twenty years later became one of the first piano teachers teaching the Suzuki method and subsequently training piano teachers in the method as well. She is my age, still teaching and still loving it.

Caroline married Patrick Gowers, a brilliant composer who had written music for the Cambridge Footlights when Bamber Gascoigne, Peter Cook and Dudley Moore were part of it. In pure Jane Austen/Mrs Bennet style, Caroline's mother invited Bamber to lunch as a prospective match, and while she liked him, it was with his friend, Patrick, who came along with him, that she fell madly in love. I was very possessive of Caroline and it rather put my nose out of joint.

Theirs was a whirlwind romance. They met in May and married in September. Patrick was doing a PhD on the French composer Erik Satie, and he seemed to live in the British Museum Reading Room. He would become well known for the soundtrack he wrote for the television series *Sherlock Holmes* in the eighties (with Jeremy Brett as Sherlock). The haunting solo violin theme was played by their daughter Kathy, a professional violinist who, while enjoying performing, has been torn between carrying on and doing something quite different, a battle with which I wholly empathise. Another daughter, Reb, my darling goddaughter, is a talented writer of both fiction and non-fiction, including an updating of her great-grandfather Ernest Gowers's legendary *The Complete Plain Words.* Caroline's eldest son is the super-brilliant mathematician Sir Timothy Gowers. It is often said that people who are good at maths are fine musicians and vice versa. I think that is nonsense. Some are, like many of the Gowers family, and some are most definitely not. Some of the best musicians I've known can't do their seven times table. And some of the best mathematicians I've known are tone deaf.

Towards the end of my second year at the RCM, I knew that I did not want to spend the rest of my life teaching little girls like myself to play the piano, either singly or in groups. I was certain that I wanted to engage with people, though I didn't know how. One day, quite by chance, I read an article in *The Times* about a serious shortage of staff in London County Council children's homes. I have always felt that this was a sign. Caroline understood immediately and said go for it, and she kindly volunteered to come home with me to Sparrows Nest to break the news to my parents.

My parents were fond of Caroline and we had a jolly time over supper before going up to bed. But we barely slept. Instead, we talked about what to say to my parents. Two years before, when I had raised doubts about a career in music, they had said I could leave the RCM if I changed my mind. Now I was doing just that. First my father and then my mother mustered all the arguments they could to dissuade me, saying that I was doing so well, that I was already qualified to teach, that I was rebelling for the sake of it. They didn't know any social workers and clearly did not think the job was for a girl like me. How, they asked, would I earn a living? I have blanked out much of the detail but I do remember that my father ended with a stern warning that I could expect not a penny more from him. And he meant it. From now on, he declared, I would have to support myself.

I got back to London, somewhat tear-stained, and went straight to the London County Council headquarters on the South Bank, clutching the piece from *The Times*. I was offered a job on the spot as a House Mother at a residential children's home in Croydon. Three months later, they asked me to go as a Housemother to Mile End, a residential approved school outside Brighton. They were like Borstals but for younger boys. I was twenty.

It was challenging work and opened up a whole new world for me. The 'delinquents', as the boys were referred to in those days, were aged between ten and fifteen, and their so-called crimes were rarely more serious than stealing buns from the back of a baker's van. One boy, Reggie, was fifteen, and born when his mum was fifteen. He told me that I was younger than his sister. As I got to know more about the boys and what had brought them here, I saw a career opening up for me, maybe in Probation Service. I discovered that LSE ran a two-year non-graduate diploma in Social Administration for applicants older than twenty-one who had earned their own living for one year. I did not think LSE would be very impressed with an application from a public schoolgirl with a flair for music and no A' levels, so I decided to broaden my work experience. After a year at Mile End, I somehow plucked up the courage to walk into Cadby House and ask for a job at the Lyons Factory in Hammersmith.

For hours at a time, I stood in front of a conveyor belt rolling Swiss rolls, three at a time if they were minis, and if they were chocolate-coated, putting a walnut bang in the middle on the top. Woe betide anyone who sneezed and missed one. Working on a conveyor belt is hellish and you could not take your hands or your eyes off what you were doing for even a second. Having dexterous piano fingers helped. On either side of me were Windrush generation West Indian women, warm and chatty companions reminiscing about the island sunshine, jerk chicken and steel bands. While earning £7 a week at Lyons, I took the LSE entrance exam. The essay that got me in was about my co-workers' experiences as immigrants in those terrible days of No Irish, No Blacks, No dogs.

I worked there for four months, until I fell off my scooter and broke my nose. My parents were abroad at the time and after a few days in hospital in Kensington, I recuperated with a lovely family I had got to know in Brighton, in their little house on Southwick village green. The father, Tock, was a pilot in the dock, bringing the boats in and sometimes bringing home fresh crabs, which he plunged into boiling water while I stood watching them desperately trying to climb out. It should have put me off crab for life but it didn't. They were delicious. It was summer and it was fun to be at the seaside, so I stayed and got a job putting soap in the boxes of the Dubarry Perfumery for £5 a week until the new term began.

By the time I got admitted into LSE, my father could see how determined I was to pursue this course; he took pity and gave me an £8 weekly allowance. Rather extraordinarily, once I gave up music, it just disappeared from my life, unless someone needed a pianist to play something to dance to, or to sing Christmas carols with.

When I married Anand and came to live in India, there was no piano in the house in Warden Road. We didn't have much furniture at all. You couldn't just go out and buy furniture from a shop in Bombay because there *were* no furniture shops. Just as a tailor made your clothes, so a carpenter made your furniture. Unless you could find it second-hand. We bought the dining-room table I still have in our house in Goa from some Swedes who were leaving India. They were also selling a baby grand piano, so we bought that too, but it is very difficult and expensive to maintain a piano in this climate. The wires slacken very quickly. My piano went down a semitone and then became completely flat. The choral symphony in D minor sounded more like C minor. By the time we moved up to the second-floor flat after sixteen years on the ground floor, the piano had become just another piece of furniture. I sold it. For nothing.

I have always loved singing. My mother was a soprano but I am an alto and, on joining Indus, a club for Indian and foreign women in Bombay, I jumped at the opportunity to sing in their choir, occasionally also singing duets with my friend, Nirmala

Matthan, at special Indus events until she moved to Bangalore. After my daughter Tara died, I joined the Cantata Choir conducted by Joachim Buehler from the Max Mueller Bhavan. I found singing very consoling, but six decades in polluted Bombay have done something to my voice, and these days, I growl rather than sing.

I know quite a lot about the theory of Indian classical music, and I tried hard to get into it when I came to Bombay. I knew that it is improvised rather than written, atonal, and everything begins with a raag, which dictates the notes and the rhythms that may be used with endless variations. It may be because harmony, the heart of all Western music, doesn't exist in Indian music, but it has never got under my skin or into my blood in the way that classical Western music did. I can listen to it and quite enjoy it, but there's a limit. I am not sure I appreciate its finer points.

Yehudi Menuhin's collaboration with the great sitar maestro Ravi Shankar in the 1960s was among the first attempts at Western/Indian fusion music. It can be clever, but I find it contrived. To my ear, the elements of each don't mesh with the other. I think fusion jazz works better than fusion classical, but while I love jazz, I would never choose to go to a fusion concert.

Naturally, I wanted my little daughters, Anjali and Tara, to understand the nuances of Indian classical music from the start. When they were very young, I used to take them to musical recitals at the Bhulabhai Desai Memorial Institute in Breach Candy, where little ones were actively welcomed and allowed to listen not very quietly and sitting not very still. Since I couldn't teach Anjali to appreciate Indian classical music myself, I arranged for a teacher to come home to teach her to sing and to play the harmonium. She isn't musical, but she can appreciate Indian music better than I can. Once Anjali and Sachin became an item, I soon discovered that he loves music, anything from

Western pop and Western classical to Indian classical, and lighter Indian classical such as bhajans and devotional songs—such a wide variety that you never know what will be on when you're in his car.

I have always loved dancing; I learnt ballet before I went to boarding school at ten. But I was from the twist generation. Anjali took a Kuchipudi dance class after school taught by Miss Rao, the very talented librarian. She had a tremendous feel for it, but when Miss Rao left, the dancing stopped. I always preferred modern dance to classical ballet because, to me, it is much more expressive. Classical Indian dancing is very formal and constricting, though Anand's niece, Aditi Mangaldas, a professional Kathak dancer, has broken a lot of barriers, true to the Mehta family tradition.

When I came here in 1966, I discovered that, except for Parsis in South Bombay, few people knew much about Western classical music. Indian Parsis, though originally from Persia, were often educated in England and had always aligned themselves closely with the British (and Europe more generally), and many knew their Bach from their Beethoven as well as I did. Not so the average Indian. So, as Music Chairperson of Indus, I frequently gave talks on music appreciation, introducing my listeners to various instruments of the orchestra or explaining the movements of a symphony. In those days, a handful of elderly Catholic ladies taught piano, violin and cello, mainly in Bandra, and a few of their students got scholarships to the Menuhin School in Surrey and became professional musicians. There was always plenty of jazz in clubs and bars in Bombay and Goa, which was where John Lennon and all the Flower Power lot gravitated, though not until 1968. In any case, Lennon was more interested in discovering transcendental meditation with Maharishi Yogi than in playing music.

For at least the first twenty years that I lived here, the few Western classical music recitals I went to were organised by the splendid Parsi ladies of the Time and Talents Club, who managed to persuade the odd pianist or violinist to stop over in Bombay on their way to somewhere else. Foreign exchange payments were forbidden, so they were given gifts instead and the recitals took place in the somewhat basic Patkar Hall near Bombay Hospital or the Tejpal Auditorium at Nana Chowk. Very occasionally, when an orchestra or dance group or the Vienna Boys Choir arrived, they would perform in the Homi Bhabha Auditorium in Colaba. Other than those, I depended on concerts by the Naval Band and the Police Band. Though fun, they were not quite concert standard.

Things began to change in 1968 when Jamshed Bhabha, a great patron of the arts, and J.R.D. Tata established the NCPA. Their first theatre, the Tata Theatre, was constructed on the land where Apnalaya had their original centre at Nariman Point in 1982. This coincided with the opening up of the economy, and Bombay was gradually able to play host to some top-flight musicians, many of whom were personal friends of Khushroo Suntook, a Bombay businessman with a great love for and knowledge of Western classical music. Membership was expensive, and I did not join until my dear friend Khushroo took over running it as vice chairman in 2000. He became chairman in 2007. I have never forgotten the thrill of hearing Zubin Mehta, a Bombay boy and a classmate of Khushroo, conducting the Israeli Philharmonic. I haven't a clue what they played, just that it was magic.

In 2006, Khushroo founded the Symphony Orchestra of India (SOI), which is the most remarkable gift to Mumbai and the first and only professional orchestra in India. It is a wonderful example of the way music brings people together, gathering musicians from more than twenty countries to play alongside a growing number of Indian musicians, all permanent residents in this truly international, cosmopolitan, multicultural city. It could only happen in Mumbai!

SOI has been a great joy to me. A couple of years ago, they played Zakir Hussain's specially commissioned tabla concerto, which somehow succeeded in making a Western orchestra into a massive Indian percussion instrument. But the high point of the season for me was their stellar performance of Beethoven's Ninth symphony. I had to pinch myself. Yes, I was here in Mumbai, India, listening to this, not in the Festival Hall, London or the Lincoln Center, New York but in our very own magnificent Jamshed Bhabha Theatre, which opened in 1999. We had come a long way from the mediocre pianist playing in the draughty Patkar Hall.

For many years after I came here, there was a baby grand on the Willingdon Club veranda where, at weekends, an elderly lady played a limited repertoire. I had always amused myself with the possibility that, if I ever fell on hard times, I would have to make a living playing popular favourites at the Willingdon. But I can imagine far worse fates than playing 'Blow the Wind Southerly', 'The Merry Widow Waltz' and Bach's 'Jesu, Joy of Man's Desiring', which the magnificent English pianist Dame Myra Hess transcribed so beautifully for the piano in 1926. I think I would make all the Parsi members very happy.

The last time I played the piano was in England in the summer of 2018, on an electric keyboard accompanying my great niece who learns the violin. If someone ever asks me to play something, I can play Mozart's slow movements or some of Bach's Preludes and Fugues. Once it's there, in one's head or in one's fingers, it never completely goes. But when I left the Royal College of Music in 1960, I left music forever, in a manner of speaking. I rarely if ever listen to classical music on the radio. When I came here in 1966, I couldn't listen because the radio signal was useless, and I didn't have any records. I didn't mind. I really only like listening to classical music in a concert hall or, if it's sacred music, in a church. I don't want other distractions. I listen to classical music in the same way that I go to see a play at the theatre or watch a cricket match. It can never be background because I know too much about it to be able to make an apple crumble at the same time. I am plugged in to BBC Radio all night via my earpiece, but exclusively to Radio Four or the World Service. Hearing the news every half hour quickly sends me to sleep. And if it doesn't, I switch to Four Extra for a replay of ancient golden radio comedies such as *The Navy Lark*, *The Goon Show* or *I'm Sorry, I'll Read that Again.*

Like so many Brits of my age, the radio programme *Desert Island Discs* has been background music for as long as I can remember. It is a couple of years younger than I am, having been first broadcast on the BBC Forces Programme on 29 January 1942. There have been gaps when I didn't hear it, but now, there is a wonderful archive where I can catch all the ones I've missed. The other day, I listened to Freddie Flintoff telling a lovely story about when he was captain of the England Cricket team playing in India in 2006 and the series was in the balance on the last day and the atmosphere very tense. Instead of making a galvanising team talk, he had a shower and walked into the dressing room to the tune of Johnny Cash's 'Ring of Fire' playing loudly on his iPod. He was wearing nothing but a towel around his shoulders, and he started dancing. And, one by one, the rest of the team got up and started dancing too, when suddenly the door opened and Sachin stood there looking at them in amazement and cried: 'What on earth is going on in here?' A giggly Flintoff proceeded to lead his team to bowl India out and win a Test match for England in India for the first time in twenty years. It's a very jolly tale, which, according to Sachin, has not a grain of truth. A modest Flintoff, just like Sachin, does not rate his captaincy highly except for this triumphant episode, which explains why 'Ring of Fire' is in his list of eight discs.

Like so many people who love this programme, I've been secretly hatching the list of discs I would take to my desert island, and the vile coronavirus lockdown gave me the opportunity to force the moment to its conclusion. To my surprise, it didn't take me very long.

My first disc would be Bach's 'St Matthew's Passion'. To me, Bach is the ultimate composer. He always has been and I don't really know why. His music is so pure and uncluttered by superfluous emotion. It is classical with clean lines and forms that appeal to the mathematician in me. Choral singing—a choir of voices—has always been my favourite form of music-making. My friend Caroline and I sang this piece with the Bach Choir in the Festival Hall. I am an atheist, and always have been, but I love religious music. Maybe it is because the strong purpose and emotion of the music are understood. What I love is the body of sound of, at best, a massed choir, with an organ or an orchestra, ideally reverberating up the stone pillars and arches to the vaulted ceilings of a church. It's a magical combination.

My second would be Beethoven's 'Appassionata Sonata No. 23' in F minor, an easy choice because it represents the pinnacle of my years of piano playing. It was one of the set pieces for my Grade 8 piano exam, for which I won the gold medal and which got me into the Royal College of Music. Much of the credit for that should go to my wonderful piano teacher, Miss Rice, during my last few years at MGC. The strange thing is that I can remember so little about her, or about the hours and hours that I must have spent with her. She was serious and very focused and she got the best out of me as a pianist for three or four years during the most important learning period for me. She must have been in her early forties, had a pleasant round face, her blouse firmly buttoned at the neck, and she cared about what she was doing. I think I have blocked her out of my memory because, during my final year at school, after I had taken my Grade 8, she left to become a nun, and at the same time, I lost what I call my musical memory, the ability to memorise music and be able to play without looking at the music. It is essential for any serious musician. Perhaps, subconsciously, I felt abandoned. I have always blamed her for this and, to be honest, I have never forgiven her. I never saw her again and have no idea who taught me when she left but it was around this time that I began to have doubts about taking up my place at the Royal College of Music and about music as a career. Surely not a coincidence?

When I listen to the 'Appassionata' now, I find it hard to believe I ever mastered it. Nowadays, one can listen to dozens of interpretations of this piece on the internet. I would choose Claudio Arrau's, a striking synthesis of force and tenderness. Beethoven knew when he composed it that he was going irreversibly deaf, and it captures his passion and anger as well as his impending fear.

As a girl, I played everything I could get my hands on, but I was less good at playing pieces by the more delicate, more subtle composers, which is how I would describe Mozart. As a pianist, I preferred the meatiness of Beethoven or Brahms. You have to be technically brilliant to master Chopin, and I didn't believe my technique was ever up to it. It was while I was grappling with Chopin and Brahms that I decided that there were things I would rather be doing with my life than perfecting a piece of piano music. Nevertheless, I brought lots of my music with me when I came to Bombay. When we moved house from Warden Road to Bandra not long ago, I gave away almost all my piano music, but I could not bear to part with my three books of Beethoven Sonatas or Bach's 48 Preludes and Fugues. They are much too beloved and I have thumbed through them too many times ever to part with them.

My third choice would be Schubert's gloriously light and flowing Octet in F major because, to me, it is a perfect piece of chamber music, and the recording by the Vienna Octet in 1958 is as near perfect as is possible. Scored for an unusual combination of instruments, a string quartet plus double bass and three woodwind, the clarinet, bassoon and horn, it maintains the perfect balance between them all, creating utter perfection. I shall never ever tire of listening to this, and if I could take just one record, it would be this. And if I am very lucky, I might find some Schubert lieder on the flip side.

My fourth choice is lieder, but from the other great lieder composer Robert Schumann, his 'Dichterliebe' song cycle sung by the baritone Dietrich Fischer Dieskau accompanied by Gerald Moore. Although I didn't understand the German (I subsequently looked up the translation), I sensed that these beautiful songs were about loss, the loss of a loved one, the devastation and utter emptiness of loss. This record was in my father's collection, and when I was staying in England after my daughter Tara died, I would listen to it over and over again, and it somehow eased the terrible pain in my heart. It still moves me to tears, both for itself and for Tara.

The film *Carmen Jones* was my introduction to opera, which I subsequently came to love, and my fifth record is 'Dat's Love' from the film starring Dorothy Dandridge and Harry Belafonte. It is their fabulous rendering of Bizet's 'Habanera' in the 1954 film directed by Otto Preminger, a very different genre of singing, but I think it's becoming obvious that I favour vocal music over most others. It also reminds me of holidays in our holiday house in Devon from where, on rainy days, my father drove us seven miles to Torquay to see films. A rare treat.

I like to think that I broke the RCM mould of classical musicians by loving popular music as well as classical music. I played pop music by ear on the piano at weekends in the boarding house at school, which all the girls loved. When I left school in 1958, popular music was opening up, and musically it was a very exciting time. I thought of choosing an Elvis number for my island, but even though 'Love Me Tender' is one of the greatest love songs ever, I was not a big Elvis fan. In my early teens, the singers were all crooners like Dean Martin and Frank Sinatra or Doris Day singing 'Que Sera Sera' and 'How Much Is that Doggy in the Window?' All very innocent and civilised. Then Elvis burst onto the scene with his slicked hair, tight trousers and suggestive gyrations, setting the stage for the likes of the Beatles and the Rolling Stones, and the advent of the electric guitar with its new, noisy, exciting and sexy sound. I came to really love some of the Beatles' songs, and have always marvelled at their musical ingenuity. I wasn't a big Rolling Stones fan. Mick Jagger was at LSE at exactly the same time as Anand and I were, though unfortunately, our paths did not cross. He came to Bombay some years ago, and we went to see the Stones live. It was extraordinary to see all these wrinkly men of our age jumping up and down on the stage.

The Beatles are more timeless, so as my sixth track, I am going to take 'When I'm 64' from the 1967 album *Sergeant Pepper's Lonely Hearts Club Band*. I almost chose 'Eleanor Rigby' because it was the first record I bought here in Bombay, but in the end, I chose 'When I'm 64' because when I was young, it was a lifetime away. It sounded really old. Which makes me laugh now that I am nearer eighty-four than sixty-four.

When I came here, the only pop music came from Radio Ceylon, which was offshore like Radio Caroline in England, and gave us a short burst of pop once a day. At first, we were able to see all the American films in the cinemas and to buy foreign records at Rhythm House, where you could go and listen to pop records in a little booth, but all imports stopped in the seventies when the economy went belly up. As far as I know, you still can't switch on a radio and get Western pop, and the legendary Rhythm House closed its doors forever in 2019.

I began to hear popular Western music again as Anjali was growing up, particularly when Sachin came on the scene because he loves it. It must have been 1992 when I heard Stevie Wonder and Paul McCartney's 1982 record 'Ebony and Ivory' being played regularly in Anjali's room. I think Sachin must have introduced her to it. It represents my reintroduction into the world of popular music through my daughter, and later my granddaughter, through these two great stars. This may sound a little sentimental, but it also reminds me of my first instrument, the piano, and of the way I have lived my life. I love the lyrics, which resonate as much today as they ever did back then. For all those reasons, that would be track number seven.

One can't live in India for more than fifty years without becoming aware of Indian pop music, which until recently was comprised solely of songs from Hindi films. These were nearly all sung by playback singers, some of whom are very famous. So, for my eighth and final choice, and to remind me of all my happy years in Mumbai, I would cheat and have three songs from Hindi films. First, '*Chal chal chal mere saathi*' sung by Kishore Kumar, from *Haathi Mere Saathi,* which was the biggest hit movie of 1971 and featured Rajesh Khanna and Tanuja. The second, '*Dum Maro Dum*', from *Hare Rama Hare Krishna,* with Dev Anand and Zeenat Aman, who plays a Westernised hippy, was another hit from 1971. And the third, '*Jai Ho*' by the great A.R. Rahman, comes from Danny Boyle's fantastic film *Slumdog Millionaire,* which I can't believe came out as long ago as 2008 and starred the wonderful Dev Patel and Freida Pinto. The first captures the full flavour of Hindi films in the early days of my time in India when films were the only form of mass entertainment and Hollywood offerings had a very limited, purely urban following. They were largely fantasy and the narrative did not matter much. The story was just an excuse for the song and dance sequences that made the film. Kissing was not allowed, though there was no skimping on the suggestive gyrations. The second overlaps with that but also takes on the hippy drug culture that was emerging then with Maharishi Yogi and Rajnish. The third is a joyous song from a movie that is very much a British view of India but powerfully illustrates my immersion in the urban poor and my hope for a better tomorrow. So I shall, metaphorically anyway, end on a note of optimism.

My choice of book would have to be either *War and Peace* or *Gone with the Wind*. I only really discovered reading after I left school and went to London and found Tolstoy in Kensington Library. On reflection, I would take *War and Peace*, and take the film version of *Gone with the Wind* as my luxury. I have always thought going to the cinema in the afternoon was somehow immoral, but on my desert island I would happily spend endless afternoons watching Vivien Leigh, Leslie Howard and Clark Gable. The luxury I really want is a radio, but I don't think that would be allowed. My radio has always been my most precious possession ever since I was a little girl, and I listened as I fell asleep. I still do, and I put it on whenever I wake at night, which I do more than ever during these terrifying times.

Studio portrait, aged two

Family group on Portscatho beach, 1949

With my sister Gillian

My father, brothers Jeremy and Richard, my mother and sister Gillian at the top of a mountain in Scotland, 1950

Playing the piano at Hampton Lane, 1953

Sparrows Nest

My best schoolfriends, sunbathing at Sparrows Nest on a Sunday out from school

A Sunday outing to Sparrows Nest, with Hetta, Amanda,
Judy and Shuttie

With my friend Amanda, wearing our fashionable fifties dirndl dresses

Caroline and me setting off on my Vespa for our tour of the Loire Valley, 1959

Anand and me in the summer of 1963

Two years later, 1965

My mother and Aunt Mare

Richard and my mother in Cornwall

My mother at ninety, 1997

The Mehta family home at
Warden Road, Breach Candy, Bombay

The day before the wedding

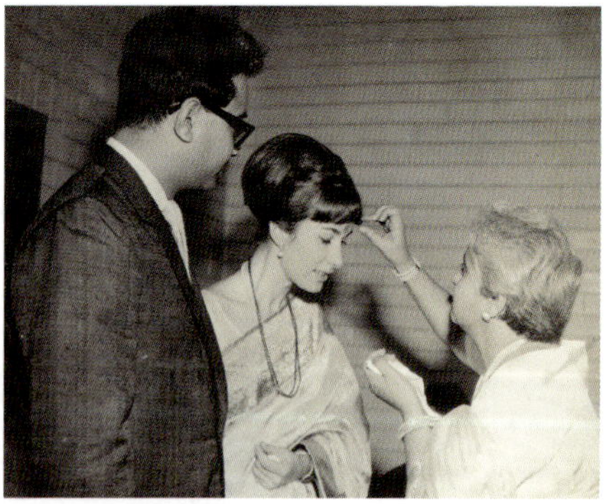

A blessing from my mother-in-law,
Amru Masi

Our wedding (above) and the wedding reception, December 1966

Proud parents with Anjali, December 1968

Anjali, aged two, in the Warden Road kitchen

Anjali and Tara at Indus fashion show

Singing with the Indus choir, Bombay, 1974

My two girls,
my favourite photo

Tulsi with her children, Radha and
Vinayak, and Anjali and Tara, 1975

As a family with Tara and Anjali, Sparrows Nest, 1975

With Anand and Anjali, 1977

Anjali, the medical student, 1987

Anand and me in Egypt, 1989

Early learning: Draupadhi and me with the children at Apnalaya

Early days at Apnalaya, outside our first shed

With Dnyaneshwar outside our Jaiphalwadi centre,1990

With a group of young Apnalaya volunteers, 2019

A royal bus-ride: Her Royal Highness, the Princess of Wales (Catherine) and His Royal Highness, the Prince of Wales (William) accompany a team from Apnalaya on an open bus in Mumbai

Receiving the MBE (Member of the Order of the British Empire) from HRH Prince William in London, December 2017

Sachin and Anjali at our home, 1993

Anjali and Sachin's engagement at our Warden Road house, 1994

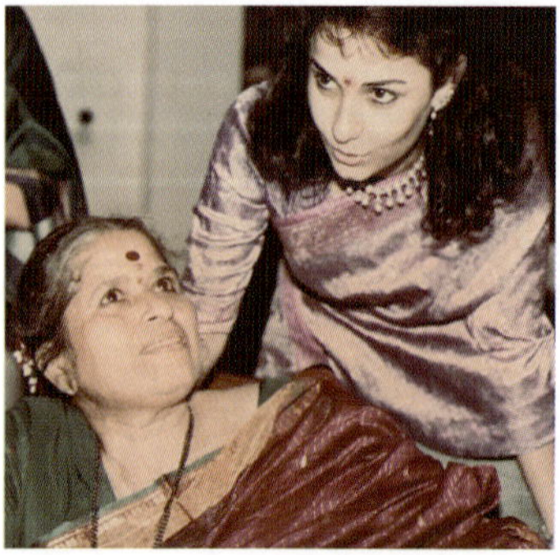

Anjali with Sachin's mother at the engagement

Anjali with Sachin's father

Richard, Gillian, Jeremy and me with our mother before Anjali's wedding

Anand and me with Sachin's parents Ramesh and Rajni

Anjali, a radiant bride-to-be

Grandmothers-in-law

During the wedding ceremony

Cousins Radha, Vinayak and Anandi had
a role to play in the wedding

My mother and Amru Masi at the wedding

Anjali and Sachin with all the grandmothers

Anjali, the Maharashtrian bride, at the reception
hosted by Sachin's parents

Sachin with newborn Sara

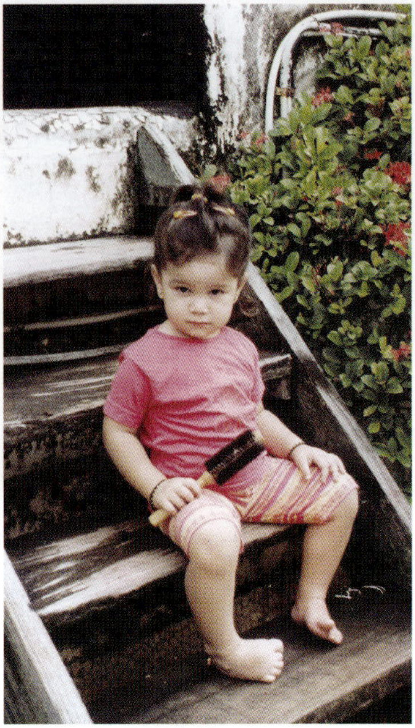

Sara, always determined

Sachin and Sara in the park in London

Anjali and Sara in Goa, 1999

With my grandchildren in Goa

With Anand, Sachin, Sara, Anjali and Arjun at Melbourne Cricket Ground on the eve of the Boxing Day Test, 2003

Arjun and Sara, 2023

Anjali with all her cousins at Aliya's wedding, 2016

Celebrating our golden wedding anniversary with Arjun, Sachin, Anjali and Sara, 27 December 2016

At Anjali's home on Ganesh Chaturthi, 2017

6

When Anjali Met Sachin

ONE AFTERNOON IN 1991, I WAS AT HOME IN MY FLAT IN THE FAMILY bungalow on Warden Road when the phone rang. 'Can I speak to Anjali Mehta?' said a young woman. 'She's not here. Tell me?' I replied. 'I'm ringing from such-and-such hotel in Bangalore,' said the voice. 'Mr Tendulkar wants to talk to her.' When Anjali got back from JJ Hospital that evening, I told her I had been mildly amused that a Mr Tendulkar's secretary had rung, hoping to find her. 'Oh, Mummy,' groaned Anjali, 'it must have been Muffi playing a prank!' Muffi—Muffazal Lakdawala—was a fellow medical student, mad about cricket. I laughed and didn't give it another thought.

Anjali was not telling the exact truth. She and Sachin had been seeing one another for over a year, a secret shared with just a handful of close friends. But not her parents.

Romance had sparked in September 1990 at the airport in Bombay. Anjali and her best friend, Aparna, also a medical student, had come to fetch me from my annual visit to my elderly mother (still bicycling in her nineties) in England. They were in the viewing gallery at Arrivals when Aparna squealed: 'That's the Indian cricket team coming out, Anjali.' 'Who's that?' asked Anjali. She was pointing to an enchanting boy with chubby cheeks and a shock of dark curls coming through from the Heathrow flight before mine. As Anjali looked at him, their eyes met, or so she claims, because the next minute she grabbed Aparna and they ran down the stairs in chase, the fact of my impending arrival forgotten. Sachin was seventeen; Anjali was twenty-one. And Cupid must have been hiding behind a column.

Just weeks before, on 14 August, Sachin, already a superstar in India, had scored his maiden Test century at Old Trafford in Manchester, dragging India from defeat. Anand had watched the match in London on my brother Richard's black-and-white television.

However, every keen Indian cricket fan would have heard Sachin's name less than a year earlier when, aged sixteen and barely five-foot-six, he played for India against Pakistan in Sialkot. The brilliant Waqar Younis, himself only a year older, and making his Test match debut, had bowled a bouncer that smashed into his nose. Sachin had famously carried on playing with blood streaming down his cute little baby-face. It was a baptism of sorts. From that moment, Sachin was christened Master Blaster.

Needless to say, Anand, a cricket anorak, had known about Sachin even earlier. One afternoon in October 1988, he had been playing in a bridge tournament at the Cricket Club of India in the card room on the pavilion side of the club. A match was going on, and during a break, someone suggested that Anand should come out and watch a young batsman who appeared to be a bit of a star. When Anand got free, the batsman in question, one Sachin Tendulkar, was still in and continuing to stun spectators with his style. The club had had to amend its rules so that a fifteen-year-old could enter the dressing room.

The next time Anand watched Sachin was at his debut innings in the Ranji Trophy tournament at the Wankhede Stadium against Gujarat, where he made a century, becoming the youngest to do so and therefore a household name in Bombay. But I can guarantee that Anjali had never heard of Sachin—or any other cricketer, for that matter—until that moment, two years later at the airport. The day after Sachin's return to Bombay, I read the story in the paper about a gang of giggly girls who had mobbed him on his arrival at the airport and clambered on to the bonnet of his taxi. It never crossed my mind that one of them was my medical-student daughter.

Anjali had had one or two boyfriends, not remotely serious and possibly only there to keep others at a distance. She was tall and pretty and had dozens of admirers. My mother-in-law was particularly keen on a gorgeous Gujarati chap who sent Anjali flowers every single day. We nicknamed him Phoolwallah. The son of a celebrity I dare not name was also buzzing around. I had created for Anjali a lovely room at the top of the house with windows at either end and a view of the mango tree, where she and her friends used to lounge about on mattresses and fat bolsters. We had more space than most people, and a garden, and there were always heaps of young ones coming and going.

As a devoted mother, I think I might be permitted to say that my daughter was quite a catch. From the moment she began studying medicine, I imagined she would fall madly in love with a dishy doctor she met fluttering ebony-black lashes above his surgical mask during a complicated medical procedure. Or maybe an Oxford graduate who had come back to Bombay to work in some Indian pharma company? Or an IT graduate with a good corporate job? I would never in a million years have predicted that she would fall for a cricketer.

How—and why—Anjali kept Sachin a secret from us for so long, I don't know. Perhaps she was waiting until she felt absolutely sure about him. Even as a small girl she was measured, sensible and organised, in pronounced contrast to her little sister Tara, who was a dreamer, scatty and forgetful. Anjali forgets nothing. She used to get home from school, go straight to her room and do her homework. She was always prepared, punctual and private. That is her nature. I suppose I didn't share my private life with my mother, either. I later discovered that when Anjali met Sachin, she wrote to her aunt Helen, my brother Richard's wife, and said she had developed an interest in cricket and asked if she could send her a copy of the *Idiot's Guide to Cricket*, which was only available in England. Anjali has a doctor's brain. She learns quickly and has a brilliant memory. She read the book in a day and then invited a surprised Sachin to test her. 'What's cow corner?' he asked, hoping to catch her out. But Anjali knew it was a particular place on the cricket field in the deep on the batsman's leg side. Clean bowled!

Anjali says it was love at first sight that day at the airport. For her, at least. The second she got home, she phoned her friend Muffi (he who was accused of the 'prank' phone call) and asked him for Sachin's phone number; Muffi had a cousin who played club cricket in Bombay, so he knew people, and the job was done. Sachin, rarely at home, happened to pick up the phone that day. Anjali introduced herself as the girl from the airport and said she wanted to see him again. Sachin claimed to remember her. 'So, what was the colour of my tee-shirt?' bowled a flirty Anjali. 'Orange,' said Sachin. A six for Sachin! The rest is history. I wouldn't be surprised if Anjali has kept the tee-shirt.

They were often apart for months at a time while Sachin went on tour all over the world. With no mobile phones and no internet, they must be among the last couples to have written actual love letters with pen and paper. Anjali always had to calculate where Sachin would be in a fortnight's time when her latest missive would arrive. Occasionally, she would phone him, but JJ Hospital is in a crowded area on the very busy Mohammed Ali road, which Anjali had to cross to get to the Public Call Office carrying bags of coins that were swallowed up at an alarming speed. Once or twice, when Sachin was in Bombay, they met at her friend Deepika's house. I still marvel at the fact that we knew nothing for two years and that their relationship remained a secret from the rest of the world for four years.

Perhaps every parent's life changes when their daughter decides she has met Mr Right. The change is possibly more dramatic if she is their only child, is all set to become a doctor, is more than four years older than her boyfriend and said boyfriend is on his way to being regarded as a living god on earth.

At one stage, on walls all over this vast country and especially in Bombay, where Sachin was born and still lives, you would find graffiti declaring: CRICKET IS MY RELIGION. SACHIN IS MY GOD. Even now, years after Sachin's retirement, having played his two hundredth Test match against the West Indies at the Wankhede Stadium in 2013, he has 36 million Twitter followers. Even now, when Sachin turns up for an IPL game at the Wankhede Stadium, the moment he tosses his unmistakable black curls, the 33,000-strong crowd starts chanting 'Sachiiiiin, Sach-in, Sachiiiin, Sach-in'. It's a heartbeat, a pulse, an invocation, an incantation, a charm. It is extraordinary. It is deafening. Sachin is a god to all Indian cricket fans, but the fact that he is Maharashtrian means that he is specially loved in the state of Maharashtra.

I discovered the seriousness of Anjali and Sachin's love affair in May 1992 when Anjali was travelling to the USA for a holiday, stopping in the UK in order to visit my mother in Cheltenham, and I rang, hoping to speak to both of them. Anjali evidently had other plans. Sachin had just become Yorkshire's first overseas signing since they had dropped the ruling that all players must have been born inside 'God's Own Country'. My mother informed me that Anjali had gone straight from Heathrow to Yorkshire to watch her friend Sachin play at Headingley, and would be coming down to stay with her in a couple of days before leaving for the USA. A true romantic who knew nothing about cricket and less about cricketers, my mother had detected that love was in the air. I breezily mentioned to Anand that Anjali had gone to Yorkshire with Muffi to see Sachin play and would be going to stay with my mother in Cheltenham in a day or two. As ever, he seemed unruffled. Neither of us had a clue precisely what was going on but we were absolutely confident that our daughter had her head screwed on the right way.

Yorkshire, too, had fallen for this sweet boy of nineteen who was happy to be photographed in an anorak emblazoned with the white rose of Yorkshire, wearing a flat cap and holding a foaming pint of Tetley's bitter. In order to keep fans at bay, he had to ask for his name to be removed from the Honda he had been given to drive from match to match all over England. Fish and chips and mushy peas proved irresistible and, as a fine mimic, he can still pronounce his order in an excellent Yorkshire accent. He had become a keen pool player too. British Indians made a terrific fuss of him. Every curry house treated him and his mates to free meals.

It was only then that I recalled that Sachin had been among a group of friends Anjali had invited over to Warden Road in mid-April. He had walked past me on his way up to Anjali's room, too shy to introduce himself. Muffi had been there of course, and Deepika, Aparna and Amelia, my niece from London. They were all celebrating Sachin's nineteenth birthday a few days prematurely. A week later, he was gone, and that was that, or so I thought.

It must have occurred to Anjali at some stage that his going to Yorkshire would give her a rare chance to see him play cricket in a place where he was treated as a normal cricketer and better still, a golden opportunity to spend time with him without anyone noticing her in the house he had been lent in Dewsbury. Not that they were alone. Sachin's cricketing friend Vinod Kambli had gone with him to play league cricket in Yorkshire and cricket-mad Muffi was there on holiday.

The moment I knew that Anjali was in Dewsbury with Sachin, I reckoned this was a potentially serious situation and I was going to have to deal with it. Luckily, I was flying to London myself two weeks later. As soon as I could get hold of her, I told Anjali that when I came over, I wanted to meet Sachin and talk to him. Alone.

Anjali, Sachin and Muffi were waiting for me at my brother Richard's house in Bayswater. I asked them to leave me with Sachin. As we sat down on benches either side of the long kitchen table, I thought how young and sweet he looked, and I had to remind myself why we were there. I told him that Anjali was our very precious only child, doubly precious because we had lost our second daughter, and I asked him what his intentions were as far as Anjali was concerned. Traditionally, in England, this would have been the father's remit. However, Anand is nothing like a traditional British male, which is one of the reasons I married him. He loathes confrontations. Moreover, he could have won Mastermind on the subject of the nineteen-year-old Master Blaster's career thus far, so he might not have been terribly objective about Sachin's suitability as his daughter's intended.

I had clocked by then that Sachin was the brightest star in the Indian cricketing firmament, but I was concerned by the possibility of him becoming a playboy like so many of his fellow cricketers. It comes with the territory. Sachin in India in the nineties was like David Beckham in England. I needed to look him in the eye and ask him how he felt about my daughter.

'We want to get married' were his precise words, sweeping the rug from beneath my feet. I was astounded. I had always imagined Anjali marrying a tall, dark and handsome man. Dark and handsome, Sachin was. But at nineteen, he was still a boy. And so small. Barely taller than Anjali, who is five-foot-five and a half. Sachin's bouncy hair possibly gives him another inch, but not enough for Anjali to wear the high heels she had always loved.

Anjali told me later that Sachin had made it clear from their first date that he was serious. She was his first girlfriend and he was convinced that she was The One. They were truly, madly, deeply in love; I could see that. And all I wanted was for Anjali to be happy. At a later stage, I would worry that he was away for long periods of time, which would test them in all sorts of ways, but all I could see at that moment was his young, innocent, hopeful, ecstatic face.

They had sensibly decided against running away to Gretna Green, which they had considered for a while. In India, men are not legally allowed to marry until they are twenty-one (a law flagrantly ignored); he was only nineteen, and Anjali was yet to complete her postgraduate medical degree. They would have to wait another two years and then they would marry in Mumbai. In the meantime, I told him, we would be happy to keep their secret.

At one level, life continued as normal. I continued to work with my charity, Apnalaya, and told no one about Sachin, though he became a frequent visitor to our house on Warden Road. Not that everyone recognised him. My sister-in-law Tulsi once mistook him for the son of our Gurkha watchman. But the man who sold chana on the street, as well as the security people at the American Consulate across the road, would definitely have known his face, and yet none of them ever tipped off the press. I can only surmise that they felt it would have been the betrayal of a superhero. I find that very touching.

So it went on, with Sachin totally taken up with cricket and Anjali with her paediatrics, living in the hostel at JJ Hospital. But she was obviously getting impatient, and one evening, when Sachin rang from New Zealand, she asked him when he planned to propose. After a short pause for thought, he instructed her matter-of-factly to go and ask his parents for their permission to get married. Sachin, a respectful son, would not get engaged without his parents' consent. If they agreed, the engagement could be held as soon as he returned home, provided of course that Anand and I also approved. We had no hesitation.

It was all rather unconventional, to say the least. Sachin's elder brother, Ajit, arranged the meeting between Anjali and his parents. We didn't meet Sachin's parents until shortly before the engagement. Despite coming from different social circles, we got on splendidly. They were solid, middle-class Maharashtrians and devout Hindus. As is Sachin. His father, Ramesh, was an acclaimed poet as well as a professor of Marathi Literature at Kirti College. His mother, Rajni, worked for the Life Insurance Corporation. Sachin's mother has only ever spoken her mother-tongue, but his father spoke English.

The engagement took place on Sachin's twenty-first birthday, 24 April 1994, at our house, with a lunch for twenty-five relations, followed by a formal announcement to the press. When Sachin had been away in Dubai, he had instructed Anjali and me to go and see our jeweller friend Sanjeev for Anjali to choose a ring. Sanjeev let her take home a simple, small diamond ring, which she judged appropriate for a medical student working in a government hospital, for Sachin to approve when he came back. There is a lovely photograph of Sachin putting the ring on her finger and kissing her, which he has never permitted to be shown to the public. He is a very private person.

Needless to say, the press went wild. Nobody had a clue who this Anjali Mehta was. The only picture they could find was a mugshot taken when she enrolled at St Xavier's College at the age of sixteen, rather different from the beautiful young woman she had become. Following the announcement that Sachin was now spoken for, it was reported that millions of Indian girls went into mourning. The fact that Sachin was only twenty-one and hadn't played the field romantically attracted considerable attention. As did Anjali, especially as she was nearly five years older.

I count my blessings that I became the mother-in-law of someone everyone loves and who has lived a blameless life and become a role model to so many. At nineteen, Sachin was a sweet, shy, soft-spoken boy of few words. When I commented to Anjali about how quiet he was, she said: 'You should meet the rest of his family; they're completely silent!' Like Anand and me, they both recognised how different their backgrounds were and neither underestimated how much it mattered.

Sachin's family lived in a small flat in Bandra with no privacy. Anjali had grown up in more exclusive South Bombay with lots of space, literally and emotionally. She had known privacy, unlike so many Indians, and she valued it. Hence the secret romance, I suppose. I had worried what would happen to her after marriage if, as most Indians must, she would have to move in with her in-laws. So, it was a great relief to me—and to her, I expect—that, well before they married, Sachin could afford to buy the flat on the floor below his parents' flat. By now, Anjali was doing long shifts in the paediatric wards at JJ Hospital and Sachin was on tour, so it fell to me to do up the flat for them and to begin planning the wedding.

I have a vivid picture in my head of Anjali in the crowded paediatric ward, going from cot to cot and bed to bed, in her white coat, hair tied back, stethoscope dangling, sometimes with a sick baby tucked under one arm, labelled NNK for No Next of Kin. Abandoned. She scarcely had time to eat; I used to send a tiffin in for her. She would come home for half a day and a night once a week and talk about her work with tremendous passion. She had routinely come top of her year, but in addition to that, she had real compassion.

Anjali and Sachin decided to have the wedding a year later, at the end of May 1995, when Sachin had a break from touring. His father was charged with finding an auspicious date and planning the ceremony. So began a year of meticulous preparations. Anjali and Sachin were consulted at every stage, though getting hold of them was often a challenge. Sachin was busy with cricket, ending 1994 as Player of the Series against the West Indies. Junior doctors don't get many holidays, and Anjali worked until two days before her wedding.

Indian parents famously spend way more than they can afford while marrying off their daughters. Not us. We didn't have much money and we were not extravagant and wouldn't have wanted a lavish bash in any case. Maharashtrian weddings are normally held in the morning and followed by lunch, and May is unbearably hot and humid in Bombay, so we needed an air-conditioned venue. The obvious choice was the Taj Mahal Hotel in Colaba, but in those days it didn't allow a ceremonial fire, an essential part of the Hindu ceremony. We were getting desperate when my friend Indra suggested the Jewel of India, a lovely restaurant on the ground floor of the Nehru Centre, in Worli. The owner graciously agreed although they had never had a wedding there before but—and it was a big but—we could invite no more than two hundred people. That suited us, but Sachin's father was dismayed. He said there was no way he could invite only a hundred members of their vast family. But somehow they managed it, hopefully without offending too many.

Sachin's family brought their priests for the ceremony, which Sachin wanted done and dusted in less than one hour. Sachin's father took the time to explain the service to me in detail. I had been to many weddings, including my own (a civil one), but until then, I had not thought deeply about the ceremony itself or what it means to true Hindu believers. One lovely aspect is that it involves close family. The bride's mother's brothers traditionally bring the bride in halfway through, so Richard and Jeremy would have their part to play, and five married women from the family are required to put a tikka on the bride's forehead. I was happy to discover that the Hindu marriage service is less patriarchal than I had feared. I have never been terribly impressed with the Church of England service in which the groom always speaks first and takes the vows first, although nowadays, the wording has been adapted to suit modern times.

For those making the arrangements, a wedding, especially an Indian wedding, can be a real nightmare, as it is much more than just the marriage service. It can go on for several days, but in Anand's family, ceremonies are kept to the minimum. Many people have a Sangeet the previous day and a Mehendi, attended by family and friends and usually involving singing, dancing and dinner, but we decided to skip that. Anjali's Indian grandmother wanted a traditional Gujarati mosalu which she hosted at home for our family and a few close friends the day before the wedding. For the mosalu the bride's mamas (her mother's brothers) come to her home, bringing gifts, saris and jewellery, so my two brothers had another role to play here, though I supplied the saris and the jewellery. I was thrilled that seventeen members of my family came from England: my mother, my sister Gillian, my two brothers, Jeremy and Richard, and their wives. It was Jeremy's first visit since I had come to live here in 1966. My aunt Phyll and various nieces and nephews made up the balance. Anand's mother also hosted a dinner for more than a hundred people on our terrace three days before the wedding, and his sister Jill and her husband Mohamed threw a more informal party with music and dancing at the Breach Candy Club for a few oldies and lots of young. Mo, originally from Lebanon, had flown in delicious Lebanese sausages as a treat for Sachin. That night is the only time I have ever seen Sachin really let his hair down and dance.

In the run up to the wedding, I had arranged a week-long programme for my family, including a visit to Sachin and Anjali's new flat in Bandra, which was a real eye-opener to them because the outside was so scruffy and so close to other buildings; it was also on the third floor with no lift. The flat was very small indeed, but was light and nicely done with marble floors because Sachin loves marble. A massive flat-screen television took up almost an entire wall.

Another day, I took them to Chor Bazaar where vendors sell old junk and the odd treasure from tatty stalls on crowded lanes shared with goats. It sounds terrible, but I love going there and have bought a considerable amount of furniture there for our homes in Mumbai and Goa. Most memorable for some was our visit to JJ Hospital to see Dr Anjali Mehta, Chief Resident Doctor, in the paediatric ward. My brother Jeremy said that seeing Anjali at work was the highlight of the trip for him.

On the eve of the wedding, I gathered my English family to share a description of the ceremony written by my dear friend Pommy Manchanda, who was very knowledgeable about all things Hindu. I found her piece the other day and it moved me as much as it did when I first read it.

I was fascinated to learn that none of the endless circles made by the bride and groom around the fire signified endless love. Love and marriage here do not go together like a horse and carriage. In the course of more than five decades, I have observed that an Indian marriage, be it arranged or a love marriage, is a world away from marriage in England.

For the wedding, Anjali wore a stunning red-and-gold Paithani silk sari and Sachin wore a simple white kurta-pyjama with an embroidered trim. Anjali looked radiant, her hair swept back in a bun with a white mogra gajra, a small teeka on her forehead, a gold necklace and matching earrings, a Kolhapuri saaj (three long rows of hollow gold beads) and gold and red glass bangles, all very restrained by Gujarati standards. For the ceremony, Sachin and Anjali both wore a typically Maharashtrian floral mundavalya, a string of jasmine buds across the forehead with another hanging either side of the face.

The guests were exemplary, sitting transfixed as the ceremony unfolded beneath a canopy of flowers for much longer than the hour that Sachin had laid down. Soft drinks and small bites were passed around from time to time, always vegetarian and with strictly no alcohol at all until the following day. Then lunch was served, but not until Sachin took Anjali downstairs to give the world's press their first view of his wife. The next day, their photographs were on the front pages of newspapers around the world. Someone sent me a clipping from the London edition of the *Asian Age* that said: 'Cricket aside, what do Sachin Tendulkar and Imran Khan have in common?' The answer was a mother-in-law named Annabel. Imran's mother-in-law was Lady Annabel Goldsmith. That day, I acquired a new label—Sachin ki saas or Sachin's mother-in-law—and a new status as a celebrity-by-association, which took some getting used to.

The wedding is usually followed by a reception the same or the following day, and the obvious place to hold it in those days if you lived in South Bombay was the Turf Club, on the race course not far away in Mahalakshmi, a glorious patch of open space in the middle of built-up, concreted Bombay. However, we quickly realised that it would be impossible to prevent uninvited fans from joining the fun. So Anand and I hosted a reception and dinner for a mere 700 instead. (The number of guests at rich Indian weddings can run to several thousands; I think two or three thousand came to mine and Anand's reception.) Held on the terrace above Jade Garden in Worli, it was a glorious gathering of our friends, Sachin's friends, Anjali's friends, and masses of people from the cricketing world. One of my favourite things about India is that invitations are often sent to 'Mr and Mrs Mehta & fly (sic).' When I first saw it, I couldn't imagine what it meant. But I was soon told that it's short for family, and can mean, in practice, children and any friends and relations who want to come along. But, on this occasion, 'fly' were not invited. No photographers were allowed in to the wedding or to the reception except those brought by us, but there is a wonderful photograph of a wall of the world's press waiting outside Jade Garden for Sachin and Anjali to arrive. We had been expecting the Indian press but we had no idea that the whole world would cover my daughter's wedding. It was quite a shock. Sachin was twenty-two, hailed as the Master Blaster, and was already a legend, but he had not yet become a living idol.

A couple of nights later, Sachin's parents threw a party in Juhu for all their family, neighbours and friends and the extended community in their housing colony, including Shri Bal Thackeray, the founder of Shiv Sena, the right-wing Hindu nationalist party, whose family Sachin has grown up with.

Sachin and Anjali honeymooned in Goa in the most remote cottage on the grounds of the Taj Fort Aguada hotel with medic friends Sanjay and Neeru in the cottage next door. They had lived in the same hostel with Anjali at JJ Hospital, so had been in on the conspiracy to smuggle Sachin into the compound to meet her whenever he was back in Mumbai between tours. In true Indian style, we went as well, though partly to check on the progress being made on the house we were building in Goa. We stayed in a nearby hotel with my mother, my sister Gillian and my sister-in-law Serena, and we all turned up to watch Sachin play in a friendly cricket match the next day.

It was a crowded honeymoon by English standards but couples in India often take others along, if indeed they honeymoon at all. Although it's rare these days for a dozen family members to accompany the newly-weds and take over a hotel, as they did for my parents-in-law and for Moti, Anand's grandmother's wedding. But Moti was only sixteen at the time, which might explain it. Close friends of ours, Didi and Shirish, got married the day before we did and went south by themselves and were so bored they came home early after just a few days.

For our honeymoon, Anand and I went first to Delhi, and from there to Agra to see the Taj by moonlight, and 'it was unbelievable, a sort of dream' just as one of Noel Coward's creations says in his play *Private Lives.* It is absolutely magical, like floating lace. After that, we went to the Maharaja's Palace in Jaipur where he still lived. Our palatial room was lined in green marble. From there, we went to the Lake Palace in Udaipur, staffed by bewhiskered turbaned retainers and most memorable for its terrible whiff of drains. Then on to Ahmedabad for the famous Kite Flying Festival, staying with Anand's cousin Devi and her husband's family of mill-owners. Be they multimillionaires living in magnificent bungalows or lowly peons living in huts, everyone flew kites. I remember thinking to myself: 'How could one possibly be bored in a country like this?' We returned to Bombay and Anand abandoned me immediately to go on a bridge tour.

When I came to India in 1966, people seldom travelled unless to make a religious pilgrimage or to visit family. Going on holiday only became an option for ordinary people once the economy opened up and people had more disposable incomes. There were very few hotels, five-star or otherwise, in the sixties. Bombay had the Taj Mahal in Colaba since 1902. The second five-star hotel, the Oberoi, did not open until 1973. When travelling, we usually stayed in rudimentary government rest houses or guest houses attached to factories for visiting customers, or we just stayed with friends. A friend went to Ranthambore National Park to look for tigers (in vain) in the eighties and the only place to stay was the Cement Factory Guest House, where they bathed in a cement bath in cold water.

After a few days, Anjali and Sachin returned to their own flat, and so began their married life together. It's a strange adjustment for a mother to make when your daughter is no longer your responsibility and her home is elsewhere. It reminded me of my anxiety when my very close friends Amanda and Caroline married all those years ago and I feared losing them as friends and losing touch with them. It took me quite a long time to realise that I hadn't lost them, but our relationship had undoubtedly shifted.

Now, our house felt empty and even my beloved dog Vij went into mourning. Or so it seemed. He was very old and he slept a lot. The very first evening when Anjali and Sachin came over to our house as a married couple, Vij decided to lie down and die, right there and then, in front of them. It was as if he had waited for their return to say a final goodbye. That first visit was also memorable because Sachin and Anjali told us that they had enjoyed the wedding so much that they wanted to have it all over again. I was thrilled to bits because I had done my best to make it perfect for them.

Anjali had yet to complete her postgraduation in Paediatrics, so she went straight back to work, but Sachin happened to have a break from cricket, so he did all the sweeping and swabbing in the flat and scrambled his own eggs for breakfast because they didn't have any domestic help. He has never been too grand to do his share of the chores. Quite the opposite, in fact. He had not grown up with servants and has always enjoyed domesticity. Even now, he prefers to do his own ironing because he thinks he does it better than anyone else. He can rustle up a delicious baingan bharta quite expertly.

As a boy, Sachin had shared a room with his elder brother Ajit in their parents' flat in Sahitya Sahawas, the writers' co-operative housing society in Bandra East. He arrived some ten years after his siblings and, by all accounts, they doted on him. I learnt that Sachin's eldest brother Nitin was a published Marathi poet and worked as a purser with Air India. His sister Savita, who gave him his first cricket bat, had moved to Pune after her marriage. His brother Ajit, who has described himself as 'literally crazy about cricket' also worked for Air India as part of the ground staff. They were a very close-knit family.

It was Ajit who spotted his little brother's astonishing ability and natural style and dedicated himself to nurturing his career. He has played a crucial role in Sachin's life, initially playing with tiny, tubby Sachin in the unusually large playground they were lucky to have in Sahitya Sahawas. When Sachin was eleven, Ajit introduced him to Ramakant Achrekar (who Sachin always called 'Achrekar Sir'), the coach for the Sharadashram School team for which Sachin was immediately selected.

We only got to know Sachin's parents after the wedding. In India, parents of couples don't usually interact before the wedding is formalised. When I suggested to Anjali we should get together with Sachin's people as we would have in England, she answered firmly: 'It is not done.' After the wedding, I often visited Anjali and would always go up to Sachin's parents' flat to say hello to his mother Rajni. Crippling arthritis prevented her from standing, and she would sit on a chair chopping onions and garlic, which she would then put into a pan on the gas stove and reach up and stir without being able to see what she was doing. She was an excellent cook, famous for her Maharashtrian fish dishes, crispy fried Bombay duck and tasty prawn curry. Maharashtrian food must be cooked with a light hand and I prefer it to Gujarati and North Indian food, which is rich with ghee and gravy. Her simple yellow dal served with plain rice, varanbhat, is the best I've ever eaten. Arjun was brought up on it, and for many years would eat nothing else.

I have always admired Rajni's spirit. She is now housebound with 24-hour care in a room crammed with pictures and figurines of Hindu gods in Sachin and Anjali's home. I truly believe that Sachin gets his guts from her, as well as his ambition and his focus. He also inherited her hair. She is two years older than me and has thick, curly hair, barely greying, which she wears in a big fat plait. When she was still working and suffering acute pain, she somehow got down four flights of stairs to get to her office because there was no lift in the building. Sachin's father accompanied her in a taxi. He was a fine example to Sachin of a devoted husband. Every day, he would buy Rajni a fresh sweet-smelling gajra for her hair. I think it was a relief to them when Sachin met Anjali, the first doctor in their family. Had they arranged a marriage for Sachin, as would have been the norm in their community, it would have been difficult to find a girl with the education, experience and sophistication to cope as Anjali has with the extraordinary way in which Sachin's life took off. But that's her mother speaking.

Anjali has seldom spoken in public about her husband or her marriage. Ajit has never said a word about Sachin. Sachin has always been quick to express his gratitude to Ajit and to his coach Achrekar Sir, but he invariably claims that his father was his greatest inspiration and his guiding light. In spite of being bookish, Ramesh encouraged his son to pursue his sporting ambitions, at the expense of his formal education. To this day, Sachin places a photograph of his beloved father by his bedside wherever he goes.

There was no money in cricket when Sachin began playing and no one predicted then that successful cricketers could become multimillionaires. Today, parents are keen for their children to become cricketers because it is well paid, even relatively low down in the chain. My grandson, Arjun, is already earning a good living playing cricket. Arjun is six-foot-three; he towers above Sachin and me, his mini grandmother. I am in my eighties and shrinking daily. Arjun's height comes from my uncles, my mother's brothers, who were well over six feet tall. There is a lot of left-handedness in my family, too, and all three of my nephews are left-handed, but Arjun might also have inherited that from his dad. Sachin writes, chops onions and cuts Arjun's hair, all expertly, with his left hand, and he bats and bowls with his right hand. Arjun tells me that being left-handed is an advantage for a cricketer and that teams try to have both right-handed and left-handed bowlers so that the batsmen have to keep adjusting.

Like his father, Arjun lives and breathes cricket. Sachin has spent his whole life in a cricket cocoon. As a precocious boy of eleven, he was entrusted to the care of his coach and sent to live with his aunt and uncle in Dadar because their flat was closer to his training ground and he could therefore spend less time on buses and trains and more playing cricket. As a gifted young pianist, I am glad to say that I was not required to spend every waking moment practising arpeggios to the exclusion of all other activities as was Sachin the young cricketer. Somehow, he passed his SSC exams, but by the time he was sixteen and playing cricket for India, school was out forever. Did I worry that Sachin's education had been curtailed? Not really, because his talent was clearly on a genius level. Once I asked Anjali what sort of books Sachin read when he was on tour and she told me he didn't read at all. Apparently, someone had advised him that reading would ruin his eyesight. Did she worry? Evidently not. When he wanted to switch off, he listened to music. There are hundreds of photographs of him carrying his little two-in-one cassette player, plugged into his earphones and listening to classical Indian music, bhajans, Western pop and Bollywood songs. It was also a sort of defence from the outside world. Sachin's father must have been pleased. He had named his son after Sachin Dev Burman, his favourite music director.

A few months after they married, Anjali qualified as a paediatrician. She was exhausted after so many exams, and she and

Sachin were longing for some quality time together. Throughout their courtship, Sachin had been in Australia or somewhere far away and she was always in the hospital. My mother used to say that if you start your marriage deeply in love, it carries you a very long way, and so it was for Sachin and Anjali. Anjali explains it as mutual respect for their different passions: 'I admired him for his astonishing talent and for going off and playing in front of the world. He admired me for studying medicine.' It took many years for them to find a single fault in one another.

Anjali's proud, forward-thinking grandfather, Anand's father, had died within a few days of Anjali first setting eyes on Sachin at the airport, bequeathing to her his office in Flora Fountain, in downtown Bombay, so that she could set up a practice there. However, Anjali quickly decided not to pursue her career in medicine. If she had worked in a government hospital, she would have had to do her fair share of nights and weekends in hospital, which would have been tough when Sachin was back in Bombay between tours. Had she worked in private practice as Dr Anjali Tendulkar, she reckoned she would be consulted for her name rather than her expertise. In any case, she didn't want to be endlessly treating the coughs, fevers and cut fingers of wealthy kids. She was interested in seriously sick underprivileged children and in helping their mothers to care for them. Anjali is an all-or-nothing person and she couldn't have just dabbled in doctoring. Moreover, she wanted to devote herself to keeping her husband in the right frame of mind to play his best cricket. Playing cricket at Sachin's level brings immense pressure and exposure, and she believed her duty was to help him through the ups and downs, the disappointments and the triumphs, to steer him through his medical dramas and his mother and father through their health issues. As I understood it, she was giving up her life for Sachin.

My daughter's decisiveness blew me away. There was no discussion, no agonising, no vacillation, no tears. Her mind was made up. It reminded me of myself when I decided to leave England and come to India to marry Anand all those years ago. Apple. Gravity. Tree.

7

At the Crease

ENGLISH CRICKET AND ALL ITS DELICIOUS CLICHÉS—THE THWACK OF leather on willow, soggy cucumber sandwiches, unreliable canvas deck-chairs—have always been somewhere in the background of my life.

I grew up with the Voice of Cricket, the revered John Arlott. In my mind's ear, I can still recall his ball-by-ball radio commentary that heralded the start of summer, and which could be heard in the background whenever I entered my aunts' flat in Bedford Square for tea. He was a poet with a Hampshire burr, cheerfully describing the gasometers at The Oval or the pigeons on the pitch at Lord's when rain stopped play for hours. I read Sir Neville Cardus on both cricket and classical music in what was then the *Manchester Guardian* and can confirm that he could wax as eloquently about Don Bradman as the Halle Orchestra. As a small girl, I had watched with great pride as my brother Richard batted for the Rugby School First XI. When Anand was in London and we were dating, he played for LSE's second team at Berrylands in New Malden, which was, I confess, too far from London's Notting Hill where I lived at the time to make me a regular supporter.

Before we were married in Bombay, I had queued with Anand and a gang of friends to get into the Cricket Club of India to sit on cement benches to witness the magnificent Test battles between India and the West Indies, in which some of Anand's friends were playing. From the moment Sachin and Anjali became an item, cricket came into the foreground. In fact, I often feel as if I have been at the crease myself for the past three decades.

The first thing I had to learn was that cricket in India is different from cricket in any other country in the world, partly because it is the country's only significant sport. It is the sport of the masses. While religion and politics and culture divide Indians, cricket unites them. You do not have to be wealthy to watch cricket or to play cricket. I love that. The poorest watch or listen and the poorest play. It is a team game in which the individual has opportunities to excel and yet, in each game, a different player shines and one player can do several different things. Special partnerships develop. Extra-special in some cases, such as the record-breaking opening partnership between Sachin and Sourav Ganguly in 136 One Day Internationals. They scored 6,609 runs together, the most successful ODI partnership ever.

Being the mother-in-law of a cricketing idol made cricket post-1995 all the more exceptional. I watched Sachin from up close as his fame grew and grew and fed on itself. It is perhaps rather surprising that we went to very few of the 200 Tests and 463 One Day Internationals (and a single Twenty20 International) Sachin played for India. Anand made a huge effort to watch every single ball on TV, wherever he was. Most of the time, I was far too nervous to watch. It was only in 2008, when the Indian Premier League came along, that I was relaxed enough to go to the ground and watch live. From then until 2013, Sachin played for the Mumbai Indians, and we were always there for the matches played in Mumbai, sitting very comfortably in the Ambani Box. It was very competitive, highly entertaining, and I thoroughly enjoyed myself. We still go now, and we are given seats in the President's Box. Fun as it is, without Sachin playing, it doesn't have quite the same appeal.

A fine journalist, Rajdeep Sardesai, the son of cricketer Dilip Sardesai, called Sachin the God of Happiness because, every time he walked onto a cricket ground, he brought happiness. I had been in England in the sixties when the Beatles became superstars, and I have always thought that being Sachin must have been like being one of the Beatles. From early on, he inspired mass hysteria among the crowds. While politicians have come and gone and let people down, Sachin has always been there and never disappointed. We have all grown older watching Sachin. That extraordinary resilience he demonstrated as a plump-cheeked boy of sixteen, batting even with a smashed nose, has never left him. That, and the hunger to succeed, backed up with exceptionally hard work, partly explains why his career was so unusually long. Being obsessed with success is not enough. Cricket is the thing. Sachin was, is, and ever will be obsessed with cricket.

He was fortunate that his arrival coincided with that of cable television, which meant that the God of Happiness/the God of Cricket could take his gospel to every home in India. In 1989, he might have been seen by a few million in fuzzy black and white, Anand being one of them. By 1995, some 70 million homes had colour television, so more than 400 million people in India were watching him. Technology was advancing so fast that suddenly, instead of just two cameras, there were multiple cameras showing Sachin from multiple angles, which allowed his technical brilliance to be amplified. Taking on the greatest fast bowlers in the world and not just standing up to them but dominating them, as they had dominated India in the past, could not fail to attract attention. Sachin was inspirational. He was aspirational. He was a fierce and ambitious competitor in the spirit of modern India. Without ever being brash. To be quite honest, I think I was a bit scared, perhaps intimidated by him in the way one can be in the presence of someone highly intellectual or fantastically famous. When he was with me, Sachin was not talkative. Our communication was limited largely to chats about the children. I left Anand to discuss cricket with him.

I transferred my cricketing allegiance from England to India the second I arrived here in 1966, in plenty of time to celebrate India's 1971 Test series triumph in England, and then again when India won the World Cup at Lord's in 1983. But the first time I went to see Sachin play in a Test was in June 1996, the year after he and Anjali married. We were staying with my mother in Cheltenham and the match was in Edgbaston, not far away. Anjali bought tickets without telling him. We took my mother with us and we sat in the stands. It was a typically English golden summer's day and my mother's first Test ever. For the first time, too, I was watching India play England with me supporting the visitors.

It was an extraordinary match. We had missed the first day's play when Sachin was bowled for only the second time in fifty-five innings. India had scored 214 in their first innings. Sachin made 24, and a century from Nasser Hussain took England to 313 in reply. We were watching India struggle miserably in the second innings with Sachin batting, desperately trying to keep India in the game. And, as if especially for us, Sachin scored a century, raising his bat to where we were sitting. He says it was a happy accident because he had no idea we were actually there. He went on to score 122, having hit 19 fours and a six, his ninth Test century, but sadly, India lost the match.

It was only then that I was reminded how much beer was routinely drunk at cricket matches in England. I had grown used to dry matches in Bombay. As the day wore on at Edgbaston, the crowd became more and more merry and started swaying from side to side, but even when tanked up, they were nothing like as raucous as the sober spectators are here in India.

I have neither Anand's nor my brother Richard's elephant-like capacity to remember every match, ball by ball. Dear Rich, now aged eighty-two, can still recall schoolboy matches in minute detail, such as the golden day in 1955 when his Rugby school team beat Marlborough by one run. I have always enjoyed Test match cricket most, the only cricket there was when I was a girl, with the battle between bowler and batsman stretched out over five days. Anand believes that Sachin is, without a doubt, at his best in Test cricket. Not that he didn't also excel in ODIs. I cannot remember the details of the standout matches that he played but I can remember the tension as the drama unfolded, the atmosphere and the anxiety felt by me and millions of Sachin's fans across the world. For me, it stemmed from knowing that the match was important to him for some personal or particular reason, or that he was carrying an injury that others didn't know about, or that the cricket world was following his innings in the hope that he would break yet another record. Watching a Test match live is quite different from watching on TV. The pressure is palpable.

Sachin was away from home a great deal and Anand and I always tried to be 'useful' grandparents, helping Anjali with the two small children. We did so through five cricketing tours, four to Australia and one to South Africa over the Christmas holiday. Goodness me, we were lucky!

Cricket in Australia is always fantastic: big crowds, nice grounds, and often the best teams in the world. I could see up-close the rivalry between Sachin and Shane Warne and Sachin and Brett Lee on the pitch—though they were good friends off it. But I do remember the Sydney Test match in January 2004 because it was unforgettably thrilling. We were there with Anjali, Sara and Arjun. Sachin came in to bat on day one and was 73 not out at close of play. By the end of day two, he had scored his third double century and was 220 not out. Unfortunately, Anjali and the children missed it because they were already on the plane back to India. The next day, Sachin took his score to 241 and was not out when India declared on 705 for seven. It was an extraordinary display of batting. In ten hours, Sachin did not play a single cover drive, the shot that had got him into trouble earlier in the tour. His brother Ajit had discussed the issue with him, and they eventually decided that he should abstain from cover drives altogether; Sachin stuck to the plan. Such was his iron discipline. Although it ended in a draw, the match was memorable in other ways as well, though I only remember Sachin's innings. Anil Kumble, one of the best ever Indian bowlers, took a total of 12 wickets; it was also the final match of the great and gritty Australian Steve Waugh. Sachin took the catch to get him out on 80 in the second innings. Waugh's last. Howzat!

But by far and away, the most memorable match I have ever been to has to be the last one Sachin played on retiring, a Test against the West Indies at the Wankhede Stadium in Mumbai in November 2013. His two hundredth Test. The Indian government launched a special stamp to celebrate the occasion. The stadium was packed. The world's cricket press was there and all of Sachin's family, including his mother who had never been to a match before. We were in the President's Box. The atmosphere was electric. I cannot begin to describe how emotional I felt, but I expect the whole of India was feeling exactly the same.

India won the toss and elected to field, which was a big disappointment for the crowd, who would have to wait longer to see Sachin bat. India bowled West Indies out for 182 late in the afternoon, and it was India's turn to bat. When Sachin came out at number 4, the whole stadium roared 'Sachin, Sachin!' louder than ever. It was truly deafening and must surely have reverberated all over Mumbai. My stomach churned, silently. At close of play, he was on 38. On the morning of 15 November, day two, he went on to make 74, in what was his last innings for India. The following day, India went on to a total of 495 and then skittled West Indies out for 187, giving India a hefty win. I am not sure anyone cared who had won or lost but everyone there knew they had witnessed history. No one left the stadium and eventually Sachin came out onto the ground. He had had to hide himself away while he cried for a good ten minutes, until he told himself enough was enough. I was as surprised as everyone else by his masterful delivery of a speech of some twenty minutes when, with Anjali, Sara and Arjun at his side, he thanked all those who had helped him throughout his career, holding a very small piece of paper on which he had written the names lest he forgot someone. Even now, if I listen to a recording, I am moved to tears. For his entire career, Sachin had seldom said a word and let his bat do the talking. As he spoke, you could have heard a pin drop. There was not a dry eye in the stadium. Our tears continued as Sachin was carried around the stadium on the shoulders of his teammates. His final lap of honour. Later that day, Sachin got a call from the office of Manmohan Singh, the prime minister, who came on the line personally to tell him that, as a thank you for serving Indian cricket for twenty-four years, he had been awarded the Bharat Ratna, India's highest civilian honour. Needless to say, Sachin thanked God before he cracked open the champagne.

Except for that Edgbaston match and Sachin's final momentous match at the Wankhede Stadium, Anjali did not go to the ground to watch him play. She stayed in her room, on her own, rigid with tension, glued to the TV. Woe betide anyone who disturbed her. Sachin's retirement brought an end to that particular stress. Now that Arjun is playing, maybe she is feeling the strain again, though he is not yet at the stage where the matches are televised live. But there was another reason why she stayed out of sight when Sachin was playing. In India, there have been occasions when an angry, volatile crowd has turned nasty because the team or a player has played badly and they have taken out their disappointment on the wives. Once, in Calcutta, fans set the stadium on fire. Apart from everything else, Anjali never wanted to be a distraction from the match itself. Wives and Girlfriends (WAGs) of cricketers in India seem more content to remain in the shadows than WAGs in England. Even now, not every cricketer playing for India becomes well known. I got to know some of the wives of those we used to travel with, but few of the players were married, and details of their personal lives never appeared in the papers. Today, there are pages and pages about film stars and pages and pages about cricketers too, but not much about the WAGs. Anjali has never been the type to invite *Hello!* magazine to wander around her house and photograph her lounging on a sofa or baking cakes. Which is lucky, because Sachin would not have wanted it. In any case, Anjali does not bake. She tells me that there is no point doing something yourself if you can ask someone else to do it for you, and she berates me often for doing things that she sees as unnecessary. I, on the other hand, actively enjoy cooking and am always happy to turn my hand to anything practical. As is Sachin, if for different reasons. He cheerfully issues videos of himself making a spicy baingan bharta and taking it into his mother's room for her lunch or giving Arjun a lockdown haircut with such proficiency that he might be flirting with a future career as a barber.

By the time I arrived here in the sixties, Bombay was well established as a fertile breeding ground for cricketers. Heaven knows why; it's hardly a city of open spaces. There is the famous Oval Maidan in Churchgate and Shivaji Park in Dadar where

Sachin grew up. On both, dozens of matches overlap with, miraculously, no confusion as to whose ball is whose. These days, fewer major players in the national team come from the big Indian cities such as Mumbai, Kolkata and Delhi, perhaps because there is more incentive for scouts to go further afield. Or maybe city boys have better things to do than to sweat it out in the dust under a scorching sun.

Anand played cricket from when he was very young. As a schoolboy in Bombay, he played with Dilip Sardesai, a great batsman, though an unlikely one because he was born in Portuguese-ruled Goa long before cricket caught on there. Anand also played with Budhi Kunderan, a future Indian wicketkeeper and later captain. Budhi was all the more remarkable because he came from an impoverished family, sharing a chawl in Bazaar Gate with six siblings and extended family. At some stage, he and my sister-in-law Jill might have briefly gone out, though this has been a closely guarded family secret in spite of the fact that he died young and she is over seventy. Until now.

One of Budhi's teammates, Bombay-born Parsi Farrokh Engineer, another great wicketkeeper/batsman, was splendidly hale and hearty when I last saw him in Mumbai before Covid. Dozens of Bombay players such as Farrokh, Ajit Wadekar, Sunil Gavaskar and Dilip Vengsarkar became big and beloved stars.

Anand charted Sachin's rise from the day he saw him play through the window of the card room of the Cricket Club of India in Bombay but, as I have said many times already, my husband just loves cricket. Anand believed young Sachin would immediately be selected to play for India, but apparently, Gavaskar decided he would be psychologically damaged if he faced fast bowling. Who knows who was right? Over the years, I must have watched Sachin's first ever televised interview in 1989 with that lovely cricket journalist, Tom Alter, several times. You can see such passion and determination, such ambition, sincerity and quiet self-belief in Sachin's open face when he says he is not scared of fast bowlers such as Curtly Ambrose, and I believe him. He had had some practice with Kapil Dev, so he knew what he was talking about. In any case, in all the years that I have known him, I have never heard him say something for effect. He obviously relished a challenge from the start. Only the other day, I heard the former England captain Nasser Hussain saying that Sachin's 'magnificent technique' had prompted hundreds of meetings to discuss strategies for getting him out. He was speaking to the Trinidadian Ian Bishop, who said that Sachin was the most challenging batsman he ever bowled to. Shane Warne was famously asked who the best three batsmen were that he had had to bowl against, and his answer was, first Sachin, then nobody, then Brian Lara.

I once read a newspaper article headlined 'Is Sachin Out?' which perfectly captured the atmosphere in India when Sachin was playing. The whole Indian nation, even up in the hills, would be watching or listening, and the news of Sachin's prowess on the field would ring from hilltop to hilltop and permeate the furthest corners of India; if he was out, India's hopes plunged immediately and tangibly. You could almost hear the collective gasp. Everyone was always looking to him. In Test cricket, he batted number four, which is a crucial spot. First, there was the tension while everyone waited for him to go in to bat. Then the tension while he was there. Then the tension, if he got out, that it was probably all over. What separates Sachin from every other cricketer is the burden he has carried on his shoulders from the age of sixteen to the age of forty, of a billion-plus people in India expecting him to dazzle every time he walked on to the pitch. The pressure never receded. He became part of the national psyche, somehow bringing relief and succour to Indian hearts. If Sachin was batting, everything was right with the world. Indians expected miracles and Sachin delivered them. In one-day cricket matches, Sachin opened the batting and the mood in the crowd was even more twitchy.

Some have said that Sachin, like Bollywood star Shah Rukh Khan, symbolises India's rise to global prominence and the great prizes that have come with India's economic liberalisation. People as old as me grew up with the name Don Bradman, perhaps the greatest batsman of all time, who did a similar thing in Australia, bringing such relief to Australians in the Great Depression when there were no jobs and no money. When Sachin's career began in 1989, India was going through great turmoil politically, the Babri Masjid row was bubbling up, and Sachin somehow brought people together, irrespective of class, caste, culture, religion and all that divides.

I shall never forget the day Sachin took us into the nets at Lord's and explained to us that, within a split second, the batsman has to see the position of the ball in a bowler's hand, where the seam is, and where the shine is, before he releases it in order to work out the speed of the ball, the trajectory, where it is going to bounce, and then make something like fifteen decisions in order to get his bat in the right place. Such intensity is unthinkable to someone like me.

I used to reflect on what—if anything at all—a star cricketer has in common with a concert pianist, and I came to the conclusion that it is tireless self-criticism. Neither is ever content with their most recent performance, be it on the pitch or on the stage. When I was at the Royal College of Music, I reached a point when I was no longer willing to spend the next four hours perfecting a few bars of music. And when perfecting one's technique stops being an all-consuming obsession, that's it. End of. For me, it had been coming for some time. I was given the ideal environment and all the support possible to become a professional pianist, but I never believed I had the talent, and my heart and my head were not in it. That disconnect is fatal.

The sad thing about so many sportsmen and women is that they have to give up when they are relatively young. It is different for musicians. Zubin Mehta, the world-famous Bombay-born conductor, was eighty-three when he retired in 2019 after fifty years as music director of the Israel Philharmonic. And he's still conducting, even after retiring. Strikingly, Sachin's sporting career began much earlier and continued much longer than most. To have the same success as a boy of fifteen, as a young man in his twenties and then in his thirties, is freakish.

Retirement is difficult at any age. My father said that what he missed most was meeting friends and colleagues made during a lifetime of working in Birmingham. Anand retired at fifty, and although he took up one or two part-time assignments, basically he had to find other ways to fill his time. Many, if not most, sportsmen and women have to retire relatively young, and I have always felt that it must be doubly difficult for them, having led such physically active lives. I think we were all nervous about how Sachin would adjust to life after retirement. At first, there was some relief that there was no more tension, and lots of time to spend with the family, long overdue. But with that came an absence of the thrills, of highs and lows, ups and downs. Sachin felt he had to do something physical, and he started to play badminton, and soon he was playing harder and harder because he always wanted to win. He played one season in the Cricket for Seniors tournament with former players, playing three matches in America, then his knee put a stop to that. He still plays in occasional senior events but, inevitably, he will have to give that up too. He works out at the gym regularly and he plays golf whenever he has the opportunity. There was tremendous excitement among the members when he joined the Willingdon Club as Anjali's husband, so that he could play golf; fortunately, they are all far too polite to ask for his autograph.

He also threw himself into remodelling our house in Lonavala and amused us all when he became an expert on the pros and cons of marble flooring versus granite. Whatever Sachin does, he does wholeheartedly. Among other things, he appreciates a good wine and is well on his way to being a connoisseur.

Having always been a team player, he was not used to being alone. When he went to his house in Lonavala, it was always with a gang of friends with whom he could play table tennis, watch cricket and have a beer. But Covid changed that, and he is happy to go just with a couple of friends or family. These days, he makes occasional appearances on TV, offering expert analysis. Having played with the Mumbai Indians from 2008 to 2013, he remains wonderfully loyal and often turns up at their matches. The other day, when they played against Delhi, he tweeted that the Mumbai Indians are 'one family. You know it's not just you, an entire force is with you!'

Sachin still cannot go out freely in Mumbai without being mobbed. Though he can in some parts of London. Decades ago, we went to John Lewis in Brent Cross, where it turns out that half the staff are Indian and every one of them wanted to serve him. In Bond Street shops, the shop assistants have been trained to ignore celebrities. Oxford Street is inches away, but a world away in terms of being pestered. Before Sachin retired, he was at a launch at an Adidas shop opposite Selfridges and the word got around. Once the event was over, he and the family came out and started walking along Oxford Street and the crowd became so dense that he got nervous and told Anjali to go on walking while he slipped away and got into a taxi. I was at home when he arrived, absolutely ashen, because he had genuinely feared he was going to be crushed. I had been with him when that almost happened before, one time in Mumbai, when he was going to run the Mumbai marathon alongside Anjali and me. The streets became jam-packed with people wanting to touch him, and eventually the police surrounded us and led us away. It was an alarming episode.

When I first met young Sachin, he was as starstruck as every other Hindi movie lover. Neither he nor I imagined that one day, he would be friends with many of the Bollywood stars he hero-worshipped. As a boy, he loved the singing of Lata Mangeshkar, the brilliant playback singer, who sadly died in February 2022. She was a great friend of Raj Singh Dungarpur, the big chief of Indian cricket who selected the national team for two terms and was responsible for introducing Sachin to the world because he was the chairman of the selection committee that put Sachin in the Indian cricket team. Raj introduced Sachin to Lata Mangeshkar, which he says was one of the biggest thrills of a thrill-filled life. Proof that even living idols can have heart-throbs. Amitabh Bachchan was another. When Sachin and Anjali moved to their flat in La Mer in Bandra when Arjun was a baby and Sara was two, the Bollywood actress Aishwarya Rai lived upstairs with her parents. When she married Abhishek, Amitabh Bachchan's son, Sachin and Anjali soon became friends with them all.

Sachin was lucky to find a wonderful agent early on in his career. Or rather, Mark found Sachin. Mark Mascarenhas was a huge flamboyant fellow from Bangalore. The son of a doctor, he had spent a lot of time working in America and his style and his thinking were American, by which I mean BIG. Mark was devoted to Sachin, and just loved being with him. They were both terrific foodies. In his way, Mark was a sort of genius, identifying Sachin as a brand and as an emblem of Indian cricket from the day he made a century at Old Trafford. He made a lot of money from getting the TV rights for the 1996 World Cup in India and Pakistan, and in 1995, he signed up Sachin for a five-year contract. He was on the point of re-signing Sachin in 2002 for a vast sum and had told the journalist Ayaz Memon, then at the *Times of India,* that he intended to have the entire Wankhede Stadium lit up with Sachin in the middle to celebrate the moment. That never happened because Mark tragically died in a car crash in Nagpur shortly afterwards. Sachin stayed with Mark's company WorldTel for four years following Mark's death, but then he set up his own company, which has its own CEO and employs at least half a dozen permanent staff.

I got to see Mark at work at very close quarters. He was an impresario like none other. He understood sport, brand-building and negotiating contracts. Moreover, he loved Sachin like a son. Sachin had total confidence in him and if Mark thought something was a good idea, he would be guided by him. Mark also spoilt him, in a good way. When Sachin said he liked Dire Straits, Mark arranged for him to meet Mark Knopfler. Mark knew everyone. Everyone loved him. He came into Sachin's life at precisely the right moment, enabling him to stay focused on cricket while Mark handled everything else, always getting Sachin's priorities right: for example, that practice sessions were more important than shooting commercials. In one of the first advertisements Sachin did, he was required to come into an office carrying his briefcase and then to sit down. Not only had Sachin seldom been into an office, but he was a stranger to a briefcase, and he also had to act surprised, then dismayed and then delighted. I am pleased to say that he is better at acting now than he was, but it took a long time. In those early days, he was the first cricketer whose acting 'career' in advertisements really took off. For quite a while, he was on every lamp post on Marine

Drive advertising Pepsi, and even these days, he can be seen on billboards across the city, endorsing something or the other.

I saw a depressing statistic the other day stating that 50 per cent of all Indian sportsmen become bankrupt five years after retirement. As soon as a sportsman makes any money in India, probably anywhere in the world, he is besieged by a thousand and one people wanting to 'help' him invest his fortune. But Anand made sure from the start that Sachin's affairs were professionally managed. And Anjali has been the main decision-maker because Sachin was always away. But in retirement, he has become quite a shrewd businessman and seems to enjoy it.

These days, young cricketers are well paid, even at the Ranji Trophy level. Some IPL contracts are worth crores because the television companies are all vying with each other to get the rights and the ads cost millions. The ads that interrupt IPL matches drive me absolutely mad, but they are helping talented young cricketers get rich quick. I am told there is one IPL player whose father drives an autorickshaw and another whose father sells eggs from the back of his bicycle, and I know that it won't be long before these boys can buy a house for their family. Just as Sachin has for many of his extended family.

Anand and I spend hours watching cricket on TV. Televised cricket really lets you get to know the characters on the stage, which I love. In a stadium, you can't see their expressions unless there is an action replay on the big screen, so you can only guess the emotions when you see the guy stomp off. Television reveals the human dimension of these superhuman beings when the camera zeroes in on the fury of someone who has been sledged or wrongly given out.

I love the build-up of rivalries in Test cricket. A good commentator or, better still, Sachin sitting next to you, provides superb insights into a player's strategy. He tells us the likelihood of the next ball being a bouncer or if the batsman is trying to block the ball rather than make runs and stay in rather than get bowled. People always think about Sachin as a batsman, but he has amassed some amazing statistics as a bowler, taking 46 wickets in Tests and 154 in ODIs. When he was asked to bowl in that famous last over in Dubai against South Africa in November 1993, he defended the six runs, giving India a win. Three years later, he did it again in Chandigarh against Australia, making him the only bowler in ODI history to defend six or fewer runs in the final over of a game more than once. 'Ice cool' is how Blowers (Henry Blofeld, beloved British cricket commentator) described him. It was a sensational victory. Not many people know this, but Sachin actually began his cricketing life wanting to be a bowler, so it is hardly surprising that his nerveless bowling has occasionally made the difference.

Sachin's groundedness, his essential normalness, never ceases to amaze me. People do not expect celebrities to be normal, because many are not, and even those who are often go through a bad patch. Sachin has, thank heavens, never lost his balance and never blotted his moral copybook. He has met everyone from the Queen of England to Nelson Mandela and the Dalai Lama, not because he particularly wanted to, though he was proud to do so, but because someone decided he should. Frankly, nowadays he would rather go to a game reserve and see tigers or leopards than meet famous people. I do know he was delighted to be invited to the Royal Box at Wimbledon several years running and I will never forget seeing him and Anjali there on television. Actually, all I could see were their heads peeping out from a great mound of purple blankets. It was mid-June, and they were freezing cold. But I think he got more of a kick out of meeting Roger Federer on more than one occasion because he is a great fan of Roger and his tennis.

I am exceptionally lucky to have such a dear, modest, caring man as my son-in-law. He has become more confident off the cricket pitch as he has grown older. And he has remained delightful. And even after batting with such greats as Dravid, Ganguly, Dhoni and Kohli, he still talks about my Anjali as the best partnership of his life.

8

Marriage, Modesty and Manners

I COULDN'T QUITE BELIEVE MY EYES WHEN I WENT TO MY FIRST WEDDING in Bombay. On a vast open ground, hundreds of people came and went, stopping to lounge on sofas, chat loudly and eat ice cream. During the wedding proper, a priest droned on incomprehensibly in Sanskrit, and occasionally told someone to throw some flowers or rice or pour water. Everything seemed mildly chaotic and lasted for hours and hours and hours.

After about half a dozen near-identical experiences, I began to find them increasingly tedious. Decades on, I dislike going to weddings unless I am very close to the couple getting hitched. My problem is remembering what excuse I gave for not attending when I meet the host many months later.

Throughout the wedding season in Mumbai, in the most comfortable, cooler months of November and December, a stretch of Marine Drive is lined with dozens of wedding marquees, in an ever-changing kaleidoscope of colours, dripping with freshly made cascades of jasmines, orchids and marigolds. These days, big fat Indian weddings are often showcases for a family's wealth and contacts, costing crores and running over several days in several different venues. The host (the bride's father) pays the guests' airfares and hotel bills. Thankfully, I am not invited to such affairs. But friends of mine are. One told me that she believes that her presence was less to bear witness to the couple making their vows and more to big-up the crowds for the video being made. She felt like an unpaid extra in a Bollywood movie.

I think the same thing is happening in England, though one rare good thing about the Covid-19 lockdown may be a return to more intimate celebrations. Even the wedding of the late Queen's granddaughter, Princess Beatrice, was restricted to thirty guests. For many people in India, a daughter's wedding is the biggest expense of their lifetime and even the poorest seem to think it important to have a ceremony and reception with food to show their appreciation of their guests' presence.

By the time I came to marry Anand, at the age of twenty-six, I had been to just four weddings, those of my three greatest friends, Caroline, Amanda and Jenie, and to the much grander one between my brother Jeremy and Serena. All of them were in and out of church in less than an hour. The reception was a bun and a run; platters of tiny sandwiches and bite-sized chocolate eclairs washed down with lashings of champagne, a couple of speeches; then a cake was cut and the bride and groom went away. End of.

Two days before my wedding in Bombay, it was Christmas Day and my first Indian Christmas. No roast turkey, no Christmas tree, no stockings. It was hot and humid. Out on the streets, life went on very much as usual with shops and street-stalls open for business. For the mosalu ceremony held on Christmas Day, my mother-in-law hosted a luncheon in Warden Road. Navnit Mama, a beloved honorary uncle to the Mehta family, turned up with a serving of Indian roast turkey with all the trimmings, which he had bought from the Ambassador Hotel especially for me. It prompted an unexpected and desperate attack of homesickness. Fortunately, I stopped crying in time for the reception three days later at the Turf Club with some 2,000 people. Or was it 3,000? It was vast. Anand is an only son, so the boat had been pushed out, with relations, friends and business associates and their families all invited. Strict prohibition and food restrictions in those days meant soft drinks only, probably that unforgettable electric-red 'raspberry' flavoured soda, boasting 'contains no fruit' on the label. As a foreigner, I had a permit allowing me to buy four bottles of whisky or gin each month, which we stockpiled for parties, but our wedding lunch itself was dry, which was normal then for Indians, rich and poor. My liquor permit was revoked the day I married.

From the start, Anand and I knew our marriage would require compromise, as mixed marriages always do. An American friend of mine married a Gujarati Jain and went the whole hog—quite the wrong expression given that a Jain will protect the life of even the most harmless insect. She became vegetarian, only ever wore cotton saris, and was happy to spend hours making papad with her mother-in-law in the kitchen. Had I been obliged to become strictly vegetarian in order to marry Anand, it would have been a close call. I really don't think I could have lived without the odd serving of meat or fish.

There has always been a play-off between Anand's wishes and mine. Even now, when I leave the house to have lunch with So-and-So, then on to the NCPA for a dance performance in the evening, I know that he would prefer it if I stayed in with him while he watches cricket. Most Indian husbands, I've noticed, like their wives to be around, but then maybe that applies the world over.

Anand retired at the age of fifty, so he has been at home a lot over the past three decades. I have not been to all the concerts I would have liked to go to. Not that Anand ever stopped me, though he might occasionally have said something grumpy about needing the driver for something else. The pattern was clear from when we returned from our honeymoon and he went off to play in a bridge tournament the next day. He has travelled the world to represent India in hundreds of tournaments and continued to play almost every evening of the week until about twenty years ago. He compromised less than I did at first, in that I came to live in Bombay. But he also allowed me more independence and freedom than your average Indian husband might have. I used to go off exploring India with my chums from Indus, an organisation for cultural exchange between so-called 'educated' Indian women and foreign women, some married to Indians living in Bombay. One of them, an American, had a devoted Parsi dentist husband who never failed to see her off on the station platform and was always there to collect her when she came back. Wherever she was, without fail, he booked a trunk call to say goodnight. He did not like her to be out of his sight.

It was on those trips that I discovered that many of my friends took little responsibility in the home except for overseeing domestic matters and the care of the children. It seemed to me that India was at least thirty years behind England in terms of women's liberation. Mind you, second-wave feminism did not hit England until the sixties. Until then, women didn't complete their own tax returns because their income was judged to belong to their husbands; it was almost impossible for a single woman to get a mortgage; worst of all, a husband could not be prosecuted if he raped his wife because, by marrying him, it was understood that she had consented to have sex with him, whenever, wherever, however. In other words, the situation then was similar to the situation in India until recently.

I'll never forget how, on a visit back home in 1970, my mother carefully hid from me her copy of *The Female Eunuch*, published that year. She thought it too shocking for me to read. But I found it, wrapped in brown paper. I had, of course, already read it. Recently, I was thumbing through the 2020 edition and was struck by Hadley Freeman's introduction, in which she writes:

'Greer's searing examination of women's oppression is a vital, passionately argued social commentary that is both an important historical record of where we've been and a shockingly relevant treatise on what still remains to be achieved.'

When women's lib arrived in India in the seventies, I vividly remember my mother-in-law saying to me: 'Annie darling, I don't know what all the fuss is about. I am a very liberated woman. I can do anything I like.' It never occurred to her that financial independence is an essential part of a woman's independence. If she had brought a dowry to her marriage (which she had not), it would have immediately been absorbed into the wealth of her husband's family. Anand's family have never given dowries. The giving of a cash dowry as well as the receiving of one was made illegal in 1961, since when more subtle arrangements, perhaps involving property or jewellery, are entered into.

My mother-in-law really did not know how to boil a kettle. No exaggeration. She had never needed to. And yet, she ran her household with great efficiency because she knew how to get things done by others. Anjali makes her own tea every morning because she gets up very early. But when we are together in London, it is often Sachin who comes into the kitchen early in the morning to make tea for her. She seamlessly runs several houses as well as Sachin's office, and it is she who plans holidays and parties. I didn't bring her up to be a tame, submissive wife, but I have seen the way in which, during his playing days, she dedicated her life to Sachin's needs and demands without grumbling. She never, ever let him down for one second. She took responsibility for the children, often alone, without consultation with him because he could not be disturbed or distracted from playing cricket. I could not have done what she has done, and certainly not with the endless patience she has shown. I have infinite respect for her. Anjali is more Indian than English. I find this fascinating if not surprising.

But then, everyone's marriage is a mystery because each couple creates their own private and peculiar world. From my limited perspective, marriage is different in India. I have said before, so please forgive me for saying it again, but that silly old English song about love and marriage going together like a horse and carriage doesn't routinely apply here. Certainly not at the start of a marriage. Though, in time, love may blossom. In the past, for the most traditional Hindus, life was regarded as having seven stages, each a duty, one of which is getting married and having a family. It was, I suppose, an unwritten convention.

In India today, if an Indian woman doesn't marry, it could be because she has made a calculated decision to choose her career over having a family, possibly fearful that her mother-in-law would make her give up her chosen course. More often, though, it is because she hasn't found a suitable partner and didn't want an arranged marriage or, possibly, because she has been saddled with an unfavourable horoscope and no one will marry her. Hard to believe, but true. Admittedly, some unmarried women stay at home to provide companionship to a widowed parent, and it is hard to know whether this is out of a sense of duty or a choice. I suspect that any single woman who can afford it would prefer to live alone, though the price of real estate in cities restricts that to the super-rich. I have met few unmarried men of my generation, though the term 'bachelor' in India is not a euphemism for gay, as it used to be in England (at least in the obituaries of the *Daily Telegraph*). When I first came here, gay men were frequently forced into marriage at a young age. Not so now, but the law criminalizing homosexuality, one of the last legacies of British colonial rule, was only scrapped in 2018—which, quite frankly, shocks me.

One of many things that surprised me when I first came to live here was that a love marriage is not necessarily the aspiration of many young people. I had assumed that arranged marriages were resented. Not a bit. Perhaps it demonstrates the trust and respect Indian children have for their parents. Many of the most well-educated, enlightened and liberated young people have told me they aren't looking for a love marriage. Several of the girls and young women working at Apnalaya say they want to find a chap with a job and prospects, who will nurture them, provide for them and be kind. Some imagine love might grow, but that is not a big issue or part of the deal, just a possibility. If a boy agrees to marry a girl—and it is always the boy who decides—it is because he finds her attractive, is confident that she will fit into his family, and everything will go from there. It sounds somewhat rudimentary, but it has evidently worked for centuries and, arguably, better than our Western way.

My English friends are fascinated by the notion of an arranged marriage. I have come to think they are a very good idea as long as they are never forced, as they were in the bad old days. The majority of marriages of Indian friends of my generation would have been arranged, and they seem none the worse for that.

My first experience of an arranged marriage was that of Ravi, our friend at LSE whose sister and brother also went to LSE. Ravi was Maharashtrian but grew up in West Africa. After graduating, he got a good job with the International Wheat Council. We used to meet as a gang on Friday evenings for a drink, but one Friday, he didn't turn up. His parents, both highly educated, had taken him to his village in Maharashtra where they had lined up three or four girls from whom he had to choose a wife. Within three weeks, Ravi reappeared in London with his new wife in tow. I felt desperately sorry for her. She didn't speak a word of English, was afraid to go out of the house, which they were sharing with Ravi's parents, brothers and sister, and she looked absolutely miserable. She and Ravi had three children and continued to live together. A few years later, Ravi and his wife returned to his village to visit his family, taking his children who had been born and brought up in London and were horrified by the country's (lack of) infrastructure, particularly the untarred roads that became rivers of mud in the monsoon. By now, we had also left LSE and seldom saw Ravi and never saw his wife, though he said she was adapting to life in London if not exactly loving it. The last time we saw her was at Ravi's funeral a few years ago, and it was hardly the moment to ask her whether she had become reconciled to living in England.

Back in the 1930s, Anand's mother, Amru, had an arranged marriage. She was the youngest of five children, one boy and four girls, which many Indians would have considered extremely unfortunate because that is a lot of girls to find dowries for. Fortunately, her parents were educated and Westernised, and didn't share this view. The family had moved to Bombay but quickly found friends in the 'right' social circles. The eldest girl, Pupul, married her sweetheart, a Maharashtrian she had met at LSE. The next one, Poornima, had an arranged marriage to a brilliant man, top of his class in the exams for the Indian Civil Service, though, sadly, he became mentally ill and rather violent; she eventually left him and returned to her parents' house.

Traditionally, weddings are useful marketplaces for showing off children of a marriageable age and finding out who might be available. It was at the wedding of Nandini, Amru's very beautiful sister, to Bhagwandas, a wealthy Gujarati, that someone suggested that Amru should meet the groom's cousin, Jayantilal. The two were left in a room together for a few minutes and that was that. Had one of them been appalled, they would not have been forced to marry. Amru's parents were delighted because Jayantilal's family had already been vetted and they knew he was wealthy and had a nice house. It was an excellent match. They seemed very happy.

Unlike her poor sister, Nandini. Nandini's mother-in-law, Tara, was a nightmare: a cold, frustrated woman who put the fear of several Hindu gods into her beautiful young daughter-in-law. 'You laugh too much. You must not show your teeth,' she said to her. Not that Nandini had much to laugh about. While Bhagwandas's family was Brahmin, Tara's was not, but Tara was preoccupied with caste. She felt humiliated by her own servant, because he was a Brahmin and, she claimed, threw her roti on to her plate to avoid touching her.

Nandini kept a diary, and it is a gripping and horrifying read. On arrival at her new home, Malabar Castle, following her wedding, her husband stood in front of a towering statue of the Hindu god Kali draped in garlands of skulls and said to her: 'Now forget your family. This is your new family. Once a girl is married, she becomes one with her husband and she must forget everything but him.'

Nandini did her best to please her husband, slipping into the high heels and chiffon saris he picked out for her to wear to the Mahalakshmi races. She learnt to play golf and joined him for morning rounds so that he could show her off. He didn't like her spending time with her mother and sisters, who lived nearby on Malabar Hill. 'Tell your family not to kiss you. If you don't, I shall tell them myself to keep their filthy hands off my wife,' he ordered. She dutifully produced three babies and devoted herself to them, as far as she was permitted. Like Amru, my own mother-in-law, she was forbidden from singing to the children and instructed to dress them only in white. Bhagwandas used to fly into furious rages with her for the smallest thing, such as a button missing from his shirt, as if it were her fault. According to Devi, her daughter, Nandini was afraid of her husband. Tara once admitted to Nandini that she had wanted to leave her husband but had stayed for the sake of her children. 'I had one in the stomach, one in the crib and one in the ghodiyu (hammock),' she told her. But in spite of—perhaps because of—her own misery, she showed no sympathy for her daughter-in-law.

Typically, Anand's family told me nothing about Nandini. I knew she was divorced from Bhagwandas and had returned to her parents' home a long time ago, but I knew none of the background drama until I read Devi's memoir, *Walking with Krishnamurti*, based on Nandini's diaries. Another fascinating read. Nandini wrote with an oblique candour about her wretched marriage and the healing influence of the Indian guru and philosopher, Jiddu Krishnamurti, to whom she was introduced by her father-in-law. It was the only decent thing that man ever did for her.

Nandini writes of her husband's 'demands in the bedroom' and his insistence on acts she found 'physically painful and emotionally agonising'. During one of their many fights, he said: 'When you married me, the contract was that I would give you money and a home while you gave me your body.' After ten years, Nandini moved out of the marital bedroom and into the adjoining dressing room. The abuse continued.

One night, her screams brought her mother-in-law to her room. Instead of protecting Nandini, she told her to get out of the house immediately and never return. 'I wonder how you as a woman do not feel for me,' said Nandini. Her words cut no ice.

I was appalled. Nandini and Bhagwandas's marriage had been arranged. Bhagwandas, a handsome, educated, sporty, charming and fabulously rich man-about-Bombay presented himself as an ideal match for Nandini, the most beautiful of the four Mehta girls. Her parents, Vinayak, a brilliant Indian civil servant who became the Collector of United Provinces (now Uttar Pradesh), and his lovely wife, Iravati, were delighted. Bhagwandas's father, Sir Chunilal Mehta, was well-regarded for his business acumen, his wealth and his antiques. Had they probed more deeply, they might have discovered that Chunilal had a foul temper and was easily seduced by dodgy holy men, and that his wife Tara was a tyrant. Initially unimpressed by his riches or status, after seven long years of courtship, Nandini finally submitted. She never reproached her parents for their part in her marriage and, to their credit, her parents did their best to make up for their misjudgement by welcoming her home when she was thrown out by her mother-in-law.

Then ensued a prolonged, acrimonious, high-profile court case between Nandini and Bhagwandas for legal separation and custody of the children. According to her diary, Krishnamurti counselled her to 'take adversity as it comes. Prepare for it. Be ready to meet it. Out of it comes maturity, a fullness, a joy that is imperishable.' She described his presence in her life as 'like rain, like a benediction'. Clearly, she found strategies for coping. She writes: 'One must love and ache wildly, feel passionately, desire and yet live lightly on life. Not cling and clutch but be like a butterfly, sitting on each flower.' Her salvation was, I believe, entirely thanks to Krishnamurti. I met him several times and he was the most remarkable man, charismatic, gentle and wise. Nandini too had an overwhelming serenity, an other-worldly aura, similar to his. I believe that their relationship was platonic, though there were rumours to the contrary.

The British judge at the Bombay court presiding over Nandini's divorce, evidently a hangover from the Raj, claimed Nandini had invented the allegations of sexual cruelty, assault and psychological torture. Her husband's lawyers accused her of being 'unduly influenced' by Krishnamurti and of revolting against 'the norm in Indian culture'. The papers carried stories about the wife of a Bombay textile millionaire succumbing to the 'hocus pocus' of a fashionable guru. Custody of the children was given to Bhagwandas. Nandini was allowed to visit them, under strict supervision, for an hour each day and to spend six weeks with them during the summer season when their father chose to abandon hot, wet, monsoon Bombay for more favourable climes.

Bhagwandas was a bully. He forced his children to record their bowel movements each day and issued rules: 'No levity, no laxity, no hilarity. I want 99.5 per cent efficiency.' To my astonishment, Devi told me she did not hate her father then or now. Perhaps, as a child, she was wholly unaware of her father's cruelty and her mother's unhappiness. Perhaps, in the vast, dark and depressing bungalow where she grew up, it had been possible for things to be hidden behind the heavy closed doors. Perhaps it felt quite normal for her to see as little as she did of her mother. Devi describes her father as a materialist who wanted to control Nandini but failed to do so because her mother did not care about wealth, jewellery or social status. With characteristic Indian understatement, she says her parents were 'not well-matched'.

There are some aspects of Indian culture I shall never understand. And one of these is the extraordinary strength of the ties that bind family members. The family as a whole is always more important than an individual. The marriages of several Indian friends of ours have survived affairs and abuse, which would have doubtless destroyed your average British marriage. Splitting up is not, historically or culturally, the Indian way. At first, I thought that this was because, by nature, Indians must be more philosophical and more forgiving. The reality is harsher: it is very difficult for a woman to leave her husband and support herself. And if there are children, even more so. Women are indoctrinated as girls that they must like it or lump it when it comes to marriage and told not to expect happiness. I see this as the Indian practice of putting the good of the family before the interests of the individual.

The monstrous Bhagwandas was brother-in-law to my own in-laws, and he was also a first cousin of my father-in-law. In India, the first-cousin relationship can be very close, so close that they are usually referred to as 'my cousin-brother' 'or my cousin-sister' or even 'my brother' or 'my sister' with the cousin detail being dropped entirely. No such closeness existed with our cousins, who lived some distance away and whom we seldom saw. During Nandini's divorce, there was considerable tension when my father-in-law dared to side with his wronged sister-in-law against his own blood family. And yet, Bhagwandas was invited to—and attended—our wedding, where Nandini was also present. Whether Nandini and Bhagwandas acknowledged one another, I don't know. Nor was it the first time that they had both been present at family functions. I didn't take to Bhagwandas and I disliked him even more when I spotted that his motor car had a special holder for his ever-full whisky glass next to the steering wheel. Nevertheless, every Diwali, the Mehta family routinely paid a visit to Tara and when she died, we went to see her body laid out as a mark of our respect. She was hateful but she was family.

When she recovered her strength and her spirit, Nandini set up a little school, Bal Anand, in her mother's house in Dungarsi Road, for poor children living locally. The lovely garden was home to its own 'pet' cobra. I was told not to fear 'him' but that did not stop me from being petrified. Nandini had a lovely manner with the children. She fed them bananas and dates, organised singing, clay modelling, yoga and meditation and encouraged them to think about those less fortunate, which I always found especially touching because they had almost nothing themselves. I suspect that her dedication to these waifs and strays was some sort of compensation for her enforced separation from her own children.

Happily, the next generation of Mehtas was luckier in love. Anand's three sisters had love marriages; of the ten first cousins, just one had an arranged marriage. Among their children, thirteen in all, there were no arranged marriages and seven married foreigners, some of whom they met while studying abroad. I know lots of people who have studied and worked abroad in England or America and not fallen in love or found a suitable partner, so have asked their parents in India to find them someone suitable. But here again, the scene is changing and, increasingly, young people are relying less on the family to make a match and more on internet matchmaking sites such as Shaadi.com. Or so it is reported in the papers. A piece in the *Indian Express* claimed revenue from the matchmaking industry reached more than $280 million in 2022. And is growing. The article also said that the young are looking for equal partnership and not a compromise. They seek partners with 'easy conversation, a non-judgemental outlook and a sense of humour', and two out of three would prefer to wait and see if their long-term relationship works before moving on to marriage. That seems pretty sound to me, but I wonder if their hopes and dreams will come true.

If I was asked—which I would prefer not to be—I would recommend finding a partner with the same values, first and foremost, and preferably from the same drawer in terms of wealth, education and religion, because the fewer compromises required, the easier the marriage. A vegetarian Hindu marrying a meat-eating Sikh (the majority of Sikhs are vegetarian) creates complications in the kitchen for the mother-in-law if she is cooking. Not surprisingly, some of the marriages between the offspring of the richest families are arranged, sometimes when the children are still very young. I am not suggesting that these couples are pressured to get married, but they will be encouraged and the financial advantages of the union made clear.

It is not just the rich who make such arrangements. Ashok, our mali, or gardener, in Lonavala, is the son of our previous mali, and one of seven children. His father died when he was still a child, but before he died, he made an agreement that Ashok would marry the daughter of his best friend who lived in their village a fair distance from Lonavala. When they reached a marriageable age, Ashok learnt that his intended could not read or write, though I think the matter that most concerned him was her lack of exposure to life beyond the remote village she came from. But the agreement had been made and the family insisted. Against his will, Ashok went through the first part of the marriage ceremony but refused to go through the next part, which meant collecting his new wife from her village and taking her back to his home. The marriage was not consummated. He appealed to my father-in-law for help and dear old Mr Fixit arranged for an annulment of the marriage; Ashok later married Sunita, a girl of his choosing, and they had three children. They now have several grandchildren I see running around the garden. The parents of the rejected girl would have had to look around for another match. I never heard if she got married.

While divorce is still relatively rare in India, I think that slowly but surely, young women are becoming less willing to put up with an unhappy marriage. My friend Sushmita is a good example. An educated middle-class Maharashtrian woman, she started working in the Apnalaya office many years ago. She lived with her father and two brothers in a decent one-room place in Bombay. She had no mother. At college, she had fallen in love with a Maharashtrian boy her father judged to be from the 'wrong' caste, so marriage was forbidden. She was miserable and vowed not to marry. But through a marriage-broker, her family found someone they judged suitable, and she submitted to their will. Unfortunately, this man had lied about the job he claimed to have. He was a drunk and he tried to cash in Sushmita's savings to pay his debts. She left him and, fortunately, her family agreed to take her back, which isn't always the case, but he soon began stalking and abusing her. Eventually, she arranged a restraining order and began divorce proceedings.

Shortly afterwards, the man was run over, having been drunk. His family blamed her for bringing bad fortune into the household, and it took her a long time to reconcile her relief with her perceived guilt. A few years later, a neighbour confessed that he had been in love with her forever and asked her to marry him. Her father approved. They bought a flat in a pukka building, had a baby and have lived happily ever after. This is a rare fairy-tale ending.

Some lessons came early; others took longer. Like all English children of my background, I had had the importance of good manners drilled into me at home and at school. Woe betide anyone not saying please and thank you. But what is good manners in England can be bad manners in India. And vice versa. When my daughter Tara was two and Anjali was three and a half, I took them to England, and my mother plucked up the courage to tell me that they didn't say please and thank you. I was more than a bit startled, but I suddenly realised that I seldom heard pleases and thank yous in Bombay. Actually, there are two Hindi/Urdu words I do hear for thank you, dhanyavaad and shukriya, but the only time I hear either of them is at the end of an airline announcement informing passengers to attach their seatbelts. When I came to India, I automatically said thank you for anything and everything as English people always do. Our servant Walji never failed to respond with: 'No saying thank you, Madam. It is my duty.' At breakfast, out of habit, I used to say to my new family: 'Would you be so kind as to pass me the butter?' They quickly told me to stop being so formal and say, 'Pass the butter!' which, to me, sounded horribly imperious. I am afraid to say that I have got used to it. To the horror of some of my English friends.

Recently, my driver moved to a tiny flat and I gave them a fridge-freezer, and both he and his wife thanked me profusely, which was a first and completely unexpected. I can't imagine what came over them. I have learnt never to expect gratitude. My mother-in-law had a delightful chap who worked for her for several years and he seemed content until one day, he went on leave and never came back. She accepted it without a murmur. It was his karma, she told me, why should he thank her for employing him for twenty years?

One of the staff at Apnalaya, a clever young woman, was always silent in meetings, and one day I gently asked her what she was thinking. She explained that throughout her schooling, she had never been allowed to ask a question or encouraged to think for herself or to express herself independently, and so she found it impossible. The same happened at home. Her father issued instructions and her mother, she and her siblings routinely obeyed without considering their own point of view. She is typical of many. It is understood—and accepted—that only the head of the family needs to have an opinion because he (we're talking patriarchy) alone knows how to take decisions. Those beneath him must defer to him, not question. This can be disastrous, as Anand found to his cost.

His wonderfully generous father had spent a fortune on his children's education abroad, which landed him in deep financial trouble. I have no complaints about this because otherwise I wouldn't have met Anand and Tulsi when they came to England to complete their education, but when Anand found out, he had the onerous task of helping to shore up the family finances. At first, we let the ground floor of the house to the American School, and Anand and I moved up to the second floor with his family. We continued to rent it out to a gym after the school moved to Bandra, and finally put the house on the market after my mother-in-law died.

It was when Tulsi's husband, Vatsal, died in 1975 and she had to return to her parents' home that I started worrying what would happen to me and the girls if Anand suddenly dropped dead. I asked him to share all the information about our family finances with me—which he did willingly, but he wouldn't have expected me to be interested.

I also had to learn that almost everything relates to where and how one fits into an Indian family, which is why forms of address are key. Anjali's friends would not dream of addressing an older person by their 'Christian' name. They call me Annabel Aunty. One, who is very close, calls me Annie Mummy. When I arrived, servants referred to me as Memsahib. Now I am Madam or Ma'am. Anjali's servants, who have known me forever, call me Granny. Anand's nieces and nephew call me Annabel Mami, even though I have known these children (now adults) all their lives, and they are very Westernised. Anand is Anand Mama. Respect exists nominally if not actually. My English girlfriend, Amanda, has always been called 'Amanda' rather than 'Mum' by her own children. In India, that would be considered sacrilege.

As would an exposed cleavage or nakedness of any sort, though this has changed in recent years. I have taken my granddaughter on holiday a couple of times where we slept in a double bed and shared a bathroom, but I haven't seen her without clothes on since she was a toddler. The Indian attitude to modesty took a little time for me to adjust to. My mother-in-law always wore exquisite saris, from which acres of midriff bulged, and yet her décolletage was always covered. I couldn't understand this at all.

Decades ago, Apnalaya benefitted from the labours of a sewing group made up of diplomatic wives, supervised by the wife of the British Deputy High Commissioner, and they met up at the residence to make sleeveless smocks for slum children. The children never wore them, running around instead in tops with sleeves but often with no knickers because, as it transpired, it is much more important to cover the arms than the bottoms of small children. I explained it to them many times but they knew better.

From the start, Anand didn't like me wearing a knee-length nightie or dressing gown. I had to wear pyjamas or a long nightie. I was permitted to wear shorts but only on the beach. Actually, I think I have become rather prim since coming to India. I don't like to see young girls in the shortest of shorts, even my granddaughter's friends. There's much to be said for modesty. In London, when I see people wearing scanty tops and mini shorts displaying yards of naked thigh and presumably thinking they look nice, it makes me feel very old and disapproving. I daresay the miniskirts that I loved to wear in the early sixties shocked the older generation in just the same way.

Like all of my generation in London in the sixties, I wore miniskirts and shiny knee-high boots à la Mary Quant. Bell-bottoms felt like liberation. The post-War shortages went on through most of the fifties, and it wasn't until the sixties that anyone had money in their pockets and the freedom to express themselves. Not that, as a student, I had much money to buy clothes. Instead, I bicycled down to Pontings on Kensington High Street and bought 'flood damaged' cloth at a huge discount and ran up dresses on my trusted sewing machine. Then came the birth of the feminist movement and the Pill. The Pill was fantastic, though to get it we all had to pretend we were married and put on a wedding ring to get a prescription. But not everything was great. Racial prejudice was rife. Occasionally, people would barge into Anand on pavements, forcing him to step onto the road. The race riots in Notting Hill in 1958—a turning point in British 'race relations'—were still fresh in our minds.

I don't remember ever discussing this, not because it would have been incendiary but because the Indians that I knew seldom felt the need to air opinions, bare their souls and share their feelings. They had a great respect for privacy in almost every department of their lives. One of Anand's great friends, Qaid, with whom he was at LSE, had several brothers, but his uncle—

his father's brother—was childless, so he and his wife adopted Qaid and brought him up as their own. Everyone knew about it but no one ever referred to it. A similar silence surrounded the fact that Anand's aunt Poornima left her mentally ill and violent husband and returned to live with her parents, taking her two small children, Asit and Shyama, with her. Her only brother, Kumi Mama, and his wife Vasu Mami, had no children and they adopted Shyama and brought her up as their own, even though her 'real' mother and sibling were living under the same roof. I once accompanied a close friend to an orphanage where she chose a baby to adopt. Over the decades, this adoption has never been brought up, in any context whatsoever. In India, it seems to me, if a person decides to keep a secret within the family, that is automatically respected. I have known of infidelities, illegitimate children, a family member with disabilities and terminal illness, the bad deeds of a black sheep, debt, drugs and alcoholism successfully hidden from the outside world. It is not necessarily a good or a healthy thing, but if the family has chosen privacy, out of grief or shame or embarrassment, then that is their right and not anyone else's business.

As for any public displays of affection, forget it. Come dusk and Chowpatty Beach is crowded with lovers with nowhere else to go, kissing and cuddling the evening away in a most un-Indian fashion. Under Section 294 of Indian law, kissing 'in a public place and to the annoyance of others' is an offence punishable by up to three months in prison or a fine. Admittedly, arrests are rare. Even now, you won't catch many couples holding hands in the street, but only a few days ago, I saw two separate couples holding hands as they walked along the pavement at Haji Ali. I remember, back in 2007, when the actor Richard Gere kissed Shilpa Shetty at an AIDS-awareness event in New Delhi, an Indian court issued a warrant for his arrest. I often think that love only reared its controversial head in India when television brought a stream of domestic soap operas into so many homes. Until then, marriages were routinely arranged.

Many of my English friends believe that India is rife with corruption and that you can buy your way out of any problem. Without a doubt, there is corruption at high levels in politics, finance and industry, and there have indeed been numerous occasions when guilty parties have fled the country leaving terrible mismanagement in their wake. But it is not the norm. I don't know many people personally who have paid bribes. You can get by without, though things may sometimes take longer, or be less readily available. I have heard that a heart surgeon in Bombay, who already charges through the nose, has been known to contact the family the night before a procedure is scheduled and demand a large wad of cash in order for the operation to go ahead. Not a common occurrence, but a depressing one.

I am also told that the traffic police can change their mind about a parking fine if you slip them a large enough note. I've never tried slipping anyone anything, and if my driver has, I have never noticed. Anyway, that is going to be more difficult in future because CCTV cameras have been installed all over Mumbai, so every minor offence is captured on film and the evidence is forwarded to the driver with notice of the penalty. You can't bribe a camera.

It amuses me sometimes to think about the Indian customs that I have unconsciously adopted. Wearing jewellery is one. I don't think I have ever seen an Indian woman bare of jewellery. It starts as babies who wear earrings, bangles and a tee-shirt. Married Hindu women are supposed to wear bangles (I don't) and instead of a wedding ring, a mangalsutra. The type of mangalsutra worn by Maharashtrian women is a thread strung with little black beads and a gold pendant. More elaborate ones may have gold and black beads threaded on gold and a gold or diamond pendant. Mangal means auspicious, sutra means thread, and the necklace symbolises love, luck and friendship and, for some women, the long life of her husband. I like this idea but I don't wear a mangalsutra, though I have one. Anjali wears hers all the time. I haven't worn a wedding ring since mine grew too tight and had to be cut off. The only thing I have ever felt devastated about losing was the chain I had made out of my darling Tara's little gold bangles after she died. I hung a locket on it containing her photo. I had taken it off when bathing in a hotel. Months later, I found it in the lining of my handbag and wept with joy.

Fortunately, I have not adopted the Indian idea of punctuality. Most people I know are late as a matter of course in their social life and would not dream of apologising for it. I hope they are more punctual at work.

But then, in my experience, sorry is a word seldom heard, though not as rarely as thank you. Usually, if something has gone wrong, it is deemed to be someone else's fault. If a report was not submitted on time in Apnalaya, it was always the fault of the junior—who then blamed *her* junior for not giving the numbers on time.

I shall never forget the first fairly disastrous dinner party Anand and I held in our flat at Warden Road. Buffet dinner parties were the norm in those days, but I had an expandable table and wanted everyone to be seated, English style. I invited ten people because we had ten chairs. An uninvited eleventh person turned up with the tenth, so the piano stool came into play. I had made soup with a chicken stock and a non-veg main course. The eleventh person was an American volunteer with an Indian NGO and she was on a special vegetarian diet, having had hepatitis. Also, I hadn't realised that my friend Malti's husband was vegetarian, though luckily not vegan, so a dish of scrambled eggs was hastily produced. I couldn't blame anyone else for my mistake but it taught me a lesson. From then on, when people

RSVP'd, I always asked them for their food choices or special requirements.

Entertaining, even for me, can be challenging. Preferences, allergies and religious rules mean many of our friends and family are vegetarian. Some will eat beef and lamb but not pork. Lamb, which is actually goat, needs planning in advance because it is so tough, it takes hours to cook well. There are also several days of fasting or days when only fruit is permitted. I seldom get it entirely right. I learnt early on that it's safer to lay on a huge buffet, which hopefully ticks every box. The marvellous thing is that nobody ever makes a fuss. As I am always saying, diversity and tolerance are the two things I love most about this wonderful country. Even if it sometimes drives me mad.

9

Apnalaya

OCCASIONALLY, OUT OF CURIOSITY, I HAVE ASKED SOMEONE WHO IS NOT Indian what immediately springs to mind when they think of India. The most common responses are colours, curry and cricket. The odd one may have muttered 'poverty', or that awful cliché, 'streets teeming with misery'. Once, the answer was 'excessive wealth', which surprised me, although it shouldn't, considering that India boasts the third highest number of billionaires in the world. Another time, it was 'Bollywood'. Often, my question has prompted a discussion about this country of extremes and an interrogation of how I can bear to live in such an unequal society. Understandably.

A recent study revealed that the average Mumbaikar would need to work for some 300 years to get a foot on the housing ladder. Real estate in Mumbai is among the most expensive in the world, even more than London's ritzy Mayfair. Which is why only 5 per cent of a population of 21 million live in what I would call pukka housing, with electricity and water on tap—quite literally—all day long.

There is a sliver of super-rich people, a slightly larger slice of the extremely well-off and a growing chunk of solid middle-class people who are doing okay. Then there are the rest, who live hand to mouth. It is easy to forget that in countries without social security or a free health service, the illness of any member of the family and especially the breadwinner will very often and very quickly cause a catastrophic decline in the standard of living.

Coming to terms with the extreme poverty in India was certainly one of the most fundamental challenges I confronted when I arrived here in the sixties and it continues on an almost daily basis. Fortunately, I never felt that I had to give up everything and devote my life to others, Mother Teresa-style. Blasphemous as it may be, I have never been the greatest fan of Mother Teresa. Of course, the work she did herself and inspired others to do is more than remarkable, but I was put off when I heard her imply that the poorest of the poor were put on this earth so that she and her fellows could save them for Jesus and, in doing so, save their own souls. Perhaps I misinterpreted her but I felt anger, and still do, that the poorest of the poor should be there at all. I suspect that my feelings towards Mother Teresa stem from my atheist self responding to an exceptional Christian. I cannot accept that all those who work with the poor are driven by religious belief. Surely, compassion is a universal humanitarian attribute.

I have visited the hospice for the dying founded by Mother Teresa in Kalighat, Calcutta, as well as Asha Daan, the Bombay home for the destitute she opened in 1976 in a Hindustan Lever warehouse. They are amazing places, filled with love and hope. When my artistic goddaughter, Rebecca, came to stay with me during her gap year, she volunteered at Asha Daan and painted the walls of the children's ward with storks with long pink legs for the little ones to look at as they lay in their cots. Her storks are still there some thirty-five years on.

On reflection, I was slow to grasp the true nature and extent of the poverty in Bombay. That first drive from the airport on a road lined with shacks should have alerted me, but it didn't, and once I reached Breach Candy in affluent South Bombay, there were no lean-tos and no skeletal figures with bloated tummies and flies crawling around their eyes resembling those in Oxfam appeals that I remember seeing in England in the sixties. In those days, poor people were hungry and thin and the rich were fat. Fat proclaimed prosperity. Now, the fitness-conscious rich are also slim, along with the poor who are still malnourished, but with a growing number who are obese because they subsist on carbohydrates and have little access to exercise. I remember discussing with Anand, a good LSE socialist, the possibility of a communist revolution in India. It was the 1970s, and we were in Benares at the time. 'It is never going to happen; just look at the skyline and the hundreds and thousands of temples,' he said. Under communism, religion must be discarded, and Anand is right. In India, religion is at the centre of most people's lives.

Back then, I imagined that all the poor people of India lived in villages and came to Bombay to find work. The twenty or so servants employed to run the Mehta household attested to that, coming as they did from Ratnagiri in Maharashtra, from Gujarat, Uttar Pradesh and far off Nepal. All lived in the house, some of them in one of six tiny servants' rooms over the garage. Others unrolled a bedding mat they must have kept in a cupboard during the day and slept in one of the many stairwells or corridors in the main house. Ayahs tended to sleep on the floor of the bedroom of the child they cared for. One ayah always laid her head on a wooden block at night because pillows were unheard of in the village where she grew up. Three of the servants lived with other members of their families, each squeezed into a tiny, single-room kholi. And by tiny, I mean tiny—6 x 12 feet or thereabouts. The others had left their family in the village and they had one month's annual leave to visit them.

I had never thought of myself as a social activist until I was called one in a press article when I received an MBE in 2017 for the work that I'd done with my charity, Apnalaya. The label stuck. I quite like it now. My motivation to become a social worker in the UK in the sixties was not some higher calling but a simple interest in people. Having been brought up in a narrow, insular upper-middle-class environment, I enjoyed meeting people from different strata of society, first the Cockney families I went hop-picking with in the summer of 1958 and then the young of all sorts of ethnicities who hung out at the Rugby Clubs in Notting Hill, a charity sponsored by Rugby School where my brothers had been educated. Sandy Holt-Wilson, a close friend of Jeremy, my brother, introduced me to the Rugby Clubs in London. Needless to say, I took a bit of a shine to him. Alas, unreciprocated. He invited me to a May Ball at Pembroke, his Cambridge College, and didn't kiss me all evening! Sandy became an ophthalmic surgeon, and in his retirement, he devoted himself to improving eye care in Gondar, Ethiopia. Thanks to the training he provided, 60,000 cataracts have been removed by nurse ophthalmic 'surgeons' and an ophthalmoscope, costing less than £10, has been developed and is widely used. No wonder he was my type.

Thanks to another chap, Archie, an incorrigible Cockney flirt I met at a Rugby Clubs hop-picking holiday, the smell of hops is another treasured memory. I specially loved dealing with the teenagers who belonged to the Rugby Clubs. Teens will always be my favourite age group. Decades on, I still find myself wondering what became of several lovely troubled lads at Mile Oak, the approved school for young offenders, outside Brighton, where I worked for one happy year before going to LSE. One unforgettably sweet boy, Reggie Partleton, was fifteen (and his mum just thirty) and his crime was stealing a bicycle. Another boy had helped himself to some buns from the back of a delivery van. How many times had I been tempted to steal—and given in—when I was younger? Countless, to be honest. Just the small change my father had left on his dressing table, but it was stealing nonetheless.

I have never been especially drawn to small children—except the special ones I know and love, of whom there are many. Had I stayed in the UK, I believe I might have become a probation officer, having hugely enjoyed a placement in Pentonville Prison, which I did while at LSE. When I qualified, I worked in the Family Service Unit in the Elephant and Castle with a small caseload of so-called 'problem' families. It gave me a glimpse into their lives, often very grim, as well as the opportunity to help them find solutions to their various challenges.

I have two friends who volunteer as Samaritans in England and I am always struck by the sharp contrast between my work with Apnalaya and theirs, listening to people in distress, often suicidal. They can merely encourage the caller to find their own way through their misery or despair. They are not allowed to advise or make practical suggestions or to know how things pan out in the end. I would find that so frustrating. While training as a caseworker in London, we were taught to help people to examine their options and I usually spent long enough with one family to have some sort of closure, even though it may not always have been the one I hoped for. The same applies to my work at Apnalaya, which makes it all the more rewarding.

When I arrived in Bombay, I knew I wanted to be of some use to others but I didn't know how best I could contribute. I felt passionately about family planning but my Hindi was rudimentary and as an English-speaking non-medic, there was nothing I could do. Then I came across the Sanjivani Trust, started by a friend of one of Anand's aunts, who had the excellent idea of finding hungry mouths for the food left over from extravagant weddings and parties. Having grown up during the war with a horror of waste, it chimed with me. At many weddings, food was served to people sitting on just one side of a table, with a banana leaf serving as a plate. If a host agreed to a Sanjivani collection, cards were placed on the table inviting guests to put untouched food to one side so that it could be collected. A group of volunteers would then redistribute it to children's homes, orphanages and to beggars on the street. Two or three times a week during the wedding season, I would pick up the food in my trusty Morris Minor and deliver it to those in need. I carried on until I was so pregnant with Anjali I could barely squeeze into the driving seat.

Unlike the England I had left behind, there did not seem to be a culture here of charitable giving. Anand's family and many others, often educated abroad, believed helping others to be a civic duty, but they were the minority. Anand's father was on the board of the Victoria Memorial Institute for the Blind and a member with the Rotary Club, which was never Anand's scene. When Anand and I lived on the ground floor of the family house, mail arrived through a common letterbox and I discovered that Anand's father was also on the management board of one of Bombay's crematoriums because each month, he received a postcard recording the number of cremations. Anand's aunt Nandini would have liked me to help her in the school she created for the poor children in the neighbourhood on Malabar Hill where she lived. But I wanted to do my own thing. I had inherited a strong sense of social responsibility from my parents, which had been further hammered home by the Christian teaching at boarding school, when we prayed for others, every morning and evening and at a church service on Sunday. Even though I became a determined atheist long before I left school, one or two teachings stuck with me, such as: 'There, but for the grace of God, go I!' and 'Love thy neighbour as thyself'. Throw in the Ten Commandments and I don't think one can go far wrong—or so I hope!

It took time for me to find a good cause I wanted to work with. My baby Tara arrived in 1970 just eighteen months after Anjali, so for a couple of years, I had my hands full with my little girls. Then I met Mithu Alur, her husband Ranjit, and their daughter

Malini. They had been living in London where Malini, who has cerebral palsy, had attended a creche for children with special needs and returned to Bombay to find no similar schools. Mithu rounded up some of us local mums, including my friend Indu, a special needs teacher, and in 1972, we became founder members of what was then called the Spastics Society of India. Sadly, we fell out with Mithu, who could be difficult to work with, but I have never lost my admiration for her achievements. When she discovered that Indira Gandhi, then prime minister, had a relative with cerebral palsy, she immediately got her involved. Since then, Mithu has been the face of what was later renamed ADAPT: Able Disable All People Together. She and ADAPT are still going strong.

A short while afterwards, I was introduced to Shanta Gupta at a party, and she told me about the Holland Welfare Centre, founded by Tom Holland, the Australian Consul General in Bombay. His office overlooked the site where land was being reclaimed for the construction of the NCPA at Nariman Point and where the workforce and their families lived in temporary huts. Tom and his wife, June, occupied a lovely spacious residence, and the sight of these scrawny kids playing in rubble under the beating sun got to him.

Tom made up his mind to do something for these children, so he talked to Jamshed Bhabha, the delightfully eccentric Parsi who founded the NCPA. Jamshed allowed him to set up a welfare centre in a tiny corner of the plot. Then Tom asked Arvind Mafatlal, whose fortune came from textiles, to donate a shed to provide shade from the sun and shelter from the monsoon. By the time I got involved in 1973, Tom had left India, the Holland Welfare Centre was registered and Shanta Gupta was running it. When she showed me the project, there were about fifty or sixty mainly migrant children racing around, all quite small, because as soon as the children were big enough to work, they were sent out to earn some money. Lined up against the wall were cradles filled with babies, being swung by slightly older siblings. Shanta's plan was first to 'tame' the children who were not accustomed to quiet, routine or discipline and then to help their families get their children into the local municipal schools. She had already employed a teacher and needed someone to look after the money side of things, so she asked me to become treasurer. I hadn't a clue about what that entailed but I wasn't frightened of numbers, so I accepted.

I had already discovered that few Indian women knew much about money because the men hold the purse strings, which made me something of a rarity. Most of my friends had no idea what their husbands earned or, indeed, what their husbands owned because, like me, they lived in extended families where bank accounts would be shared with parents and siblings. Meher Banaji, the principal of another local charitable school, The Happy Home and School for the Blind, kindly introduced me to her elderly accountant, Mr Rao, who taught me the ancient craft of double-entry bookkeeping. I remain mystified as to why one has to write on both pages but learnt to do so. I remained treasurer for years until, thanks to the computerisation of our accounts, which finally happened in 1993, my handwritten accounts were no longer necessary.

I began going once or twice a week to keep accounts and also help out with the children. We had three or four staff by then and we thought we knew what we were doing. The children learnt to write with chalk on slates. When we found them chewing the chalk, we realised they were deficient in calcium. Our good friend, Yusuf Hamied, whose father founded Cipla, donated calcium pills. Another benefactor supplied us with powdered milk. We gave the children a banana twice a week. Each Saturday, Rotaract volunteers from South Bombay's Cathedral School came to play with the children.

In those days, people assumed that the centre was funded either by Holland or Australia because of Tom. The truth was neither. At some stage, someone had the bright idea to rename the charity Apnalaya, which melds the word 'apna' meaning 'our' and 'alaya', which means 'place' or 'space'.

Two years later, in 1975, when actual building work got started on the NCPA, Jamshed Bhabha gave us notice to vacate. Until then, our focus had been the children, but we began to realise that in order to help the children, we had to work with the mothers as well. The problem, as we soon found out, was that all major decisions were taken by the men. We knew we had to reach out to them too. The transition into community work had begun. That we would continue to work with children was a given, but where could we take our massive shed? As a group, we decided that we would have to start working in a more settled slum community. My good friend Adi Dubash, a local councillor at the time, helped us with the introductions that led to us setting up not one but two community centres in slums in Tardeo, the first in Datta Mandir, the other in Jaiphalwadi nearby.

By that time, Pratima Panwalkar from the Tata Institute of Social Sciences had joined as a member, and she was able to guide us into the modern, non-directive approach to community work, and to help us find and then supervise our first professional social workers. Using this approach, we first asked the community leaders in what way we could be of help to them. In Datta Mandir, they wanted us to start a clinic and gave us the use of their temple until we could build our own shed. In Jaiphalwadi, they wanted us to start a balwadi. No sooner had we settled in our Tardeo centres than we were offered space to start a third in a very backward slum community in Malad and then a fourth in Shivaji Nagar, Chembur, both distant suburbs. We set up our fifth, in Chickuwadi, also in Chembur, two years later. Pratima volunteered with us for many years and she and I became close friends; so it was a great loss for both Apnalaya and for me personally when she passed away in 2008.

Tardeo is a mixed but relatively affluent residential and commercial neighbourhood in South Mumbai. Somehow, we were able to persuade Suresh Salvi, a delightful government official with the Slum Improvement Board, to allot us a big enough space in Jaiphalwadi to erect our big shed, but only after the improvement work had been completed. In the meantime, we created an office in a temporary shed and built some loos which were plumbed into some sort of drainage, though not a proper sewer, and here we started our first balwadi offering two years of pre-primary schooling to children who would not otherwise have had any. Our volunteer Arnie Antia, a teacher, believed this was the best way to prepare children for the first standard and would, hopefully, reduce the drop-out rate of 60 per cent, which occurred by the time the children reached the fourth standard in municipal schools.

We soon found out that it was difficult to recruit trained teachers to work in slums, so Arnie set up a training model consisting of a dozen weekly sessions for women from the community to become pre-school teachers. The sessions included both basic theory and how to make educational equipment such as counting rods, puzzles and puppets, out of waste materials. Arnie's workshops eventually became the model for training all our Apnalaya teachers and many others working in other NGOs all over Bombay and beyond. We continued running them for many years until the government introduced its own compulsory six-month training for pre-school teachers.

We were mad really to take up the Malad community. They were mainly Waddaris, traditional stone-cutters from Karnataka, but the community was very poor, many living in huts made of straw. We were offered a small plot of land in the community to buy for only Rs 20,000 by one of Nusli Wadia's charities. It took time to build a shed, funded by the Associated Cement Company, and we entered into a partnership with the local Rotary Club to run a clinic and a balwadi there. The same year, through Pratima and a local councillor, we opened our fourth centre in an already existing shed in Lotus Colony in Shivaji Nagar, Chembur, the second largest slum in Mumbai, on the edge of the Deonar dumping ground, with a population of 3,00,000, with two-thirds of that number younger than twenty-five. This is the area in which we are still working nearly fifty years later, but we had no idea this would be the case at that time. The population has doubled since we began in 1976.

Even now, four out of ten girls in Shivaji Nagar are married off before the legal age of eighteen, and one out of two boys married off before the legal age of twenty-one. I worry a lot about this. In India, considerable effort is being put into empowering girls, which is wholly a good thing, but too little attention is paid to working with and educating the boys these girls will marry and who will take on the roles of husbands and fathers.

My own grandchildren have had such blessed and privileged starts in life. My granddaughter, Sara, now twenty-six, has completed her Master's in London and is back in Mumbai. My grandson, Arjun, is twenty-four and is playing his heart out on the cricket field. But these two lucky young ones are far from typical. Few Indians of their age in Shivaji Nagar are truly literate (one in four having never been to school), and the majority are unskilled and unemployed or semi-employed and already burdened with children. In our communities, the average age for a first pregnancy for girls is nineteen, but even worse in my opinion, for boys, it is twenty-one.

In 1979, in order to celebrate the International Year of the Child, we opened our fifth centre in Chikuwadi, a remote, impoverished slum inside the Bhabha Atomic Research Centre colony in Chembur, where the construction workers were housed. The

Chikuwadi huts were the worst I had seen, a patchwork of cloth, plastic and bits of tin sheet with mud floors, no windows, water or power. In most, the 'roof' was so low I could not stand upright. In this entire community, just one man, Shankar Jadhav, was literate, so getting the children to school was their priority and ours. By then, Rippan Kapur, who was an airline purser, had founded the charity CRY (Child Rights and You) and he was keen to sponsor the education of the Chikuwadi children. We discussed this with the community, and they responded that if we could provide the bus fare to get the children to school, they would find the money for the return fare. I confess I was stunned. And to this day, it still moves me. The community could have asked for so much more than a one-way fare. We paid this and a lump sum at the start of the school year, which helped toward buying schoolbooks, shoes and raincoats for the children.

From the very early days, most of the employees of Apnalaya were recruited from our communities and trained by us. I felt so privileged to be able to visit their homes and share in their ups and downs, and I'm sure I learnt much more from them than they might have learnt from me. When I look back, they crowd into my mind. One of them is Balaiah, who also lived in Chikuwadi. He was an alcoholic, so we referred him to our residential treatment centre in Malad. Having successfully completed the programme, he became staff, eventually training as a counsellor and then joining the training team. Sadly, he developed AIDS in the early days of the virus when treatment was difficult to come by and beyond the reach of poor people like him. We helped him as much as we could, but he died, leaving a young widow and a baby. She moved back to Hyderabad and died shortly after, also of AIDS. What was so unusual about Balaiah was that he was not afraid to speak out about his alcoholism and AIDS and ways of preventing both, which made him a highly effective force for good within our communities.

But it is with Deepak that I formed the closest bond when he became the office assistant and gofer in our Tardeo headquarters. Deepak was the only child of two mothers. As is often the case, his father had taken a second wife when his first wife failed to produce a child. His father died before I met him, but his two mothers lived together in a hut in Jaiphalwadi. One of them was the first person I had ever met with leprosy, and through her I learnt that leprosy can be treated and even cured. Deepak was not especially bright, but he was willing and cheerful. When computerisation came along, we tried to train him, but failed. Then Deepak fell in love with a neighbour's daughter, but because he was a Dalit and she was of a higher caste, her family disapproved. We helped them elope and to live in an undisclosed location until her family relented and the couple returned to Jaiphalwadi where she gave birth to a son and they were all very happy. Until she suddenly became ill, went to the nearby municipal hospital and died shortly afterwards. Deepak was distraught. I took him to identify her body in the hospital morgue, which was one of the most distressing experiences of my life. I have blanked out much of the detail. I think it was underground, because I remember the darkness and the uneven stone slabs wet with water and blood. Unwrapped bodies were heaped on a step. Two ghostly attendants, clad in dhotis, their arms and legs bare, sat in silence. Someone subsequently told me that mortuary staff in those days were heavily drugged, otherwise they would have found their work unbearable.

Deepak continued to work for us and look after his son because his wife's family refused to take in their lowly grandchild, and when the slum was redeveloped, he was allocated a one-room tenement. He eventually sold it and returned to his own family back in his village. Though I am no longer in touch, I think of him often.

Among the first batch of community teachers was Draupadhi, a woman I came to admire more highly than almost any other. Married with three daughters, her husband not only routinely abused her but regularly brought other women to their hut in order to punish her for not bearing him a son. Every day, she came to work immaculately dressed in a fresh sari, her hair tied back in a long plait. Her extraordinary air of calm and dignity, as well as her quick grasp of all subjects, made her stand out from the other trainees. She rose through the ranks of Apnalaya and ultimately became in charge of all teacher training.

All three of Draupadhi's daughters wanted to be social workers, and when the eldest gained admission to the training course, we decided to give Draupadhi an ex-gratia payment toward the fees. I handed her the cheque, beaming and expecting her to be similarly delighted, and to my surprise I saw tears in her eyes. Not tears of gratitude but tears of hurt. She thrust the envelope back at me. For years and years, she had been saving up for her daughters' education, and she was insulted that we had assumed that she needed financial assistance. We had completely misjudged how much her independence meant to her. I felt ashamed—but it taught me a valuable lesson.

We often got things wrong. Early on, while still in Nariman Point, we decided to wash the children's hair with an Ayurvedic preparation to get rid of lice and nits and, to our astonishment, some of the mothers were very angry. We should first have asked them if they thought lice were a problem and if they would like to know how it could be treated. These women took our interference as a criticism of their inadequate mothering, and the awful thing was—or the good thing was—that I knew exactly how they felt because I remembered that day when I had come back to the house in Warden Road and discovered that my mother-in-law had tidied up my little bit of backyard, presumably because she thought it was a mess. She was just trying to help me but I felt judged. Just like these mums. The nit incident left me humbled.

A less personal lesson learnt was that the more we spent on preventive health education, the lower the bills for medicines that I saw since, as treasurer, I had to write out the cheques. I realised this when we wiped out scabies in Datta Mandir, thanks to the Community Health Workers. Over the years, we have trained dozens of women to work as community health workers, focusing mainly on maternal and child health, spreading information on immunisation, childcare and nutrition as well as to register a pregnancy early and to go to hospital for delivery. Many diseases are a direct consequence of poverty and poor nutrition. Recent studies that we have done confirm that household expenditure on healthcare is anything from 30 to 60 per cent of family income and savings. In the early years, we held clinics in most of our centres, some just for women and children. We did what we could at Apnalaya, but running clinics is expensive and should be the duty of the municipality. Although community health remains a large part of our work, our objective now is to work with the municipality for better healthcare delivery in Mumbai slums. We used to describe our work as putting sticking plasters on gaping wounds. Not a cure, but better than nothing. Just about.

On reflection, our journey from one centre at Nariman Point to five spread across Mumbai within the space of two to three years is rather remarkable, and sometimes I wonder how and why we did it. The why is easier to answer: we did it because we were given the opportunity to expand, almost without a second thought. As we expanded, so did the number of volunteers who helped in the running, many of them as volunteers in the clinics. The planning and implementation were carried out by a smaller group. In the early years, we used to sit in a circle on the floor for meetings, Shanta from Delhi, Pushpa, a Kutchi, Pat, an American Christian, Fakhira, a Muslim married to a south Indian, Arnie, a Parsi, and me, an atheist born in the UK, all united in one common cause. And each contributing a different expertise and experience to the discussions. Meanwhile, the work on the ground was being done by an increasing number of staff, both professional social workers and our locally trained balwadi teachers, health workers and paraprofessional workers, headed from 1992 onwards by Leena Joshi, our director. Leena joined Apnalaya in 1979 and stayed at the helm until 2011. She and I worked very closely together with almost daily phone calls and frequent meetings, and I learnt a lot from her, particularly on how to engage with and involve community members. Within one decade, from 1990 to 2000, our staff strength tripled from thirty to nearly ninety, including seven or eight social workers.

I arrived in Bombay knowing lots about both the theory and the practice of social work in England and quickly discovered that India was a very different world. Having learnt about the non-directive approach from Pratima, we used it when venturing into new communities. To our surprise, the first thing they wanted in Shivaji Nagar was a post-box. So, Medha Patkar, our first social worker in Shivaji Nagar, helped the youth to get one, and in the process established a relationship that enabled us to work together to address some of their other needs.

Our community health work took off thanks to another volunteer, Pat Gass, an American friend of ours, who was married to Eric, a third-generation missionary in India. Pat was a trained nurse and she and Eric had worked in rural India before coming to Mumbai. She contacted Raj and Mabelle Arole, a husband-and-wife team of doctors running a pioneering project in Jamkhed in rural Maharashtra, where they were training local women to become health workers within their own communities, and they agreed to guide us in setting up a similar project in our communities. The two Doctors Arole had both been to Johns Hopkins University in the USA, and on starting the Jamshed project in 1970, persuaded Johns Hopkins to analyse data collected from their villagers in order to devise a strategy for improvement. The analysts sent back a report saying that on the basis of this information, the entire population should be dead because their diet was insufficient to sustain life! Their project became the model for village community health and continues to this day.

I was once helping at a clinic in our Chikuwadi health centre when a thin, frail woman came in to ask how to treat her husband who had TB. The health worker told her to give him milk and nourishing food. The woman exploded: 'How can I give him milk when I have no money to feed my children?' Of course, the health worker meant well, but her advice was as absurd as instructing people to boil water to kill germs in order to stay healthy when they could barely afford to buy water, never mind fuel for a fire. Apnalaya's mission, from the start, was to work within the existing system, to help people and communities to help themselves, to equip them to manage their lives so that our intervention was no longer necessary. But in such deprived communities, this takes a long time; in my experience, at least fifteen to twenty years or one generation. We were able to withdraw from four of our five communities only when the slum dwellers had been rehoused.

Helping our communities get better housing was not something we could do ourselves but, fortunately, four of our communities benefited from the SRA scheme. However, we were able to help people get access to government schemes, such as rationing, by helping them obtain ration cards. But it is difficult to acquire a ration card or a voting card or to admit your child into school without a birth certificate. So, in 2007, when Plan India asked us to take on a project called Mapping the Nowhere Children, Apnalaya embarked on the huge task of helping people to get birth certificates for their new babies and their older children. Many women return to their villages to give birth, which makes registration, meant to be done within twenty-one days of the birth, quite a challenge. To my mind, a birth certificate has a truly existential significance. It gives a human being self-respect, a value, a voice. It is only when someone believes they have rights that they can become responsible. The true number of the poor in India is unknown because many are not registered. We have seen this in what is widely considered to be the under-reporting of Covid-19 deaths. These people were always at the top of my list of priorities at Apnalaya—an increasingly crowded position as time went on.

Because the voting register is based on the list of those with ration cards, I was mistakenly given a voter's card back in the mid-seventies when Indira Gandhi had declared a state of Emergency. As a foreign national, even though I am a permanent resident in India, I am not allowed to vote here. I felt so passionately about the horrifying state of the country that I voted for the first and only time in India. I broke the law. Would I get arrested? I hoped not. I would not survive long in an Indian prison.

The only time I ever voted in a UK general election was in 1964, in Paddington North—naturally, I voted Labour. The comedian Jimmy Edwards was the Conservative candidate that year, which was already a great joke because he didn't have a snowflake's chance of winning in such a strong Labour-held seat.

From the late seventies, I went to work every morning. Apnalaya was expanding rapidly. As the only trained social worker, my role became more prominent. Helping to raise funds was very much a part of my work too. In the early years, it was customary to hold a film premiere or cultural programme to raise funds, so we would do it once every two or three years, and the money raised would get us through, with sporadic help from local trusts or philanthropic friends. One of these events was organized by Kit Peters—a member of our initial group of regular volunteers—who was married to Bill, the British Deputy High Commissioner. They lived in Jinnah House, and agreed to host a performance of Indian classical dance in the gardens. We sold tickets to friends and relations and persuaded companies to buy advertising space in programmes and brochures. Ten years later, the British Foreign Office decided that their foreign diplomats were living too royally and costs should be cut. The current DHC's Residence, though grand by Mumbai standards, is on the fifth floor of a block of flats with no garden to stage big charitable functions.

Frankly, fundraising is my least favourite part of the work. In the early years, I asked the same people and the same companies for money over and over again with ever-increasing embarrassment. Sachin has come to our rescue on more than one occasion and continues to support us. Occasionally, I get an unexpected windfall. When I turned eighty, a friend gave me eight lakh rupees. I knew he was going to give us something, but eight lakh was more than I had dreamed of. As I have aged, so have my friends and well-wishers, and there are fewer people left to ask for handouts. Fortunately, as our needs have grown, so has the availability of grants from trusts, funding agencies and corporations under CSR, but it is extremely difficult to secure, and it is a relentless struggle to keep up.

When I got to Bombay in 1966, of a population of 5.5 million, some 30 per cent lived in slums. By 2019, the population had tripled, or even quadrupled according to some figures, and more than half lived in slums of sorts or on the pavements. My idea of a slum when I arrived here came from what I had heard about the Gorbals in Glasgow or the back-to-back housing in Birmingham that my mother visited as a volunteer with the NSPCC after the war. Living in India, I learnt to use the word 'slum' differently, because here it refers to any unauthorised area where people have created shelters. Many of these homes are adequate if very small, but many are indeed unsafe, deplorably overcrowded, unhygienic, without access to sanitation or clean water and often under threat of demolition. To put it into context: the Dharavi slum in Mumbai is spread over 2.1 sq. km, has a population of a million people, 5,000 businesses, 15,000 single-room factories and a thriving informal economy. That is at least forty times more crowded than Tower Hamlets, London's most impoverished, most densely populated ward. Dharavi is the biggest slum in Mumbai, Shivaji Nagar the second biggest, but much less attention has been focused on Shivaji Nagar.

I was also very surprised to learn that there was no equivalent of Council housing here, no subsidised housing for the poor at all. However, since the 1990s, alarmed by the steadily increasing sprawl of slums, the government created the Slum Rehabilitation Authority (SRA) to implement a scheme to encourage private developers to construct new properties to rehouse slum residents free of charge on part of the plot they had encroached upon. The builder could then use the remaining space to build much fancier apartments for commercial sale. In some communities, the SRA has been responsible for great improvements. Up to a point. Water still does not flow 24/7, but many new blocks have storage tanks and, if well managed, there should be enough water for everyone throughout the day.

It was not until I had been working with Apnalaya for two years that I entered a slum for the first time. Since then, I have been into hundreds. What struck me when I was first invited in was not just the size, averaging 10 x 15 feet for a family, but the meagre number of clothes hung on hooks on the wall beside kitchen pans, steel thalis, jars filled with dals, pulses, rice, atta and sugar neatly lined up on shelves. I couldn't help comparing this with the dozens of cupboards and drawers full of my clothes, and my airy kitchen, often in a state of relative chaos.

Four of the five slum communities where Apnalaya has worked have been rehoused, two in Tardeo, one in Malad, and one in Chikuwadi in Mankhurd. The hutments have gone, replaced by twenty-storey blocks in Tardeo and ten in the other two. After moving in, Janabai, one of our helpers, showed me the modern one-room tenement in Malad she proudly called home. It had a tiled floor, a living-room, kitchen area, running water and a loo. She was delighted with the raised platform for cooking on, though disappointed it wasn't marble, which made me smile.

Tourist visitors to Dharavi, Mumbai's biggest slum, are always surprised to see tiny pockets of relative prosperity amidst the poverty. You would find this in many slums, particularly those in South or Central Mumbai where schools and colleges are more accessible and jobs available. In Jaiphalwadi, where we started work more than forty years ago, many of the men were porters at Bombay Central station nearby. Now you will find the majority in better jobs, possibly teachers in a college or employees of a bank or the police force or even working abroad. They would love a bigger place and could afford one, but none is available except in the far distant suburbs, maybe 40 or 50 km away.

Admittedly, when some are moved into new tenements, if they can't afford the outgoings, or don't like it because they miss living hugger-mugger with neighbours in the way they had become accustomed, they rent it out and move back into their old slum, if it hasn't already been bulldozed. I have no problem with that. I have the right to choose to live where I want, so why shouldn't those with less? My dream is to see the government rehouse every single slum dweller into simple one-star flats in skyscrapers, which is the only solution given the prohibitive cost of land in Mumbai. Prime Minister Modi launched an ambitious scheme in 2016 to provide affordable housing to all those living below the poverty line by 2022. It didn't happen, and there appears to be no real political will to deal with Mumbai's ever-worsening housing crisis.

Over the years, Apnalaya got involved with many different areas of concern—education, community health, HIV/AIDS, drug addiction and rehab, domestic violence, sport, financial literacy, gender issues, slum sanitation, youth training—but to my mind everything begins with housing. To live in a stable building with a water-resistant roof over your head is life changing. Education plays a part in improving lives but it is not, alas, an end in itself. Basic schooling, passing the twelfth standard and even going to college only takes someone so far. After that, who will provide employment? But nothing counts without a roof. Only with a roof can a person find dignity. Only when a person has a sense of their own worth can they begin to hope. If I were to start again, I think I would work for an organisation dedicated to improving housing for the poorest, but there aren't many such organisations that I know of.

Having worked with the poor in India for nearly fifty years, I have become quite unshockable, but the abysmal conditions in Shivaji Nagar still make me weep: malnourished, anaemic children living inches from a mountain of squalor, garbage and a cesspool of a nullah. There is no privacy and no ventilation, and too many bodies are packed into tiny spaces. They deserve better. I ask myself several times every day, how appalling must life in the villages be for these people to have chosen this instead? I know the answer. The alternative is near-starvation. They believe they will find work of some sort in a city slum. Rag-picking is probably not what they had in mind. What amazes me is that they sort rank and reeking garbage day in, day out. And instead of howling with despair, they smile and get on with it.

Recently, the much-loved Mumbai celeb Twinkle Khanna, brand ambassador for Save the Children, our biggest donor at the time, visited Shivaji Nagar to see what Apnalaya was doing.

A group of young girls and boys demonstrated their knowledge of menstrual hygiene (courtesy of our team at Apnalaya) with confidence and poise. I felt inordinately proud of these youths—and proud of Apnalaya for taking care of people failed by governments over many decades.

Sometimes, when feeling particularly bleak, I question what we at Apnalaya have actually achieved. In Mumbai, there is still grinding poverty, desperate disease, mass illiteracy, though much of this hidden from view. The quality of education, particularly in municipal schools, is actually deteriorating, and that was before Covid shut schools during the lockdown, which greatly impacted the education of millions. When we started working in Chembur, some of the municipal schools were so crowded that they ran in two-hour shifts throughout the day with two classes held simultaneously in one classroom, each facing a blackboard at either end. The noise of the children waiting outside for the next class was deafening. From an Apnalaya survey of aspirations of teenagers done quite recently, we learnt that some teachers actively discouraged children from continuing to attend school, telling them they would be better off joining their parents scavenging on the garbage dump.

A few years ago, I went to a talk by Bill Gates, one of my heroes, when he came to Mumbai. He told us that the Gates Foundation does not fund education in this country because education should be the task of government, choosing instead to concentrate on health and sanitation. We see from the other end the ill-effects of government lethargy. The Mumbai municipal corporation is the biggest municipal corporation in the world, and I understand that they can't wave a magic wand and instantly solve the city's problems, but it would be nice to see them work more purposefully. New municipal commissioners arrive, filled with good intentions, and then they are replaced, having got nowhere. Meanwhile, the daily growth of the population means that before a new flyover has come up to cope with the increased traffic, another is already necessary. There will never be enough space, enough housing, enough schools, enough hospitals in Mumbai. Controlling the growing population is necessary. But how?

It has been proved conclusively that as school attendance increases for girls, so the birthrate declines. And we have witnessed that firsthand in Apnalaya. Nobody of my age, or who has read Rohinton Mistry's magnificent novel, *A Fine Balance,* will forget the gruesome campaign to sterilise millions of men during the 1975 Emergency spearheaded by Sanjay Gandhi, son of the former Prime Minister Indira Gandhi, when thousands (many of them young, unmarried men) were forcibly sterilised. Many died from botched operations. That was unacceptable, intolerable, wrong. India is a free country, a democracy, and I am proud of that. Nobody should tell us how many children we can or cannot have. There are incentives in place to limit families to two children, but there are no laws in force.

The dream of almost every aspiring Indian was, and still is, to have a government job, which comes with housing benefits and pensions. Even for the most educated and privileged Indians, becoming a top civil servant in the Indian Administrative Service (IAS) used to be highly competitive and extremely desirable. No longer. Instead of wanting to be civil servants, or even doctors, lawyers or engineers, they now want highly paid, big-bonus jobs in the corporate or financial sector. Few go into politics. The same thing applies in the UK, I think. The world over, politics is not seen as public service but a dirty business.

Part of the price one pays for moving to another country is that one has to live with its politics. Had I still lived in England, there is no doubt that I would have been a Remainer and not a Leaver, but I would have accepted Brexit Britain because it was the will of the majority and I respect democracy. Apnalaya has collaborated extensively with both the municipality and the state government, so I could not afford to be a critic. Now that I am in my ninth decade, I sometimes wonder if, had I been more willing to put my head above the parapet, I might have improved the lives of the poor more effectively. But that's a pointless exercise because it's simply not in my nature.

It is only since I have stepped back from day-to-day operations at Apnalaya that I can see how far we have come from the first shed in 1973 when three of us managed everything. I am proud to say that I have helped build Apnalaya from a traditional, low-key, rights-driven charity into what is now an exceptionally professional, evidence-driven, results-oriented, financially sustainable NGO, recognised in the sphere of urban poverty for its approach, research and achievements and expanding beyond Mumbai into other regions. I have been told that I led with love, which moves me to tears.

The truth is that I have always believed in my team and encouraged them to find answers and they have never let me down. The board is still made up of unpaid volunteers, which is the law in India. Some staff who began as community health workers and balwadi teachers have worked their way up. Many have stayed with us for more than twenty years. Indeed, Dnyaneshwar, who joined us in 1987, is still with us, though threatening to retire soon, or so he told me recently. Now we have more than ninety people on the staff, including a well-paid CEO, and four directors, senior managers and assistant managers, an HR department, health-workers and junior staff, all of whom earn a good salary. There are many more unpaid community volunteers, such as Shefali, who was one of the first rag-pickers I ever met. She was working on the dumping ground nearby and we suggested that she and some of the others got together to form a group so that they could have some bargaining power with the municipality, and she responded magnificently to the challenge. Her son is now an active youth volunteer.

We often found that when a person took on responsibilities outside their normal boundaries, it gave them a new sense of purpose. Our intention was always to train local people so that they could negotiate directly and effectively with the government about local issues such as water connections, garbage collection or setting up a classroom for children with disability.

I put my faith in youth and the programmes we have developed to give them the confidence to achieve this, as exemplified by Saleha. She lives with her family on the edge of the dumping ground and joined her first Apnalaya programme at the age of twelve. A couple of years later, she managed to persuade her father to let her stay on in school, although he wanted her to leave. She soon began taking classes for groups of boys and girls in Apnalaya, discussing sanitation and menstrual hygiene. She became a mentor and a role model within her community, which culminated in her being chosen to speak on behalf of the girls of India at the United Nations General Assembly in New York, where she met Bill and Melinda Gates. Exceptional by any standards.

I worry about what I call the corporatisation of philanthropy. Too many new terms such as impact, return on investment, sustainability, replicable models and exit policies have crept into the donor vocabulary, and it often seems to me that less and less attention is paid to the people needing help. I think we have avoided this at Apnalaya.

When I was awarded the MBE in 2017, I questioned whether I deserved to be honoured when so much work on the ground was done by a large team of people. I was neither the founder nor the leader of Apnalaya, though I know I was looked upon as the leader following Shanta's departure for Delhi in 1981. The progress that we have made over the years is due to those people, staff and community, backed up by partners and collaborators, donors and supporters. I have learnt more from them than they have from me. And it wasn't what I did but what I helped them to do. They were also my window into their world, and for that I am eternally grateful.

I have always thought of myself as a good number-two person, happier to follow than to lead. I have also been aware that it is near impossible to change big things in intractable India and that the best I could do was to enable others to effect small changes from within their communities. But the truth is that I devoted my time and energy to Apnalaya not out of some sort of vocation, but because I was so interested and absorbed by the people we were helping. Through Apnalaya I met the late Queen of England, princes and princesses, multibillionaire philanthropists, corporate leaders and those without a rupee to their name. And I have met literally thousands of wonderful people in the not-for-profit space who are far more deserving of a medal than me.

My life has been very different from the one my parents might have mapped out, teaching small girls to play the piano in smart schools in Hemel Hempstead or elsewhere. I have been warmly welcomed in slums in Bombay and never made to feel like an interfering foreigner. Indeed, I never felt that myself. I could have become an Indian citizen but I never wanted to because my Britishness is somehow very much part of who I am, and I did not want to give it up. Had I been forced to in order to continue to live here, I would have done so.

Now that I have retired, I look back with some satisfaction. I am confident that Apnalaya will survive me and continue on the same path, ever thriving, for many years to come. But it will only truly have succeeded when we are no longer needed.

10

Changing Places

MY MEMORY IS LIKE THE RAVA DOSA MY NIECE, ALIYA, ALWAYS CHOOSES when I treat her to lunch at the Willingdon Club. Crisp round the outside, soft in the middle, and full of holes! Memory is a strange thing. Weeks after my daughter Tara died, I couldn't recollect her as a living, moving creature at all. I have been told that there are two ways of recalling things: visual memory and cerebral memory, both helped by photographs. I am not so sure. Some things have dropped out of my brain forever, and even if I see pictures, I can't retrieve them.

Yet, a handful of happenings remain crystal clear. Especially the times of transition, or dramatic news. The memory of having my ears pierced in Torquay the day after we arrived in Devon, when I had left school forever, is as fixed in my mind as the holes in my ears. As is the room in which I was standing at LSE in November 1963 when I heard of Kennedy's assassination. The whole place froze. I rushed off to find Anand and we cried together.

Going off to live in London when I got into the Royal College of Music is another sharp memory, possibly because it was a huge step that I had taken rather carelessly. I chose the Royal College rather than the Royal Academy for no better reason than that I fancied living in Kensington. I was eighteen and eager to spread my wings. I had a weekly allowance of £8 to cover everything. I had a bicycle! I had my freedom! I moved into Queen Alexandra's House, a student hostel with practice pianos in rooms upstairs, a stone's throw from Albert Hall and the Royal College, which made it, as far as I could see, the ideal place to be. I have always lived on the bright side.

Later, when I went to LSE, my friend Ruth and I shared a flat in Durham Terrace, in Little Venice, now rather smart but then Rachman-land (Peter Rachman was a Polish-born landlord in Notting Hill in the fifties and early sixties, notorious for his exploitation of tenants). We had a bedroom each, and a kitchenette, and enough room on the floor of the living-room for Tulsi, Anand's sister, to camp during the holidays; in those days, she was an undergraduate at Oxford, reading PPE. There was no space for my piano and I didn't miss it one bit. Those were happy days. I worked hard, shopped for vegetables and dangly earrings in Portobello Market and made friends with a lovely group of young men, many of them Indians, all studying economics.

LSE was a revelation. It was so refreshingly multicultural. There were very few of the public-school types I'd been surrounded by my entire life and no posh English girls like me. The first person I befriended was Bert, who came from St Kitts. He told me that whenever he played cricket and hit a six, the ball invariably landed in the sea. I don't think he was joking. We used to go to the Friday evening hop at the Three Tunnes Bar, and one foggy night—2 December 1962, to be precise—I met Bert's friend Anand Mehta. They used to go to India House for lunch together, where a meal cost a half-crown and I joined them. It was a thali with rice, yellow gravy and mixed vegetables and tasted pretty awful, but it filled us up.

The Indians were the chaps I was most drawn to. We had the same sense of humour. But Anand had a wider group of friends, including Hassan from Pakistan, Sami from Iraq and red-haired

Barry Scott, whose father was a plumber in Leeds and remains a close friend to this day; Reg, too, was working class; Ravi was an Indian from East Africa.

Once I got stuck into LSE, my parents forgot about their crushed musical ambitions for me surprisingly quickly. Indeed, I hadn't been studying for long when my mother began to share my interest in criminology, so much so that she leapt at the invitation to sit on a Parole Board alongside a judge and a psychiatrist to decide if criminals could be safely and responsibly released from the new maximum-security prison nearby. She loved it. For her, too, this was a taste of freedom and independence from my controlling father.

Three years later, I told my parents that I was going to marry Anand and live in India. To borrow a phrase from my beloved P.G. Wodehouse, if they were not actually disgruntled, they were far from being gruntled. They were silent. No surprise there because Lancasters don't scream or shout and, in any case, it would have made no difference. I had presented them with a fait accompli. I was sorry to have none of my family or friends at my wedding. My father could easily have afforded to fly the whole family out, but that sort of extravagance was not his style. I was resentful, but I didn't dwell on it. I am not a dweller. That way madness lies.

It wasn't that they disapproved of Anand, or so they told me later. They were concerned because they didn't know what my life was going to be like in India and they were afraid. Just as they were when I decided to leave the Royal College of Music to become a social worker. They didn't know any social workers. Girls like me became teachers, nurses or secretaries.

As an English girl, I was much less strange for Anand's family than Anand was for mine. Generations of his family, daughters as well as sons, had been educated at British universities. In the sixties in general, Indians knew much more about Great Britain than the British knew about India. As children, my mother-in-law and her sisters had an Irish governess. They had become familiar with the British way of life because, during Empire, the British had brought their customs, lock, stock and barrel, to India. Servants to the British learnt how to do things the British way, such as laying the table with cutlery and glasses; for people like the Mehtas, those ways became their ways. However, the British, I am sorry to report, were reluctant to take on the Indian practices and habits that the climate and conditions dictated. I have never forgotten my visit to a museum in Chennai filled with army uniforms from times gone by when the British soldiers in India wore navy serge high-necked woollen coats. The single compromise to the heat was a solar topee, worn only by officers. Those in the ranks just sweated.

My parents knew little of India or Indians, though my father had travelled to Madras on a business trip, which was quite an undertaking in those days, with planes making multiple refuelling stops. There, he struck up a lifelong friendship with an Indian businessman named Arunachalam, and together they set up TI Cycles of India. Every time I see a Hercules bike, I think of my father.

I, too, knew little about India, but I was curious and unafraid. I was young and in love. Years later, my parents explained they had been worried about the life I might have. In England, they knew no Indians personally. They had never met any. There were no documentaries about India on the television in those days to help them. Sitcoms such as *It Ain't Half Hot Mum* (which is now, rightly, considered racist and homophobic) didn't appear until 1974. *The Jewel in the Crown* came in the eighties. Both were set in colonial India, rather than India post-Independence. My parents had read Rudyard Kipling's *Kim* and E.M. Forster's *A Passage to India*, but we weren't a bookish family. They had lived through two World Wars and knew about Gandhi and Nehru and the socialist path that India had taken, and that India didn't try to be friendly with any countries except Russia, and that they led the Non-Aligned Movement with Egypt and Yugoslavia. And they may have been alarmed by the continuing tension between India and both Pakistan and China. It was indeed odd for me to find myself living in a country that was so chummy with Russia, which, to us in England, had always been the Big Bad Wolf.

Still, failing to attend the wedding of your youngest daughter, the only daughter to marry, was quite a big deal for all parties. It must have been tough for my parents-in-law too, but that never crossed my mind.

Traditionally in the UK in the sixties, the bride's family played the major role in arranging and paying for the wedding. I wonder now, how the Mehtas explained to their family and friends that none, yes, not one, of my family would be present at my wedding?

I was very fortunate that my mother-in-law was unfazed and treated me as if I were her own daughter, planning every single detail, from my saris and jewellery for each different lunch and dinner, to where each party should be held and what we should eat.

On reflection, I wonder if my parents were punishing me for my self-determination. I wonder if they ever regretted their decision. I shall never know. Whatever else, they must surely have known that when they said goodbye to me, it would be a long time before we saw each other again.

When I told my father I was going to India in 1966, my father generously gave me £500, the amount he said he would have spent on my wedding in England. I bought a white Morris Traveller, a station wagon with wooden strips on the rear, sort of half-timbered, to take to Bombay with me because Anand's father had warned me there was a seven-year waiting list to buy a Fiat, the only small car you could get in India. My trusty Morris became known as my dowry. It was one of the best decisions I ever made. It gave me my independence from the start. There was much less traffic in Bombay then and I loved driving, always with the windows down. My car had a high-pitched, musical 'poop-poop', different from everyone else's, which changed to a less distinctive 'beep-beep' when, having worn it out, my father-in-law found a replacement at a shop in Chor Bazaar that specialised in second-hand, re-conditioned car horns. The woodwork went next, and he had that replaced too. Only in India! Even today, people still go on mending and mending and mending things.

Had my parents seen me off weeping and waving hankies, leaving might have been tougher. They didn't. Dear Aunt Mare accompanied me in the Morris to Marseilles, where I boarded the Messageries Maritimes liner bound for Bombay. My brother Richard had given me £20 as an early wedding present, which I spent on three good Swiss saucepans with lids that I am still using. An Indian friend had pointed out that saucepans in India had no handles, which sounded very unlikely but turned out to be true. To lift a *dekchi*, a handle-less saucepan, one needs a large tong-like instrument, or asbestos hands, strong arms and total concentration. I also packed a traditional Coalport china tea-service with delicate blue flowers. All gone now, and I don't miss it. I brought some crystal tumblers too, because they were not available here. The first time I rather proudly took them out, my new servant, fresh from his village in Uttar Pradesh, dropped the tray and smashed the lot.

I also bought some LPs of my favourite music and a sewing machine, my sister's reject, an ordinary Necchi, which came in handy for running up curtains for the flat, and clothes for my daughters. I was a practical seamstress, not a creative one. Nearly all my possessions fitted into my old school trunk and a small tea chest. On the journey, Aunt Mare said not a word about me leaving England for good. All I remember of that last night in a French hotel is the ferociously noisy gas-fired geyser in the bathroom that kept me wide awake in terror that it would explode and I would never get to India.

The boat journey itself was a big disappointment, nothing like the Doris Day movie, *It's Magic.* No luxury swimming-pool, no deck-recliners, no dishy officers. I shared a cabin with a silent, elderly Swiss woman and we were put at a table with two Japanese girls who didn't stop nattering in Japanese. We passed through the Suez Canal and I couldn't believe how skinny it was.

When we docked at Ballard Pier, Bombay, my Morris was whisked away, to my great alarm. It reappeared days later, but only when Anand's father forked out another £500 duty, plus a further 10 per cent as a bond to ensure I would not sell the car for another ten years.

Small cars were not the only things in short supply when I arrived in Bombay in 1966. The economy was overcontrolled and underpowered, resulting in terrible food shortages. Basic supplies were rationed and there was an acute shortage of milk and butter, and no cheese at all, except for the smuggled tins of Craft in Crawford Market. I didn't mind for myself until I was pregnant and felt I needed to drink milk. I certainly didn't mind that I couldn't bake a cake because the piped gas to keep the oven alight was so unreliable. We had piped gas, which was supplied by the Bombay Gas Co Ltd, established in 1862 by the British, who laid 400 km of pipeline to distribute coal gas to South Bombay. Having faded into oblivion with the advent of cylinder gas, the company has risen from the ashes in the last ten years because that same pipeline is being used to carry fibre optic cables delivering a seamless broadband connection instead.

It was only when I got married that I realised that Indians are not present-givers in the way that the British are. Instead of giving a new couple a toaster or linen monogrammed sheets, we were given money, in an envelope, with the amount ending in one, so Rs 101 or Rs 1001 or, very occasionally, Rs 1,00,001. Only Christians tend to exchange presents at Christmas. On birthdays, older people gave presents to the younger ones, but the young were not expected to give presents to their elders.

When my sister and I were clearing my mother's house following her death, we found all sorts of little hideous things that we had made for her and she had treasured. We learnt as children what it is to give and receive. Traditionally, in some parts of India, when a woman is seven months pregnant, she invites her friends and relations for tea. Having performed some sort of puja involving coconut and rice followed by dancing and singing, each guest lines up to bless the expectant mother and give her an envelope containing cash. In England, people give baby clothes and teddies and *things*. Not money.

These days, there is very little I need or want that I can't get here. Almost. Until recently, I would ask visiting friends to bring a blonde Bobbi Brown eyebrow pencil and good old-fashioned marmalade, preferably homemade but Frank Cooper's Oxford as second-best, but now I can buy both here, if at a price. I would make my own, but Seville oranges do not routinely arrive in India in January and February as they do in England. Not even in supermarkets. Now we have a growing number of supermarkets in Mumbai, albeit small compared to those abroad, as well as markets, street stalls and pavement vendors. Since 2017, I have been able to buy Marmite and Italian olive oil from shops such as Nature's Basket. It opened in 2005 and slowly, the odd things that blow-ins have wanted have found their way to the shelves of Nature's Basket, albeit at wildly inflated prices. There's been a Marks & Spencer in Mumbai for even longer, but it is more like the M&S in Solihull in the sixties, selling basic underwear and frumpy clothes. No Rosie Huntington-Whitely silk lingerie and no food at all.

Nor could I find any antenatal information even in India's most sophisticated city. Even in London at the time, according to my best girlfriends, antenatal care was only just starting. They were put under the supervision of a midwife, many of whom who were still dashing around Kensington on bicycles, just like in the television programme *Call the Midwife!* But most of them relied on their mothers and each other. My darling mother-in-law had had four children but wasn't exactly hands-on when it came to things antenatal or newborns. She was thrilled to hear that I was having a baby, and told me to find an obstetrician and to eat for two. I bought a subscription for *Nursery World* from the UK at the suggestion of my mother, who also sent me nappy pins and the childcare bible by the legendary American Dr Benjamin Spock, which I followed to the letter. 'Don't worry if your toddler is sitting on the beach eating sand; it can't do any harm' was a particular comfort. I had a great deal to learn. In urban India, babies are delivered by doctors, not by midwives and, according to my mother-in-law, few doctors choose to specialise in obstetrics because most women go into labour at night, which plays havoc with a doctor's busy social life. I think she was teasing me. There are so-called 'midwives' in India who work in hospital delivery rooms, but their job is not to take care of the mothers but to clean up the mess.

Only when I became pregnant did I realise how little I knew about childbirth and about babies in general, so I read up assiduously about natural childbirth, which was becoming popular at the time. I opted for a method involving four levels of breathing during labour through singing. Since I can seldom remember the words of songs, I chose one of the few that I could, The Seekers' hit: 'Close the door, light the light / We're stayin' home tonight'. When the time came, needless to say, nothing went according to plan, as I recall with hideous clarity. Anjali arrived occiput posterior, sometimes called 'sunny side up'. Episiotomy, forceps and stitches. No one's fault; I was just unlucky. The consequent urine retention and infection kept me in hospital for a fortnight and made breastfeeding difficult, but I kept going for a further six weeks. Every second was a struggle. There were no district nurses making home-visits to see how I was coping or to weigh the baby to reassure me that she was growing. I felt a bit desperate and longed for my mother. Eighteen months later, Tara was born in about three minutes, this time a perfect experience of the natural childbirth method, and I fed her for nine months. Very different story.

When I eventually took Anjali home, our wonderful ayah, Julie, introduced me to the healing and medicinal properties of neem leaves soaked in water, which I used for my bucket baths. I took quickly to bucket baths when I first encountered them in India. They are so economical with water, apart from anything else. Anand has always believed that British-style baths are a very dirty way of washing oneself. He was disgusted to learn that when I was a small girl, I often left the soapy, tepid bathwater for my brothers to get into. While at LSE in the sixties, the flat he was renting didn't have a shower and he refused to use the bath, going instead to LSE squash courts, not to play squash but to shower.

Indian standards of hygiene—or the lack of it—was a problem for me, particularly loos. Though there has been a sea change since the sixties, I'm pleased to say. I have had my fair share of tummy upsets over six decades, but nothing serious—and, as I see it, all good for the waistline. I did have a serious bout of jaundice, which was vile. I knew exactly where I had got it. While working with Apnalaya, I joined a meeting to promote healthy living in a hut jam-packed with women. One of our hosts presented me with a cup of water, which I politely turned down. When we were offered juice instead, my friend refused, saying it was her fasting day, a handy excuse. I felt I couldn't say no, and a child was dispatched to get sugar and a packet of crystals, and the granules were mixed with water to make orange juice. A precious stainless-steel glass was filled with this dubious-looking potion. Days later, I turned yellow and felt absolutely rotten and took to my bed. I was brought a television, and everyone kept coming in to watch it with me, which was the last thing I wanted. It took me a whole year to recover fully.

It also took me some time to come to grips with the politics of my new country and to understand that even hygiene standards were laid down largely by government through planning and budget allocation. I was not very interested until Mrs Gandhi, then prime minister, imposed the Emergency upon us in June 1975. All elections were cancelled and civil liberties suspended. It was like living in a police state. But India in 1975 wasn't that much fun anyway, with shortages and scarcity across the board and very little gadding about. On reflection, the most eerie thing of all was that, for people like us, life went on as usual, but with an underlying current of unease, alarm and anxiety that no one discussed. Our girls were still so small, Anjali seven and Tara five, and I certainly didn't want to scare them with talk of what was going on. Censorship changed the way we read newspapers, and we were horrified by the arrests of journalists, civil rights activists and anyone who dared criticise the politicians. We became wary of voicing opinions at the club, or anywhere in public, in case we were overheard and reported.

Our work at Apnalaya remained unaffected until Sanjay, Mrs Gandhi's son, announced his intention to remove slums. It began in Delhi and reached Bombay in 1976 when more than 40,000 people (some say 70,000) were forcibly moved overnight from Janata Colony to Cheeta Camp, 'supervised' by 12,000 police, in order to make space for the expansion of the Bhabha Atomic Research Centre. It sent shudders through the slums, with everyone fearing that they would be next.

I was even more appalled by Sanjay's plan to control India's expanding population with his unforgivable foray into family planning in 1976. More than six million enforced sterilisations of the poorest people took place. It was almost ritual butchery. This was the one and only time that I considered returning to England, though very fleetingly. I knew that Anand would not have wanted to go, so I didn't even raise the subject with him. However, I must have conveyed my unease to my father because he wrote to me, assuring me that as long as the bullock carts continued to plough the fields as they had for centuries, India would survive as a democracy. It was because I felt so strongly about the Emergency that I voted, illegally. I put on a salwar-kameez, covered my head with a dupatta and went to the voting centre, keeping my eyes down. My finger was marked with indelible ink, which lasted for a week, and no one ever asked me why.

I was in a conference at the Tata Institute of Social Sciences when we heard that Mrs Gandhi had lost the election in March 1977 and the Emergency was over. No one had foreseen that she would lose, not even my friend Bill Peters, the British DHC and an astute diplomat. It was probably the compulsory sterilisation that did it, and a great example of democracy in action. Mrs Gandhi had massively misinterpreted the mood of the nation when she called a hasty election, and she was shocked by the result. Having fallen so far from grace, she and the Congress Party swept back into power in January 1980. Staggering stuff, but such are the vagaries of the Indian political scene. I am so anti-dynastic that I wouldn't vote for the Congress now.

I don't recall much mourning following the death of Sanjay Gandhi, later that year, while piloting a small plane that crashed. He was a renowned daredevil, and he had lost control of his plane while performing an aerobatic manoeuvre, possibly because he was wearing Kolhapuri chappals and a kurta-pyjama, not the recommended kit for the cockpit. Mrs Gandhi was assassinated in Delhi in 1984 and her surviving son Rajiv succeeded her as prime minister. He, too, was assassinated in 1991. I would have thought that was enough of politics for one family, but Rajiv's widow Sonia took over the presidency of the Congress Party in 1998, a post she held for twenty-two years, with a gap in 2017, while her son Rahul took over for two years. He continues to take a leadership role in the party. Like me, Sonia is a European, and I cannot for the life of me imagine how she has managed to integrate herself so deeply into the very fabric of modern India.

My life in India was very different in a million ways, but I never for one second considered it to be inferior to my previous existence in any way. At the time, there was little evening entertainment available. No West End theatre, no Western classical-music concerts, and not much money around nor many fancy restaurants to dine out at. The cinema was very popular and all the big Hollywood movies came here, with the kissing scenes cut out by the censors. We often went to scruffy cinemas, the Regal, the Metro, the Strand or the Eros, once gorgeous Art Deco buildings already in a crumbling state. Rats scuttled beneath the seats from which arms were often missing, particularly in the Strand, which closed its doors permanently many years ago.

Television came to Bombay in 1972, but most cities in India were without it until 1975. I didn't miss it at all as I had hardly watched any in England. We didn't have a television in the Mehta house for another five years and then Anand and I seldom watched anything except sport. Every Sunday, a Hindi film was shown—to many, the highlight of the week. In our extended household, the television was in what was called the Lift Room. The servants were strictly forbidden from watching unless there was a family member present, so Anjali would sit with them for the film on Sundays. She learnt Hindi from watching these films.

Colour TV came in time for the Asian Games in1982, and soon after that the number of channels mushroomed; eventually, we could watch the BBC world service channel and CNN and, sometimes, good films in English. Nowadays, we watch very little apart from the news and sport. In a single day Anand sometimes watches up to three cricket matches played in different parts of the world. That makes him very happy.

These days, the pace of change seems to be accelerating even faster, thanks largely to the internet and social media, and I have difficulty keeping up even with my mobile phone. India is way ahead of most Western countries in embracing and adapting to the digital world, including the UK. More and more tasks can only be done online, such as admission to municipal schools, which is challenging for people living in poverty and with no access to the internet. During the pandemic, I did all my banking and shopping online and continue to do so.

Even in my eighties, I continue to embrace change. My father always maintained that he did too. One example that has stuck in my mind is the ease with which he changed his enthusiasm for the incumbent prime minister, going from Labour's Harold Wilson to Conservative's Edward Heath and then back to Wilson. When I returned to England from India every three years, I confess I found his altered allegiances somewhat confusing.

The change I have most longed for, and worked hard for, is a reduction in the numbers of people living in poverty. Statistics can always be found that suggest this is happening, but I do not believe them. I must have been despairing about this to Anand early on because one day he told me that when he left Bombay for England for the very first time in 1960, the vast majority of people walking the streets in Bombay were barefoot. When he returned five years later, the majority were wearing chappals or footwear of some sort. He could see the difference. Change is not always immediately obvious. You have to look out for it. I am keeping my eyes peeled.

11

The Sense of an Ending

A CHILD'S RAVAGED BODY, CRUDELY STITCHED FOLLOWING A POST-mortem, is laid out on a bamboo stretcher in the garden of our house in Warden Road. Little Divyan, barely five years old, was my husband's cousin, the middle son of Anand's aunt and uncle, who lived on the first floor of the family house. Born with a hole in his heart, his anxious parents had taken him as a toddler to Texas to be operated on by the legendary heart surgeon, Denton Cooley, who gave him a new lease of life. A year or two later, while staying with an aunt in Madras, he felt unwell. She wanted to take him to a conventional allopathic doctor, but his parents insisted that he should see their homeopath in Bombay. He died on the journey home. In those days, women were not welcome at Hindu cremations, so I couldn't attend, which felt strange to me. I should have liked to have been there.

But the first death that affected me deeply, more deeply than I can say, was that of Vatsal, the husband of my sister-in-law, Tulsi. I had loved him from our first meeting, which was why I chose him to be one of two witnesses at my wedding. He was extremely clever and an exceptionally fine human being. After college here in Bombay, where he became friends with Anand, he had gone to Stanford University, but his father died suddenly, and a shortage of money brought him back to India to earn a living to sustain his family.

Vatsal worked for Hindustan Levers, which made Lifebuoy, Pears soap and Vim—such familiar products to me—and he had been posted to Madras, now Chennai. Just one week following his annual medical check, having got a clean bill of health, he didn't feel like supper and decided to have an early night. He never woke up. Heart. The next morning, his servant knocked on his door, got no answer. He and Tulsi had a wonderful marriage, two little ones, and he had everything going for him. I have no doubt in my mind that Vatsal would have done something remarkable for humanity.

That happened in 1975, absolutely out of the blue. Vatsal was just thirty-five, a year younger than Anand. Tulsi just thirty-two. It shattered us all. Soon after his death, Tulsi talked to the legendary Indian guru and philosopher Krishnamurti, who was a close personal friend of the Mehta family. He told her to leave the past behind and only look forward. At his instruction, she put away all but one tiny photograph of her beloved husband. Krishnamurti somehow empowered her to move on, just as he had enabled Anand's aunt, Nandini, following the collapse of her marriage. Tulsi returned to the family house in Warden Road with her children, who started going to school with both of mine. Tulsi, a talented writer, taught for a while at Elphinstone College and wrote two history textbooks before joining a company as a copywriter and 'comms' person in the very early days of communications. Suddenly, I had my hands full supervising four children. Caring for Radha, aged two, and Vinayak, five, was the single silver lining in a very darkly clouded time.

As I have often noted, as a family, the Mehtas have always eschewed Hindu ceremonies, and seldom go to a temple, but that does not mean they are any less Hindu. It took me some years to understand that there is no correlation between how much a

Hindu does in terms of celebrating festivals or praying, and how pious or devout he or she is. I liked that each person's relationship with their gods is private and personal. Anand's father died in his seventies, a week after Anand's fiftieth birthday, when Anand was on his way back from Switzerland. Papa had been diagnosed with an aneurism, which he had chosen not to mention to anyone or have treated. When Anand discovered that Papa had kept it a secret or had been, perhaps, in denial, he was furious. In the crematorium, I, a 'Christian' atheist (if that makes any sense at all), sat at one end of the stretcher carrying my Hindu father-in-law's body while Mohamed, my Muslim brother-in-law, sat at the other end. Not for the first time, I marvelled at our multi-faith, multicultural, liberal family, and thought how appropriate this was for Papa. A Muslim man and an atheist woman, neither often spotted in a Hindu crematorium, were there because of our respect and love for our father-in-law. He was a fine example of an Indian patriarch, endlessly generous to family and friends when help was needed, regardless of their faith or lack of it.

There's little privacy at your average outdoor Indian crematorium, though these days there are electric crematoria in most towns and cities. But even then, the body, on its bamboo stretcher, is laid on a slab, where anyone who wants to can perform any last rites while they wait for the furnace to be ready. It is stark, and I can understand why, in the past, it was not thought appropriate for women to attend. Eventually, the stretcher is put on a conveyor belt, and it rumbles off into a furnace where the flames engulf it as the iron door slams down. A very final sound. The next day, the family collects the pot of ashes, which often includes alarmingly large bone fragments. I collected Tara's ashes in London, but from the registrar's office some days later, and held in a very nice wooden box.

Traditionally, the ashes are then poured on to running or sacred water. On Marine Drive in Mumbai, there's a special place where people consign ashes into the sea. We scattered the ashes of both Papa and, later, of Amru Masi, in a stream near our country home in Lonavala. We cast the ashes of Chicken, Anand's sister, into the lake there. Despite my lack of belief, I am always moved by the scattering of ashes because of the notion of ashes-to-ashes, dust-to-dust. By contrast, Hindus believe that a spirit is reborn after death, so the end is also the beginning, which is a tricky thing for me to wrap my head around. The death of a loved one is of course a loss and source of grief, if not quite the *end* in the same way as I think of it.

To my mind, the wording of the traditional Hindu death announcement in newspapers, which states that So-and-So has 'gone to her heavenly abode', sounds wonderfully regal. As everyone knows who knows me, I know I am here and one day I shall die and that is it. End of. When I went with Anjali to the Valley of the Kings in Egypt, I was bowled over to discover that ancient Egyptians spent their *entire* life preparing for the afterlife, which meant taking dogs, cats and kitchen utensils with you to your tomb. Does anyone have real proof of what happens after death? No. Unless one believes in ghosts. Which I do not. But I think I am right in saying that Hindus believe in an infinity rather than a finality.

Not that that thought protects those left behind on earth from grief. Sachin was devastated when his father died. He had recovered well following heart surgery, but he lived on the fourth floor with no lift, and one day he staggered up all four flights, sat down and died in his chair. Anand and I, Anjali and the children were all in Cheltenham visiting family while Sachin was playing cricket in Bristol. That evening, we had dropped Anjali and the children to their hotel and returned to my mother's house. Anjali then got a phone call from India telling her the sad news. She knew she had to tell Sachin face to face, so a friend drove her to Bristol. The moment she appeared at his door at 2 a.m., he suspected the worst. He got the first flight back to Mumbai in time for his father's cremation and then returned immediately to Bristol, where he scored a century which he dedicated to his father.

I have always found it quite challenging to get friends to talk openly about any personal matters, including death. Whenever a death occurs, friends and relations go at once to the house to offer sympathy and to help. No one has been able to explain to me why food is not cooked in the house for a few days after a death. Visitors bring it with them, and it's always vegetarian. Sometimes, on the thirteenth day of mourning, the grieving family hold a puja to help release the soul of the deceased for reincarnation. This is all in stark contrast to customs in England, where the funeral is often not held for days or even weeks after someone dies, and the bereaved family is generally expected to get back to normal life very soon.

Hinduism is a wonderfully complex, all-encompassing religion, and what I like most about it is that it is never strictly prescriptive about what should or should not be done. From the day Anand's grandmother was widowed, she chose only to wear white; she left an extensive wardrobe of white saris. There are no rules or sense of propriety about how long a person must remain single following the death of a spouse. I have known men marrying the spinster sister of the dead wife after her death in order to provide a mother for his children. There is no shame in such an arrangement but, in a characteristically Indian way, it is seldom openly discussed. Soon after Vatsal's death, Tulsi met her partner, Kiran Nagarkar, the celebrated writer and a very dear man. Within a year, Kiran had moved into Warden Road. They never married, but they shared their lives very contentedly until his death in 2020. Tulsi always kept that one little photograph of Vatsal on her table.

In sharp contrast, I have photographs of my daughter Tara everywhere, and she remains very much part of my life more than forty years after her death at the age of seven. I still weep for her. It happened very suddenly. Following a few days of coughing, her temperature soared alarmingly, and she was admitted to Breach Candy Hospital. Agranulocytosis, a life-threatening blood disease, was diagnosed. A bone marrow transplant was the only possible cure, and since that was not available in India, we decided to fly her to London. On landing at Heathrow airport, an ambulance was to have taken us directly to the haematology unit at St Mary's Hospital, Paddington, where my doctor brother, Richard, had arranged for Tara to be treated. She never made it; she died at the medical unit at Heathrow. Why is it that I remember so clearly my mother arriving at the hospital having pranged the car and her being so terribly afraid of what my father would say?

Everyone deals with death in their own way. I didn't want to see Tara dead. I want to remember her alive. An undertaker took her body away within hours. Anand and Anjali flew in from Mumbai on the next flight. When my father arrived—and he was obviously not in the least bit angry about the car—we went for a walk together along the Paddington canal. It was probably the closest I had ever felt to him. We talked about death and faith and how to give Tara, a Hindu, an appropriate send-off, given that I didn't believe in God. Obviously, we were going to cremate her.

There were many twists of fate around the time when Tara died, not least that my close friend, Shanta Gupta, the first president of Apnalaya, and a devout Hindu, just happened to be in the UK. She agreed to read a Hindu prayer at the service, which took place in the local crematorium. My brother Richard read from T.S. Eliot's *The Four Quartets.* My sister-in-law, Serena, the only committed Christian present, read a prayer. It is so strange that I can't remember some details while others remain etched in my mind forever, such as singing 'All Things Bright and Beautiful', which would not feature in a list of my 50 favourite hymns, but we chose it because it was the only hymn Tara had known. My close friend Caroline played the organ, a Bach Prelude, I think. I shall not forget the sight of the heartbreakingly small coffin slipping off soundlessly into the dark. My intention was that some part of the service should resonate with the faiths—or lack of faith—of all those present, and I think we achieved that. We had left Aunt Mare and Anjali making egg sandwiches at her flat for all of us afterwards, a detail I recall more clearly than who was present.

It was a blessing that Tara died in England. I could not have borne the hundreds of kind and curious visitors looking at me in the way I find people do when something tragic happens in India. In England, I was able to come to terms with Tara's death within the loving arms of my family, who somehow knew how to care for me. The day Tara died, Aunt Mare cooked roast lamb for supper. I hadn't eaten since I had left Bombay, and it was so delicious and comforting. As were the hundreds of telegrams, messages and letters that arrived so quickly from all over the world, so much easier to cope with than an invasion of people. Perhaps I remain, deep down, very British in terms of what I want to share and what I want to keep private and within the family.

Being in England with some of my oldest and closest girlfriends, three of whom had daughters of the same age as Tara, helped too, because their empathy was extraordinary. I wept for days. Frankly, I wanted to die myself. I was desperate about how Tara was going to manage all alone without me, even though the rational part of me believed there was nothing after death. I tried to comfort myself by telling myself that Vatsal would look after her. And it worked to a certain extent.

Anjali barely left my side. Anand had to return to India after a couple of weeks, and Anjali and I went to Norfolk with my parents and brother Richard and his family. They swam in the freezing cold sea while Anjali and I sat on the windswept Holkham beach, watching; there was so much warmth and life within the family that slowly, very slowly, I began to feel human again.

I have a theory that it takes between nine months and a year after the death of a loved one before one can begin to think beyond that deep, deep wound. Time truly is a healer. I was once again ambushed by grief when Anjali and I returned to Bombay, to the house where we had lived as a family of four and were now shrunk to a threesome. The two girls had slept on bunk beds in their room. We moved Anjali into a different bedroom. I threw myself into my work with Apnalaya. Of course, Tara's death changed me. It made me think more about what I was doing with my life. I hope it made me more empathetic. I hope it mellowed me. One is never quite the same person following a trauma but, unfortunately, one is not necessarily changed for the better.

Call me Pollyanna, but in time I came to realise that things could have been worse. Shortly after I returned to Bombay, a friend arranged for me to meet a woman who had gone out one day, leaving her two small children with her maid. In order to get a better view of a procession going on outside, the boys had climbed up on to the balcony railing. Both fell and both died. That she had survived this double tragedy in an entirely preventable accident completely amazed me. It drove home to me that others had endured even more devastating losses than mine. I still had my darling Anjali. I tried to count my blessings. I've seen marriages pulled apart by the death of a child. Anand was similarly broken by Tara's death, but we were able to comfort one another. Our marriage became stronger. Some forty years on, as a remembrance for Tara, Anand and I funded a bone marrow transplant centre for children in the new children's hospital in Mumbai.

I had set out to be a strict mother, determined not to spoil or overindulge my girls. My ways were rather English and old-fashioned. Unlike every Indian child I have ever known, my girls were forbidden, in principle at least, from coming in to sleep in our bed with us. Nevertheless, Tara used to creep into our room in the middle of the night with the rag doll I had made for her, and she was so still and sweet that I let her stay there. I am so glad about that now. She was such a softie, such an exceptionally loving, clinging little thing. Everyone adored her. As a child, Anjali never had a best friend in the way that most children do. After Tara's death, nearly every single girl in her class at school came, one by one, to tell me that she had been Tara's best friend and that she had loved her and she missed her.

Everything in life goes back to the nature/nurture thing. Anjali had been the first grandchild in the immediate family, and she was everybody's first grandchild or first niece and everyone seemed to claim her as theirs. Indeed, so much so that I sometimes felt she was not my very own baby. When Tara was born, she was the second girl for a start, so was largely ignored. Had she been a boy, she would have had a lot of attention. I breastfed her for nine months, which I hadn't managed to do with Anjali because I'd been so ill following her birth. Tara was the most obliging baby. From the start, she slept through the night. She didn't mind if I went out to dinner and she got a late feed. She was an angel.

I used to say that everyone is born equal, but when Tara was born, I realised that is simply not true. Being born Anjali's younger sister wasn't fair. Even as a baby, Anjali was the doer, in control. Very like Anand. She still is. She manages Sachin and she manages me. She adored her little sister. What I missed most was hearing the little girls giggling together. Anjali has never once spoken of Tara's death.

We shall never know for certain what started the chain of events that led to Tara's death. At the time, we had a driver, Shivaji, who was on medication for TB. Tara had had a series of nasty coughs and the odd fever and Dr Tibriwalla, a leading paediatrician (and also Anand's bridge captain), had put her on Anadin and a prophylactic dose of an anti-TB drug. It might have been an adverse reaction to this drug or even to a common analgesic such as Novalgin which, along with Anadin, has subsequently been banned as it can—very rarely—cause agranulocytosis. Often one hears people say: 'If only I had done this or that, I could have saved her.' I had to stop myself from thinking that Tara's death was a freak accident, but I don't believe that there was anything we could have done or should have done differently. Obviously, had we lived in England, where my brother Richard would have arranged first-class treatment by the best doctors, she might have survived. But we lived in Bombay, at a time when the facilities weren't quite as robust as they are now. When we left for London for treatment, we knew that it was probably too late and already hopeless, but this very ill little girl told me very clearly that she wanted to go to London. I shall never know if she knew that her wish had come true.

—w—

As I am writing this, it is May 2021, and I am in the middle of India's unfolding Covid catastrophe; death is everywhere around me. More than a year ago, when Covid-19 struck and the city went into lockdown, I wrote the following to a friend: 'The silence of this usually seething city is sinister, broken only by the crows cawing heartlessly as they always do, but much louder, and by the bright green parakeets doing acrobatics on the tangled overhead cables. The Sea Link is ominously empty. Today, I got the news I have been dreading: ten cases of the coronavirus have been reported in the slums of Shivaji Nagar where Apnalaya is most involved. Despair? Not yet. One has to have faith that the brainiest scientists the world over are coming closer to finding vaccines and cures.'

Covid has brought us all so much closer to death as individuals and also as a nation. Actually, as a world. If prime ministers such as Boris Johnson can get it, then truly no one is immune. I have certainly become more aware of my own mortality. Haunting photographs of flames rising from the mass funerals on India's cremation grounds, in operation day and night, have been on the front pages of newspapers across the globe. Hospital beds are being shared by several patients from the same family because there is no spare capacity. Doctors and medical staff are at breaking point. Many have died. Hospital wards have more dead patients than live ones. People are dying in hospital corridors, on roads and in their homes, with rotting bodies piling up everywhere. Crematoriums in Delhi have run out of firewood and the forest department has given permission for trees in the city to be felled for funeral pyres. City parks, car parks and quarries are being used as cremation grounds. New 'markets' have opened up with staff in hospital mortuaries taking bribes from those desperate for a final glimpse of the bagged body of a loved one. Priests are charging huge sums to perform last rites; so-called medical consultants are ruthlessly ripping people off with 'oxygen', which is not oxygen. Sick people are selling their homes to pay for bogus treatment. I wonder what the final death toll will be. Without a doubt, a small fraction of the official count. Those who die without a test and without treatment do not feature on any Covid list.

Our numbers are few compared to the UK per capita. So far, there have been 4,00,000 deaths in India in a population of 1.4 billion. In the UK, there have been 1,27,000 deaths in a population of 60 or 70 million, which makes the situation in the UK much worse, relatively. What is so distressing in India is that people are dying in such horrible circumstances, from a lack of oxygen, or while waiting hopelessly for aid of any kind. If there was a better supply of oxygen and more ventilators, deaths could be prevented, just as they have been in the UK. Thousands of children have been left orphaned when both parents have died within days of one another. What will become of them?

We are so fortunate to be living in our country home, shielded from the reality, and this is probably the case for most well-off Indians who can stay within the confines of their comfortable, cool apartments and limit their exposure to Covid. The media has at last forced our prime minister, Modi, and other political leaders to acknowledge the gravity of the situation. But faith in Modi is waning and anger is rising. Unless the promised aid, from our government and abroad, reaches where it is needed throughout India more quickly, I don't know what will happen. Life is cheap in India, and as long as it is only the poor who are dying and there is no threat to the rest of the population, few of the assurances of aid and improved facilities translate into action. Because prominent politicians, film stars and cricketers have been affected, a little more effort is being put into curative and preventive measures. But not enough. And, as Anand keeps telling me, Modi has chosen livelihoods over lives, and is not going to impose another tight lockdown. It is convenient that he can pass the decision-making to individual states so that they are to blame if things go wrong. In addition, there is talk of preparations for a probable third wave later in the year, in order to distract from what is *not* being done now. It is a grim and alarming picture. The High Courts and the Supreme Court are in on the act, issuing orders that are impossible to fulfil, and generally making a mess of an already messy situation. The single thing they have achieved is to overrule Modi's attempt to stifle publication of the facts, and one of these is that only 2 per cent of the population have been double-vaccinated. So few in the country where so much of the world's vaccines are produced.

We had a brief but desperate time when Sachin returned from a Seniors cricket match and started coughing. Sachin was not even fifty years old, and he was fit as a fiddle. He was taken to the best hospital in Mumbai. But even he admits that the doctors themselves were not completely confident of the treatment they were giving him and appeared to change their mind several times. I was hugely relieved that he had got to the hospital just as his lungs were beginning to be affected. I put on my bravest face and kept telling myself that he was in the best possible hands because the chief minister's wife was in the room next door, being looked after by the same medical team. On day three, Sachin spoke to us on the phone, and we could hear how breathless he was; he couldn't talk for long. This was a youngish, healthy man with all the money in the world for any necessary treatment.

I began to panic, silently and especially at night, terrified that his condition was worse than the doctors were admitting, never daring to voice my concerns to Anjali or to Anand, who also remained mute on the subject. Fortunately, by day six, his condition improved dramatically, and suddenly he was back in his Mumbai house, though still testing positive, so in isolation. When he eventually came to recuperate in Lonavala, I couldn't quite believe how much muscle he had lost in just a few days, and I was pretty horrified by the strange, scary, almost out-of-body experiences he had endured when his fever was highest, which he described in nightmarish detail. He was wretchedly tired and ravenously hungry for days. A month later, he was fully recovered and enjoying a quiet life, thanks to lots of good food and, between monsoon downpours, lots of fresh air. Thank heavens. Only last week, the husband of a good friend of mine, much younger than me, died in her arms.

We had another big scare when Sara, who was staying with us, found out that her personal trainer had Covid and might have infected her. She left immediately for Mumbai. Meanwhile, one of Sachin's drivers, who chauffeured us here a fortnight ago, has Covid, as does one of his daughters. His wife recovered from it a little while ago. Every day, we are hearing of new cases among friends, relations and staff. Ashok, our gardener, lost an old school friend last night, a man who had been perfectly well a couple of days ago. Death can be very fast. While Covid does not take caste or class into consideration, I am certain that many more of the poor have died than we will ever know. The journalist Barkha Dutt, from the top echelons of society, wrote movingly about the death of her father in the capital, Delhi. She believes he was failed by a 'combination of complacency, callousness and incompetence.' I am sure she is right. Political rallies have carried on as usual, which is shameful, but the politicians cannot resist. Weddings are restricted to twenty-five people (almost zero by Indian standards), but many are breaking the rules. Vast numbers of police are dying, and without the police nothing happens.

Covid has certainly changed the pattern of my life. I do more domestic tasks for a start. This morning I stripped my own bed. Normally, a maid would have done that. While drinking my two cups of light Darjeeling tea each morning, having finished reading the *Hindustan Times* on my laptop, I have always read the *Washington Post, The Times* and the *Guardian*. Not today. Instead, I and my sister-in-law Jill, who is staying with us, have already planned the day's menu and made a shopping list. I made cream of broccoli soup and ratatouille for lunch and, because there is another full lockdown in Pune and this district for six days, have ordered stores and fresh vegetables for the whole of the next week. We have several fridges, all in use. Sunita, Ashok's wife, used to do most of the cooking but it is more than usually complicated right now because Jill and Anand are vegetarians while Sachin can't have a meal without meat, fish or eggs, and Sara and her cousin Aliya are on a keto diet with no carbs and no sugar, so no fruit, in order to get what they call the 'beach-body-ready' look. They also insist that they must eat at noon and at seven in the evening. We have always preferred lunch at half past one and dinner at nine, so everything is out of synch. Furthermore, we are reorganising the servants' quarters with proper beds with mattresses because the weather here in Lonavala is getting quite cold and a bed is much cosier than a bedding roll on a stone floor.

My most important task this morning was an unusual one, however: clearing a shed down by the well to house a cow which is arriving tomorrow from Surat, a present to Sachin from the cricketer, Irfan Pathan. Sachin has wanted cows for years, but we have always managed to dissuade him. This time, he gave us no warning. He is quite mad. Cows—even one cow—take a lot of looking after. Their food is difficult to come by and expensive. And she is having a calf. I think we are all indulging him, and he is indulging himself because he was so ill. When I came to Bombay in the sixties, I remember the cowshed in our garage where Anand's grandmother stabled the house cows supplying daily fresh milk for the household. I don't know why Sachin wanted a cow, but he was thrilled to be given one, especially a pregnant one with a high pedigree.

Jill and I have developed a new vice. After lunch every day, we skip off and watch television. Our current addiction is *The Morning Show*, a sharp, smart American series starring Jennifer Aniston as a top news anchor. Having tried—and usually failed—to restrict ourselves to one episode, we get on with organising the next meal. Tomorrow, Anjali and Sachin are going to Mumbai to visit Sachin's mother, and they will return with two friends who, being Muslim and it being Ramadan, are fasting during the day but will need a large dinner. In the meantime, I must help Anand set up his new iPad so that he can have a Zoom meeting with his financial adviser, tune in to Radio Four for the Today programme and order a book for him on his Kindle. The book is *Fake Law: The Truth about Justice in an Age of Lies* by the Secret Barrister, a welcome change from the economics books to which he is addicted. There is much to do and we all get through the day, but that is just about it. Getting through it. Real life—living—seems to be on hold, and it feels as if we are in some sort of limbo.

At some stage each day, I catch up with work emails in a rather desultory fashion. Sometimes, Ashok and I discuss various gardening and practical matters, such as what to plant in the new pots I bought on Amazon and how to fix the new railings. I feel dead tired by the end of the day and tend to fall asleep during the film that Anjali puts on in the home theatre to entertain us now that the IPL has been cancelled. I stayed awake a couple of nights ago for *The Dig*, with gorgeous Ralph Fiennes as the archaeologist leading a find for Carey Mulligan. *My Octopus Teacher* was just as wonderful: part wildlife documentary, part moving tale of a man finding joy and purpose through his relationship with an octopus. Nothing like as silly as it sounds, and truly magical on a big screen. Or have I just become intellectually idle and easy to please in these terrible times? Or am I just growing old and sentimental?

Talking of growing old, Anand and I arrived in London in October, and having quarantined in our little flat not far from Lord's, I set about catching up with my relations and old girlfriends. It has been deeply depressing. Dear Caroline is well and still teaching, but the others are in a bad way. Amanda's husband fell down the stairs a few months ago and was lucky to survive. He can go to the loo but he can't talk and he will have to breathe through a tube and whisper for the remainder of his life. Yesterday, I had her weeping on the phone. My heart bled for her. She has always worked and is really struggling with being at home as a full-time caretaker. Jenie's husband died a year or two ago, since when Jenie had moved to a village near Devizes; she, too, is finding the adjustment quite difficult.

Amanda and I went to a school reunion for our year held in a smart room in the RAF Club on Piccadilly, the first I have been to and definitely the last. I knew three women, apart from Amanda, of the twenty-seven present. The rest were a complete blank. Nothing in their faces sparked a memory, and seeing their names made not a jot of difference. I regret to say that I felt as if I had been trapped in a care-home.

Whenever we come to London, Anand and I arrange a get-together for our LSE chums. Only Barry and Reg could make it this time and both were frail. They are the only ones left from Anand's original group. All of a sudden, we feel very old, and very afraid of Covid despite being double-vaccinated. Whenever I hear a cough, I fear the cougher's days are numbered. Money counts for nothing. Look at Colin Powell. This 'long Covid' thing scares me to death.

It was Bette Davis who said: 'Old age ain't no place for sissies'. Huge understatement, in my opinion. But it is much easier growing old in India than it is in England. There is great respect for older people. When the elderly mother of a British friend of mine came to stay in Mumbai, my friend's maid, who did not live in, slept all night on a mat outside the old lady's bedroom door, just in case she needed anything.

That attitude stems from the way in which Indian children grow up in multigenerational families, as close to their grandparents as their parents, and sometimes even closer. The concern my granddaughter Sara has shown for me and her grandfather during Covid has touched me deeply. She would be happier if we went nowhere at all and saw no one while we are here. She caught Covid when she came to London, in spite of being wary of crowds and wearing a mask.

I am torn by the way in which India has been portrayed by the British media. Uddhav Thackeray, Maharashtra's chief minister, has been very conservative, strict and done his best. But in a country as big as India with such limited resources, nothing will ever be enough. The British don't know how lucky they are to have the wonderful and well-funded NHS, and look how stretched it is. Under Modi, politicians have been cutting back on healthcare expenditure and trying to bring in private money instead.

I feel this personally because as a result of Covid, much of the progress we have made through Apnalaya in terms of encouraging women to go to hospital to have their babies, to get vaccinated for this and that, and keeping children in school has gone backwards. I read today that the number of stillbirths in India has gone up by 20 per cent, which is a truly terrible figure. The biggest mistake India made was allowing the Kumbh Mela, attended by 3.5 million pilgrims, where many got Covid. The same happened here in the UK with music festivals in Cornwall, where one of my nieces caught it, but the scale is so very different.

I had a realisation of sorts this morning, and it has shaken me very hard. Last week, I spent two days with Ruth, my clever friend from the LSE days, of whom I am so fond, and who is now a widow. She wasn't feeling well, and she has just rung to tell me that she has been diagnosed with pancreatic cancer with further complications because the tumour is pressing on an artery and a blockage in her bile duct is causing jaundice. The outlook is grim. At best, three months. Ruth nursed her husband, Mark, through stomach cancer. He was given a five-year prognosis but lived for another twenty, so Ruth knows miracles *can* happen—but she is fundamentally a realist. Ruth is one of my four closest, core friends from my school and college days, with whom I have never lost touch. For years, she and Mark lived in an old barn they had converted on the edge of Dartmoor, which I really loved. She moved recently to a lovely Art Deco house on the Penzance seafront. Following the death in California of her problematic only son, she has no surviving family. A kind Penzance chap has been ferrying her to and from the hospital. Life is lonely and difficult with neither family nor friends nearby. As is death. The realisation that one of my closest friends is to die imminently is unsettling. What can I do? Ruth needs someone to hold her hand but neither I, nor Caroline, can do that. Caroline lives in London, I live in Mumbai. Ruth has never been good on the phone. Anyway, what on earth is there to talk about? Like me, she is an atheist. So there is no comfort there. I feel strangely hopeless. Having gone through this traumatic pandemic, I should have thought that I can cope with almost anything. It is not the case. (Mercifully, Ruth did not die; in fact, her tumour miraculously shrank and disappeared.)

The way I feel takes me back to the day, long ago in the year 2000, when Aparna told me that she saw Anand's face, lost, afraid and forlorn, as he sat outside the ICU following my brain haemorrhage. I realised that he had been expecting the worst. The brain haemorrhage had come as a bolt from the blue. We were taking care of the grandchildren while Anjali and Sachin were on a trip to Germany. Eight-month-old Arjun had woken up crying about a tummy ache in the night; as I bent down to scoop him out of his travel cot, my head exploded. I abandoned Arjun and went to find an aspirin and became aware that this was not a normal headache. The next thing I knew, I was in the intensive care unit of Breach Candy Hospital and a day later in Jaslok Hospital because it was the only place in Bombay with the right sort of scanning equipment. I begged for my feather pillow from home and for ice to be pressed on my burning forehead, which a nurse did very gently—until my skin turned raw. The next fortnight is a blur. I never entirely lost consciousness but I barely moved. When I recovered, I had to be taught to walk again and I felt desperately fragile for weeks but I also felt very lucky to be alive and with no lasting ill-effects or disability.

Strangely enough, when I was told I had breast cancer in 2015, it didn't feel like the death sentence I had always imagined that cancer would be. Perhaps that was because Anjali was with me when a routine mammogram revealed a white baked-bean shape amid a sea of grey tissue. Within minutes—or so it seemed—she had arranged further tests, assessments and hospital admission, and before I knew it, I was recovering from a lumpectomy in Anjali's house where she was caring for me with great love and tenderness. Following a month of radiation treatment, I was cured. Hey presto! I have regular mammograms and take a pill daily; cancer never crosses my mind. Months later, I learnt that my sister, Gillian, in San Diego, had had a mastectomy at the same time. Neither of us had told the other until it was all over, possibly because we knew we were too far away to be of any real help. Or was it that Lancaster stoicism at play again?

All one can be sure of in life is that death will come. Maybe I shall last as long as my mother, who lived until she was nearly ninety-nine. But again, who knows? I have said I want my body to be chucked on the dumping ground, but I know that it won't happen. I hope I shall be taken to the electric crematorium with as little fuss as possible. I scattered half of Tara's ashes around an overgrown champa, a gorgeously fragrant magnolia tree in the garden at Lonavala that she loved to climb, the other half around a weeping wych elm where she had played in my parents' garden at Sparrows Nest. The champa has long gone, but I should like my ashes to mingle with hers in Lonavala. In India. My home.